(Not) PMO-in-a-Can:

Pragmatic Management of Strategic Objectives
(As told from the trenches)

D. Andrew Buck, PMP

(Not) PMO-in-a-Can: Pragmatic Management of Strategic Objective (as told from the trenches)

Table of Contents

Introduction and Foreword:

This work began as one thought, a single idea. My journey toward authoring this work began in examining my life and work over the course of 3 decades. It began as a search for answers, and revealed much about the approach that all of us take in thinking through our biggest challenges. Like many reading this book, I also at one time struggled to find answers, so let me start near the beginning.

Over two decades before the first publication of this book, I found my career evolving into the Software Development Life Cycle. Through many years in the technology sector, I'd eventually lived through the entire end-to-end product lifecycle and during that time, I'd transitioned into project management. I became what was commonly termed an "accidental project manager" – while I was called a Project Manager, I learned partly by the mistakes we all make along the way and initially without the benefit of formal education to bridge experience.

There are benefits and drawbacks to the manner in which I became a project manager.

Experience is a tough taskmaster and an enduring teacher. Once you've suffered the ritual hazing that comes from an embarrassing outcome, you won't be prone to make the same mistake again. Mistakes become the lessons of our history – as we fail to learn from them, we're doomed to their repetition. As I've evaluated and hired project and program managers over my career, I've asked one key question to understand them as an individual and suited for the role: Tell me about your largest failure as a project manager, and explain what you learned or how it affected you. Remarkably, the candidates that showed the right degree of humility and honesty about their earlier failures, and how those affected their behavior, were the ones I found intriguing and would more likely hire because they exhibited one key trait: Learning.

With that in mind, I've translated the lessons of 3 decades in the trenches in all facets of the technology/business lifecycle into an understandable perspective. If I was prone toward making a certain mistake, others might be prone to the same thinking that has guided our views on how projects should be managed, even though many of those adages are ineffective when applied in real world scenarios.

About me – I'm an experienced program and portfolio manager who has developed and built project and program management centers of excellence (some may call them Project Management Offices or PMOs) in a variety of organizations. It's a career that has spanned multiple responsibilities but has always been close to Program/Project/Portfolio Management, and it has been a global career that has imbued me with a rich set of life experiences. I've gained a very broad perspective on cultures, people, and formulas for project success that avoid dwelling into theory by placing that knowledge in the hands of the practitioner where it can be easily and directly applied.

I take a "contrarian" view of the world, a view I've gained through personal faith, professional experience, and understanding interactions. Part of my career enjoyment has been working with other people as both a friend and leader, helping to build their careers and competencies. My advice was not always conventional, and sometimes surprising to those I've managed; a number of them have been thankful that I haven't been the prototypical "manager" but rather exhibited leadership that they've in turn carried into their own careers. I'll touch on this concept as you read through the book, but understand that much of my advice comes from a different and perhaps unconventional thought process. Being "contrarian" is different from being "contrary"; it means breaking through the conventional wisdom to reveal a more comprehensive thought process. That's a badge I wear proudly.

Throughout this book, I'll suggest examples on how to view various project elements from a pragmatic standpoint. I'll explain why some conventionally held views in an academic respect might not translate to the corporate world where personality and fiefdoms are routinely held with higher regard. I'll also outline the thought behind practices that result in improved success criteria.

My approach is irreverent. It's also unapologetic. Through 3 decades in various organizations, my perspective underscores some basic attitudes toward what works and what doesn't. For instance, you'll see many books talk to the approach of "Establishing a PMO", viewing a "PMO" as an amorphous administrative function adding little direct project value other than placing academics in positions of review and criticism, and suggesting that this will automatically improve project performance. I've seen too many organizations try and fail with this approach because it simply didn't translate to the key success criteria for such a function. This is but one example, and while some of my writing appears to deride the traditional approaches, I'm in reality challenging their very nature by ushering a change-oriented thought process that is largely nonexistent in many organizations.

This book will **not** be a "How-To" for setting up a traditional, Inward-Facing, and Coaching/Reporting/Teaching PMO that is based on "people, process and tools". The current business climate demands more than that, and there is considerable discussion around the relevance of the very traditional PMO model originally employed by many organizations as being "past its prime". So while that approach has been very well documented -- a quick look at any bookseller will reveal countless titles on the subject -- I won't simply walk down that trail. Rather than that, my goal is to present a few objectives:

- Challenge our thinking.
- Challenge our goals.
- Challenge our approach.
- Challenge process versus strategy.
- Challenge common business-alignment versus proper strategic alignment.

The last point is important, since a common buzzword is to focus project-based efforts on supporting the business. I believe we need to go a step beyond that and ensure that we align with the strategy of the organization. The difference is not just in wording, but in the concept of "Business-Unit-Aligned" versus "Enterprise/Strategic/Organizational Alignment". This book will seek to challenge individual business unit behavior that may often be counterproductive, and suggest an approach based on collaboration toward the strategic vision. The goals of the larger company are more viable -- no one will remember how well a small business unit performed if the larger company failed in its mission.

I will discuss key points behind methodologies. Keep in mind that this book is not a short course in methodology selection or application, nor does it recommend any single approach over another. However, I'll suggest a framework that places quality at the focus of any methodology to provide end-to-end results – it's up to the reader to decide how to employ those teachings. My purpose is to provide a pragmatic guide that applies concepts and views into actionable items that yield immediate value. Through each chapter, I'll explain how terminology matters very little at a business or organizational level, but that an outcome-focused view of initiatives should be central to the Project Manager's efforts.

During my career, I've seen too many PMO Managers and Directors become marginalized not because they've achieved their goals, but because they've forgotten their charter: **Projects drive an organization**. Projects do not exist merely for an organization to provide executive level reporting, although important. Projects are measured mainly by their impact on an organization, and the view of technology, automation, efficiencies, workforce globalization and so forth are all included within a project manager's expertise. All should be recognized as strategic initiatives in how they benefit an organization.

Thus, I'll routinely use the term "Initiative Management" – an initiative can be as small as one project; it can encompass related projects into a comprehensive program that produces a common results; it can be the entire portfolio of work when weighed against the organization's stated goals and strategy. This view does not run counter to project management teachings and methods; it neither negates nor contradicts any of the best teachings of the project management profession. My goal in this book is to show how those teachings can be pragmatically applied to achieve that strategic direction.

Who is the Audience for This Book?

This is not a primer for new project managers learning about the discipline of project management and looking for applicable writing. While the topics introduced will find relevance and application in that work, this is not a "how-to" or teaching guide on the fundamentals of Project or Program Management. The topics of "Introduction to Project Management" or "Project Management for Beginners" are worthy subjects for discussion, but best left to many other authors who have phrased and framed it more eloquently[1].

The audience for this work consists of experienced project and program managers, corporate managers and C-Level Executives who have struggled with delivery challenges for major initiatives in their organizations. Rather than recite chapter and verse of authoritative texts from professional certifying bodies, or introduce topics as diverse as specific structured delivery methods in process-centric environments (i.e. PRINCE2[TM]), the objective is to provide a canvas for ideas driven from a strategic end-to-end view based on the product of an initiative. My objective is to propose a framework for the product lifecycle. As the book progresses, I'll dissect issues commonly found within current delivery processes that often result in failure to realize objectives.

Building on the knowledge gained from case examples and evidence of project successes, the traditional views behind delivery cannot begin and end at project sign-off, but must consider the entire product life cycle. Many organizations will discuss the question of Return on Investment (ROI) for their initiatives; ROI shows only a limited picture of the CFO's/CIO's and business-owner's overall equation. Rather, we need to look at the cradle-to-grave initiative costs that are embedded within Total-Cost of Operation/Ownership (TCO) and other approaches. While many of these lessons are staples of Information Technology project management, they have similar application to other ventures. To that end, I've included considerations in the lifespan of a product, such as approaches to quality that reduce development time and parallel activities to be considered when undertaking either traditional or iterative product implementations.

The underlying objective is to begin a conversation allowing organizations to undertake strategic approaches to managing core initiatives and delivering improved results. More controversially, I hope that the views and approaches inspire a dialog toward raising project management to a strategic align-

---

[1] Kim Heldman's "Project Management Jump Start", ISBN-978-0782136005 is a recommended reading as a primer to Project Management practices.

ment rather than a tactical competency. As such, I will provide a framework that can be applied within nearly any organization to help increase collaboration, provide seamless interaction, and improve overall customer satisfaction, quality, and productivity.

Acknowledgements

I would be remiss in not acknowledging the good work of my many mentors and inspirations along the way, and my more formal educators:

- Therese Eldred (ex-CSC), Ron Crepack (ex-Independence Blue Cross), Paul Metson (Thomson Reuters Markets Division), John Railton (ex-AXA) and Thomas Quinn (AXA) -- Five of the many managers during my career from whom I've learned much, and individuals I respect to this day for their integrity and for the range of opportunities to which they've entrusted me. I hope I haven't completely disappointed them.

- Steve Jones and Nneka Onwuemene (Thomson Reuters) – two people who stand as testament to the ethics of pragmatism in project management, and professionals I've had the privilege of managing over my career that embody truly ethical behavior.

- …And the many organizations and professionals with whom I've worked and conferred to make the findings contained in this text possible.

Every moment is a chance to learn, flourish, and expand our thinking. With that said, I'll propose considering the following thought:

"Rather than questioning whether we're thinking 'outside the box', maybe we should question whether there should have been a box at all."

Chapter 1:
Strategic Initiative Management as a Core Strategy

Why Project Management is needed as a strategic discipline

In the introduction, I mentioned my contrarian views. Those are largely productive when conventional thinking yields the same non-working and dysfunctional results. Contrarian thought examines the conventional reasons for suboptimal results and considers extraordinary ways of challenging that thought process. Here's an example of how this works in everyday practice:

Case Study #1:

I was privileged to work for a manager that confounded the trend toward offshore outsourcing by consistently structuring proposals to include precisely the work being delivered by his onshore US-based group. When the outsourcers asked the pivotal question of "How many people do you have doing the work now?" he would respond by keeping them honest and telling them to base their estimates purely on how many people they require to perform the same work based on the very detailed information he'd provided. This kept the process very honest by getting an assessment based on effort, not based on what the competitor thought would win the bid. As you might suspect, the results were very surprising.

He routinely received bids that recommended between 34 to 42 offshore resources, plus necessary overhead, plus an onshore project manager (or two) to manage the ongoing and planned work. His technique underscored how efficiently his operation functioned with a mere 8 employees, and demonstrated that an organized group with strong processes and expertise could be very cost-effective for the organization. For years, no one could challenge either the financials or efficiency of his team.

The above view challenges conventional wisdom, and it's been upheld by a number of organizations that formulated outsourcing and off-shoring plans quickly as simple cost-cutting measures without considering all ramifications. It was supported by a clear business case, metrics, and competitive bids that clearly detailed the increasing costs inherent in the decision.

I used the example of outsourcing, as it remains a popular direction with many organizations, despite many finding that the experiment hasn't worked for a variety of reasons:

- Failure to provide agreed deliverables on time or within budget/approved variances;
- Failure to address quality standards;
- Inability to address scope;
- Inability to deliver value for money (financial governance, ROI) or escalating costs due to ar-

tificial deflation and invalid financial models;
- Ineffective or inadequate communications, or poorly structured communications;
- Inadequate stakeholder/sponsor/executive support;
- Poor management, implementation, and leadership;
- Incomplete success criteria;
- Poor understanding of organizational intersects and how to manage within the organization;

Momentarily, I'll review the outcome of some well-known project audits, as well as frequently cited reasons behind those failures.

The overall rate of failure behind technology-based projects is currently projected at 68%[2]. This is a staggering number, when you consider the billions of dollars that businesses invest in projects expecting an end business benefit. In dollar terms, for every $3 spent by a US business, they would expect that around $0.96 would be properly spent. $2.04 isn't planned as a wasted investment, but it certainly could be if those statistics held consistently. As project managers, this is a number that we should especially keep in mind, given its reflection on our profession.

Now to the significant reasons why most projects fail:

- Failure to deliver on time or within budget/approved variances;
- Early abandonment, or cancellation before completion;
- Failure to address quality standards;
- Inability to address scope;
- Inability to deliver value for money (financial governance, ROI);
- Inadequate stakeholder/sponsor/executive support;
- Poor management, implementation, and leadership;
- Poor sense of charter (i.e. What is its success criteria?).

The similarities I've demonstrated behind general project failures and outsourcing failures are striking when you consider that few organizations view outsourcing strategies as projects before they become part of an organization's process landscape. The link conjoining these is that both fall within a category of initiative management. A CIO or CEO is less likely to be concerned about the arcane practices of project management taught through the years; they will more likely ask how any specific business initiative is progressing, and what issues may jeopardize the likelihood of successful outcome.

Whether an organization is undertaking a strategy to globalize their work force, streamline back-office operations, or implement a new customer relationship management software package, all have the commonality of being initiatives undertaken by the organization.

For anyone who cracked open the pages of this book believing they might find some underlying secret in "becoming a better project manager", I'll dispel that rumor now. As project managers, the belief of being evaluated solely on the management of implementation is an archaic and irrelevant view. The view we should be taking is that our worth is based on the value we contribute to the strategic direction of the business. While technology can be used as a tool, processes and business initiatives that revolve around the final product can also be considered.

Our value is increasingly judged on the overall success of the initiatives we've managed. Specifically:

- Have they reduced costs?

---

[2] Statistic taken from the June, 2009 edition of the Standish Report. The report defines 32% of projects as delivering their expected value or operating successfully. The remaining 68% of projects were defined as either "failure/stranded" or "challenged".

- Have they increased overall efficiency?

- Have they resulted in market leadership?

- Have they improved market share?

I mention these as a few; others can be contributors.

For the purposes of this book, all can be classified as initiatives. To digest these, and for the project management audience reading this, let's do a quick compendium of terms and how these might apply in the "Initiative-based" realm I've begun defining above.

Projects – Projects have traditionally been considered as temporary endeavors that deliver an end product. Over time, projects have evolved beyond the finite aspect defined by the word "temporary". Many organizations have over-time construed a project to be a complete flow from phase to phase, often continuing the lifespan of the work across a much longer iterative or phased approach. Here, we begin to enter an entirely different realm:

> *Scope Management*: Projects have a defined span, and the project charter defines their expected outcome or product. This includes the processes required to ensure that the project includes only the work required to fully and successfully complete the project, and concerned with defining and controlling the inclusions and exclusions from the project.

> *Change Management*: The vast majority of projects are subject to some degree of risk. While we'll discuss Risk Management in a future chapter later, Change Management is expected within the execution and ongoing controlling of a project. It's often very poorly described to most stakeholders, despite the essence of communication and success it is designed to achieve.

Having mentioned these, and indicated that the term project is often a poor description for an ongoing effort broken into phases, let's progress into the next definition that seeks to somewhat resolve this.

Programs – Programs are groupings of similar or related projects managed to provide improved control and other synergies not available from managing individual projects. Generally, these are multiple heterogeneous projects or sub-projects that are grouped to efficiently coordinate these into one larger goal. When I referred to the "phase-to-phase" approach taken by many organizations regarding projects, this is where Program Management should be prevalent since the resources and expertise used between phases will generally be the same, perhaps working on development deliverables or elements of a longer-term deliverable in parallel to the deliverable of one project or phase.

Most definitions are silent on Program alignment in a silo manner versus a cross-functional manner, especially if one program might have an impact on a wider set of business needs or form a supporting structure that can be leveraged and used as common tools or infrastructure. With that said…

Portfolio – A collection of work that serves a common strategic objective. That may include Programs or individual projects. Confused yet? Let's clarify. Where Programs typically provide synergistic behavior and benefits, Portfolios generally exist to address a business or strategy goal, and may include non-synergistic work.

Commonly, in the business world, a few different things happen:

1. Programs and Portfolios are used interchangeably. This is a contradictory viewpoint since a Program serves to best manage the resourcing, alignment, and overall management of several similar projects. A Portfolio aligns at a strategic business level to ensure that objectives are

achieved. By the way, this may or may not involve the management of individual projects, as noted above.

2. It leaves little room for the management of common elements that have universal use, irrespective of program or portfolio. A company's data center assets serve both constituencies, but do so neutrally whether the initiative is program-based or portfolio-based.

3. A Program – say one to replace a 100-Base-T Ethernet Network with a 1000-Base-T Ethernet network – is just that. However, multiple Portfolios of work will need to consider how this Program of work will have an impact on their strategic goals.

This applies in the real world, and I'll provide an example out of a prior organization.

I was a Global Program Manager managing the activities of 7 different business units, most with few common strategic goals between them at their individual business unit level. To make things more interesting, I managed two other individuals who were called Program Managers. Several of my project managers were actually managing significant programs of work. So was I managing projects? Programs? Portfolios? All of the above? Should I have been called a "Portfolio Manager" versus "Program Manager"?

In truth, we were managing all the above regardless of how they were named or organized. Common to all was that we managed individual initiatives, and the role I held was to bring focus around the communications, reporting, and investments being made to ensure that each initiative was successful (and those that could never achieve success were "euthanized" accordingly).

"So why aren't we viewing these as projects?"

In fact, we are. Project managers see their disciplines as project related – ensuring that the correct rigors around Charter, Scope, Communications, Stakeholder Management, Risk Management, Resource Management, and overall Change Control are effectively managed and controlled to create a a successful outcome, regardless of it being a project or initiative. So yes, these are projects, but there's a bit more than a clear beginning and end.

Managing initiatives implies a difference in view. It implies that we be more acutely aware and involved in the strategic view of an organization. The definition of "portfolio" indicated that we are seeking to achieve a "strategic objective". At a project-based level, the vision of how each individual project manager's effort or "initiative" has an impact on the overall strategic direction of the organization doesn't exist because the work is compartmentalized at a tactical level: There is no "big picture view", just work streams involved in achieving the simple objectives of that project.

At the Program Management level, the picture becomes somewhat more focused in that the pieces become clearer as they're assembled toward the strategic vision outlined at Portfolio level. Unless that vision is effectively communicated downward and laterally, it may never be understood and a single project may not be consistent with the strategic operational goals.

The Portfolio Level view provides a closer seat to the overall picture, but is often too far removed from the individual project efforts to understand the complete impact.

Just as the commonality within all of these examples are the individual projects, each element within the concept of Initiative Management is viewed as an initiative aligned with the strategic objectives of the organization. The goal of this chapter is to focus on the top down view of all of these as initiatives, organizing it using the elements of Project/Program/Portfolio Management, while adding the elements of Governance, financial benefit and oversight, quality assurance as a process, and an underlying framework of initiative management to focus on ensuring that strategic level goals are not lost at the tactically focused level.

In a separate chapter, I'll discuss experiences with **Chartering a Project/Program/Portfolio** or "Initiative" Management Organization (PMO/IMO) as well as the positive and negative views around PMO perceptions.

Case Study #2: PMO Chartering

In the introduction, I mentioned the Project Management Office that has an amorphous value to the organization, and spends most of its effort evangelizing process and reporting. In the process, it creates a sense that the project manager is a hindrance to achieving alignment with organizational strategy. As a Project/Program Manager in a company that had such a PMO, when the decision came from executive management that the PMO was not useful to the organization, the handwriting was on the wall that the value of a PMO had been removed. There was no eventual career path as a Director of their Project Management Office, or at least one based in the Information Technology Group.

Having partnered on occasion with that PMO, there was sufficient anecdotal evidence suggesting their reputation was likely deserved. Its charter was to address reporting needs, executive status, and provide advice, not to actively manage initiatives. My own experience suggested that it was mediocre on one count, and I'll refrain comment on the other 2 charters.

Root cause analysis to understand the underlying causes for the failure would be a normal course of action. In this case, the results would have likely been unremarkable and revealed a very faulty charter for the existing PMO, as well as a lack of authority or structure for its mission. As a result, no one really knew or understood the role of the PMO and it was largely dismissed as a failure. In the cases where I had interacted with the PMO, it was completely unclear what to expect from them as a value proposition. Sadly, the PMO became a source of continued comedy, and it was fair to say that no one missed its lack of presence.

Case Study #2a: PMO Chartering (an enlightened approach)

I mention this particular case example because of a role that I had taken later in my career in establishing a Project Management function for another organization.

As part of that remit, I was responsible to both a series of business units as well as a group of technology partners. Unless I asked one pivotal question and listened to the answers, my objectives would have failed before they even began. That question:

- *What are your expectations from the PMO?*

Most people insist that "success criteria" should be the driver for determining the actions and influence of the PMO role; however, that would be wrong until we had consensus on what that role would be. Only after we've gained consensus on the expectations could we ask the next question:

- *What are your success criteria?*

We must understand the envisioned role of a PMO before we decide how we can judge it as successful and place criteria around that. By creating a PMO where none had existed, we determined their expectations:

- *Governance – understand where they're spending money, how much they're spending, and whether that has the correct impact on the business units.*

- *Active Involvement – this organization expected a hands-on leader of the function.*

- *Command and Control – lead by providing visibility, expertise and implementing processes.*

- *Foster partnership – create a foundation for IT partnership with their business units by agreement on processes and interactions, methods and procedures that standardize the flow of information.*

These were four fairly simple goals. Along with those goals, the organization had some projects that were in flight but lacked leadership and management to control them, so landing or abandoning those efforts was critical. We – meaning I – suggested that we focus on getting in-flight initiatives to production before deciding on any new initiatives; then create the business case for each new project.

Later in the book, I'll discuss Study 2a and the outcomes since it serves as a good example for further information on establishing governance processes, risk management processes, formal change management, and other essentials within a Project/Program Management function.

As we progress, I'll look to share information about the functions that Project, Program and Portfolio Management serve in the context of overall Initiative Management for organizations, whether there is formal charter given to a "Project Management" function.

Q&A

The following question was posed publicly before publication in this book through public forums, and from time-to-time throughout the book, I'll share some responses I've provided to help crystallize the thought process I've used to achieve results throughout my career.

Question: P3M3 http://en.wikipedia.org/wiki/P3M3 - (Short form for Project, Program and Portfolio Maturity Management Model) Given the current economic climate is it more/less important for companies to focus on developing this PM maturity model? In other words, can you use P3M3 to target the quick wins that lead to long-term gains?

Answer: My answer may be a bit contrarian to the norms but I'll try to elaborate as best I can.

In a difficult economic climate, project management becomes more critical in a couple of key senses: (1) to promote time-to-market initiatives; (2) to effectively demonstrate how project governance can yield financial savings for the organization (prudent project selection, proper resource alignment, prudent application of process controls for financial control, etc.), and (3) navigating the tricky waters that help drive a project to the "right" level of process versus implementing something too onerous. I've noticed that too many organizations hunker down the wrong way on #3 and implement unnecessarily onerous processes that cause organizations to recoil against the notion of project management yielding positive outcomes and when times eventually turnaround, people are left with that vivid yet negative memory. A relevant project management competency within an organization needs to show how it can drive to the whims of management and the markets and deliver results best aligned with #1 and #2 above.

Sadly, in challenging economic times, there are too many organizations that don't receive the right message and communication about where PPPM fits in and the benefits derived, and tend to view the traditional PMO model as something that will slow progress and present overly bureaucratic controls with no tangible benefits, and PMO Managers as a result become vulnerable to the chopping block versus being viewed as vital to the success of efforts that otherwise not left within a reasonable degree of agile controls would run off the rails.

Part One:

Foundation Understanding

Chapter 2:
Scope, Change & Risk in Initiatives

The goal of this section is to impart insight on fundamental aspects of Project Management that are often overlooked, examine various Case Studies, and relate Q&A throughout to inject some levity into the reading experience. Let's examine some fundamental understandings before undertaking a more complex approach to navigating project waters.

Scope:

For the sake of brevity, let's pragmatically discuss the nature of a comprehensive Scope Statement and a Scope Management Plan.

Scope is a product of the description of the desired product, the charter for the initiative, as well as any constraints and assumptions. Ideally, it should include the Strategic Plan, the background pertaining to the product (e.g. is there historical information?), and the criteria for how the project was selected. Emerging from the process should be a clear definition of scope, a plan for managing it, relevant detail that will help the project team to support the scope and objectives, and a formal document outlining the project (sometimes referred to as a "Charter") which should identify an empower the Project Manager.

Having said all of that, let's discuss how scope is viewed in real-world terms, and how it relates specifically to the changing face of initiatives. In an ideal world, the Scope Statement is all-inclusive and does not change. Managing an initiative would be much easier if this were the case and everything was planned; however…

You were probably taught conventionally that changes in scope could force changes in time, cost and quality, routinely referenced as "The Iron Triangle". And that may also be the case, but…

You were likely also taught that initiatives have a finite goal and a defined product that should not change at project conclusion, but…

…"change" is the universal constant.

Think of any reason imaginable – something overlooked, unforeseen, unplanned (no matter how intensive the planning), risks overlooked – as well as factors outside of our control.

Suppose in 1999, when fuel prices in the US hovered around $1/gallon, you went into design on a new off-road vehicle that had amazing all-terrain capabilities, but a drawback of getting only 11 miles per gallon on average. In 1999 terms, that wouldn't seem so bad. In 2005, it would be disastrous with crude oil prices hovering around $140 a barrel. External factors can change the context of a project very quickly, and a change in project scope should not be viewed as a negative but as a logical reaction to market forces. If you continued with no scope change, the result would have been project management success – you produced the original product according to stated scope – but complete market failure in finding consumers as willing to buy the product.

The lesson to be learned about the "Iron Triangle" is that it is missing at least one side: Customer Satisfaction. In considering the big picture view of Initiative Management, market forces and market conditions are among them, and they can heavily influence changing customer needs. We'll discuss that shortly:

Case Study #3: Changing Market Conditions

A digital web development consultancy had spent years courting what seemed to be a prime customer who was a market leader in their industry segment. Instead of taking a very pragmatic view of Scope and Change control in managing the work for this customer, that was pushed aside to suit the whims of the customer. Compounding matters, the customer had incurred heavy losses due to a downturn in the financial markets, a series of bad investments, and a stock price that plunged to historic lows. However, management of the consultancy still felt there was a long-term strategic direction with this customer despite market conditions indicating otherwise, so they deferred other new business development.

This story doesn't have a happy ending. The project was never completed because the customer couldn't decide on scope at all, and wouldn't engage in productive dialogue on suggestions. The consultancy was paid a fraction of their fees despite massive cost and time overruns due to lack of high-level management of scope and change control. The customer wasn't able to parcel out new business when they were effectively "broke". And what was the result of the decision to court then as strategic business versus other prospective customers? Without other business in the pipeline, the firm furloughed much of its staff.

In the case cited above, no one walked away satisfied from scope discussions, because there was no support for changes in scope or flexibility that considered creative suggestions. Staff morale on the project was also demoralized. The situation was compounded by customer perceptions about their engagement that were not conveyed to the project team, besides changing a project manager mid-project without knowledge transfer.

If this sounds like the definition of your organization's normal project, let's work on changing that.

I spoke in the first chapter about the failure rate of projects, and a component of that is failure-by-design as well as failure-by-choice. Organizations often choose to strand a project asset due to changing economic conditions; in the future, they may reuse the elements of one initiative for another purpose (known as repurposing).

When considering scope for any initiative, you should take several items under advisement:

1. Review the overall impact of the scope change in line with overall strategy. What are the costs? How much time will be required? Will this have an impact on resource availability for other initiatives (this is often missed)? What is the opportunity cost or opportunity loss?

2. Is the change immediately needed, or could the product be released and the change included subsequently? In short, is there another point during the initiative where the functionality can change without adverse impacts?

3. Is there a clear business case behind the scope change?

I'll talk more about Change Management and Governance shortly.

Rational Communication of Scope Change

It's critically important that the project team and sponsors understand the precise scope of an initiative, and how Scope Changes are prone to have an impact, sometimes undesirable, on the outcome. When I discuss Change Control, I'll provide some further contributions on this important topic.

Keeping in mind that market conditions can alter the desired outcome of an initiative, and that other considerations need to be reviewed, it is reasonable to cite changes in scope when these will have a cost impact to a project. Third parties may often take one extreme or another – one is to hold the line on any scope change, and outline implications from the outset; the other may be reluctance to discuss the cost impact of a scope change, especially if there is a high-level view that the change resulted from unintended error or omission. In either case, it's critical that you establish a relationship with your initiative sponsor that permits open discussion of scope change, and include that in the Change Control policy we'll discuss shortly.

Third parties may negotiate the actual costs of a change differently than the initiative manager to negotiate future business.

It is for this reason that within the project charter, I strongly recommend that provisions be made for scope change discussions. While it's human nature to fall back on the adage of "I thought it was clear" or "I meant", verbal agreements are worth as much as the paper on which they're written. And a firm yet sincere approach – indicate that change should be expected without assigning accountability – is generally a more productive way of resolving the issue.

Helpful Hint: Discussions and documentation of Scope Changes should usually be followed in writing; the written communication can and should be captured as a project artifact.

Change Control:

I've already hinted enough about the importance of a defined Change Control process, so I'll begin with a case study to underscore the importance:

Case Study #4: Change Control

A project manager enters an ongoing effort that has been underway for roughly 18 months, managed primarily by an outside consultancy on a time & materials basis. As he quickly reviews the processes used to facilitate product changes and enhancements, he discovers a few issues. The first is that anyone with access to the Request Database can request a change. The second is that only a development lead and the change requestor ever discuss the change if there are questions or something is unclear. The third is that there is generally no business context for the change, meaning that anything can be requested for any reason, and does not undergo scrutiny. The Project Manager has soon found himself sorting through well over 1,000 change requests, most never reviewed, many lacking a clear business case, and nearly all lacking enough supporting detail.

The project sponsor is initially impressed only by the numbers, rather than the impact, and isn't comforted by the new Project Manager's desire to change the process to focus on business impact, especially when the consultancy has been focused on the customer's needs.

Now I'll continue this Case Study momentarily. What we notice above is a change in the project team forcing the new project manager to take a step back and examine whether these changes are essential. Since the sponsor is removed from the process, he or she don't see the net impact of the changes, that some may be contradictory, or that development time is being spent on areas that have little or no impact to functionality or business gain. With over 1,000 open changes and growing, there's no good way of sharing the bad news that the existing process is far too expensive to maintain, and a new process must focus on both the impact of a change and cost containment for the project.

> *The project manager goes through the changes with a designate from the business sponsor, who has a pragmatic perspective and understands the business flow. They review and rank changes, discussing their priority and impact. They begin with 2 approaches:*
>
> 1. *Address Critical priority changes, then address High priority changes.*
>
> 2. *Group changes by their functional area, and address the most business critical in order of priority to exhibit a business result.*
>
> *The business ultimately understands that 1,000 changes requires significant work, much of which yields little value, and that organizing based on business impact will yield the most tangible results. They select the second option. Remaining requests that will not be addressed are closed.*

In the case above, the initiative Manager and Sponsor/Stakeholder representative have taken an approach to thoroughly review and organize the change requests – while a painstaking process, it's one that yielded useful information – and sorted these into 2 methods. The first simply corrects things in order of a relative priority; the other that taps directly into the sponsor's pain points. The second approach held more direct appeal to a sponsor, since it recognized that many requests were meaningful, but offered a solution targeting these and focusing the development team and business group on functionality that addressed individual groups, promoting business value, and implementing logic around changes.

In a moment, I'll talk about how this impacts process quality. To continue...

> *The Project Manager proposed a process with controls around change requestors, the information required, and reviews by both business and development groups for implementation. The new process, while lengthy at first, provides an end-to-end view of the change, demonstrating the current condition, the desired condition, and the conditions that would help validate the change. Any relevant documentation and business logic would also be included.*
>
> *The process was socialized as one that would reduce the overall impact of change on the customer while providing a better baseline for quality improvement He stressed the ongoing process and cost controls that the sponsor or designate would have over changes. With minimal discussion or modification, the process was seen as a major improvement and adopted.*

At the beginning of the Case Study, we noted that the process allowed for change to occur without control, without regard for cost, and without clear business logic. The sponsor was informed that some of these changes were contradictory in nature – one change counteracted another – thereby rendering the effect of money spent in different cycles to undo development. It provided a clear example to the sponsor that resources were being wasted and the business objectives were jeopardized.

It underscored the need for a process with specific controls and approvals before development review. This resulted in cost savings on development resources and prioritization of work to target only requirements having a desired impact.

The new process also set a foundation through which Quality Assurance could be a focal point using a principle of "Test Driven Development". I'll discuss this in a later chapter on methodologies and how this can be easily applied. Business Requirements were received complete, understood, and logically organized, along with clear methods of validation. So let's resume the Case Study to its completion.

> *The revised Change Management Process provided a complete transparency trail for changes, and a documented method for developers and Quality Assurance to test the functionality before it was introduced to a customer. It also created a development environment that centered on defect reduction. Once the process was implemented, defect ratios that had been in the 40% range had reduced to 4 Sigma levels and were fast approaching Six Sigma.*

In a standard Aesop's fable, I'd be suggesting a moral behind this story. Rather, I'll outline the steps behind creating a functional change process. Some qualifying caveats are necessary:

The process I suggested does not guarantee full compliance with ITIL™ or CMM™, and is presented as a foundation framework only, or where an organization lacks a formalized change framework. This is not designed to replace an existing process, but provides a foundation for an organization instituting Change Management around critical initiatives.

Some key points to consider:

1. Ensure a standard document and procedure have been socialized for capturing changes within the initiative. In lieu of a document, electronic media can be substituted, providing access to all who need it along with prompting to review it. Specifically, the document should detail the following aspects of the change:

   a. Requestor.

   b. Priority of the request

   c. Documentation for the request. An adequate synopsis of the request with detail suitable to begin work if the change is adopted.

   d. Request rationale (market driven, regulatory, functional, technical, etc.)

   e. Parties or business groups affected.

   f. Impact of change versus impact if not completed.

   g. Parties or business groups responsible for estimating and implementing the change (those who will respond to items h-j below)

   h. Impact of the change

   i. Level of Effort – time, cost, resource.

   j. Constraints affected. This should indicate also whether this increases costs, increases resources, or extension of the initiative's delivery.

   k. Signatures for approval, denial, or deferral of the change by Project Sponsor.

2. Develop a Change Committee, and ensure that all committee members are aware of their roles. The committee should include:

   a. Representation from key stakeholder groups

   b. Project sponsor or authorized delegate

   c. Key groups responsible for estimation and delivery of tasks.

   d. Project or Initiative Manager.

3. Create a submittal process for the Initiative Manager to review changes before the Change Committee meeting. This permits a high level effort to determine ownership and impact before the committee meeting.

The following statements do bear repeating for those who are unaccustomed to formal processes around Change Control or Change Documentation.

1. Change Control is not designed to prevent or halt change. In fact it causes the entire project team to think more pragmatically about change implementation once their impact to the initiative is clearer.

2. Change Control is not designed to be onerous. Rather, it's designed to document a process that fosters initiative quality, creates an audit trail, and avoids the nagging question of "Who approved that?" within any initiative. It creates transparency and accountability.

3. It creates awareness that certain changes may be critical and worth the risk of delaying an initiative's launch; it also creates a mechanism to prioritize or defer deliverables into a subsequent phase of work, or become a recommendation for a v1.1 or v.2 of a product.

4. It fosters awareness of market forces by improving awareness of change impact against a time-to-market priority. (e.g. "Is this a feature that we need for launch, or can we add this later?")

Change Control has never been designed to be a guard against change, but a control to ensure it's done according to requirements. I mention these in later sections because they are so interrelated.

Let's introduce the next Case Study to illustrate the impact of Change Control.

> *Case Study #5: Change Control as a new implementation*
>
> *A financial information provider had been developing a product for their EMEA (Europe, Middle-East, Africa) markets for more than a year. The project showed no signs of completing since there was no rigor around Change and Configuration Management. The project managers had grown tired of tracking emails as a request audit trail to make minor adjustments to the project. The main stakeholder in Europe had been absent from the process, and took a hands-off view as long as he got what he wanted. The funding sponsor in the US was growing weary of an ongoing engagement with no end-date in sight. The development team wanted to move on to other delayed work. The new lead project manager on the effort quickly noticed that there was no change control around the project, and that virtually anything and everything was done or approved.*
>
> *Recognizing the failure, the Lead Project Manager spoke with each of the affected parties to implement reasonable controls. The goal in mind was to release a product to demonstrate value, then determine whether any further changes would be needed. The process would simply control change, not ban it altogether.*
>
> *As a result of the effort and focus, the number of changes decreased from 10 per week to only 2 for the remaining 4 months of work on the project. The difference was not that changes were viewed as negative, but they were considered based on impact; the question was asked: "Is this essential for launch?" Only 2 were deemed "launch-essential" and factored into the remaining project effort. Costs, communication, and confusion were immediately controlled, and the product was released on the date specified by the lead project manager's projection. There were no further delays.*

Why Change is Important:

As managers of any initiative, I've mentioned that the one constant in the universe is change. We should expect that the nature of a product between inception and release could undergo some level of revision. Features will be added, functionality may change, features will be cut, and the purpose of the entire project may become something entirely different.

Imagine if you were to walk into an automobile dealership and see that year's models on the show-room floor. You open the driver's door, slip into the leather seats, notice how the experience contours to you as a driver, review the performance specs, pricing sheet, options, and even take it for a test drive. This is precisely the car you want, and you're ready to sign the deal and close today.

What if this was your response from the salesperson: "Great, this gives me exactly what you want and need, and I understand all of your requirements now. I'll come back to you in 18 months with your brand new '*prototype*' that you can drive, and a few months after that, you'll have your new car if all goes well."

The expectation of immediacy and the rate of change have changed. In the example above, if you'd been on the receiving end of that, you'd probably say, "Are you kidding? You churn out hundreds of these a day, you know how to do it, all you need to do are add my options and paint it my color. Why does that take over 18 months?" They may like the car but they won't like the wait, and your customer will go elsewhere.

Change is inevitable. We should expect it, embrace it and prepare for it to happen. The customer will always change their mind. Just expect that the change may not be a negative one and may result in a breakthrough that accelerates the project, or leverages components that might have been waiting for some future use. Thinking creatively about how to meet the challenge behind change is part of the black art behind managing initiatives. As an initiative manager, here is one specific challenge in socializing change common to all: Gaining agreement ("buy-in") from your team.

Reading those last few words may have deflated the balloon or lessened the initial euphoria you had in mind, because not everyone is so adaptive to change. The challenge is to change the mindset of your team to expect and promote the thought process about change, and foster an environment where open dialogue about change is encouraged. Part of your role as an initiative manager is to use your knowledge, enthusiasm, and management capability to encourage your team to think outside typical constraints.

I introduced a term common to project management: constraints. They will always exist; just because we can dream it won't always mean that we're resourced to do it. But it doesn't mean that the constraints cannot change or be negotiated. Initial solutions might be too rigid for the new thought process. As an initiative manager, it's your job to separate the realistic from the unrealistic, and encourage the flow of information to think of new solutions.

Consider the following examples that are common in today's world:

1. Aspartame (the common sweetener known under the brand name of "Equal") was originally a candidate to be an anti-ulcer drug until a mistake led to a research chemist discovering the sweet taste of it. It's today one of the widest selling artificial sweeteners worldwide.

2. Minoxidil was originally a drug that was patented to treat hypertension, but its side effect in many patients was that it was found to slow hair loss or re-grow hair. Today, it's marketed worldwide as "Rogaine".

Both of these also employ the example of "repurposing" I mentioned earlier. By just thinking about one problem, solutions may emerge for others. Keep this in mind when explaining to your teams why you've just given them examples of artificial sweeteners and male-pattern baldness solutions.

For yet another play on words, ask your team to come up with words they could spell from the word "challenge". One of those will be "change".

Risk Management

Among the aspects often overlooked within the Project Management discipline is a thorough discussion of Risk Management. It's not that reference guides or information are unavailable on the subject, nor is the existing information on risk management insufficient.

Simply put, the belief that Risk Management is something done reactively is far too prevalent, and the profession of project management does little to assuage that concern. The result is that we de-emphasize risk within projects, give an overall passing glance toward their treatment and focus, and then are surprised when risks are realized and present issues to the project.

There was a comic strip some years back that depicted a senior manager making a statement typical of how project management tends to perceive risk. His statement? "I want advance notice of any unplanned outages." While his statement doesn't make sense on the surface, you'll probably guess – yes, I'm going to say it – that most of us have dealt with a similar such scenario when the frustration of unplanned events impacts our normal planned routine and we lack an explanation.

For a period during my career, I was designated to sit in a weekly session we coined as the "Monday Blame-Storming Meeting". The purpose was to engage a wide conference call to review outages and service failures, with a partial eye toward root cause analysis (RCA). In perhaps 3 of 10 cases, the RCA would be known in time for the meeting. When it wasn't, or for the remaining cases, the focus of the meeting quickly became a tirade of who should endure 40 lashes with the bullwhip (or worse, the verbal wrath of a company Senior Vice President). Some of us looked somewhat skeptically when that Senior VP made the following statement: "We need to get to a place where we have better forecasting of these unplanned events."

Her frustration was poorly phrased. Despite that, some of us sitting in the room understood the context behind the statement, which pointed to both a lack of risk management planning throughout the organization, and flawed contingency planning. It reminded me of that comic strip, but her point stuck with me: We needed to incorporate increased planning for known and expected risks, as well as plan contingencies.

I'd be remiss if I didn't point to the existing guides and methods for viewing the cost of a risk to an organization based on the following formula:

$$R = P * I$$

Where R = Risk Costs, P = Probability and I = Impact when the risk is realized. The Risk Costs should be factored within the overall contingency provided to your project.

How an organization manages and provides for risk events will vary typically based on the organization's penchants for budgeting and overall financial position (i.e. how tightly budgets are organized and maintained, whether budgets are routinely cut by an arbitrary number each year based on historic indications, etc.), as well as their tolerance for risk (i.e. is the organization accustomed to first-to-market initiatives where risk is common, or are they conservative in approach to new ventures).

Importance of Risk Management Planning

The central theme from this section is that Risk Management is underrated, and it's generally handled accidentally. A novice Project Manager will generally enter a project with a sense of bravado in thinking, "that won't happen to me", and that bravado will last until his first failure. It's also a very good interview question when asked about your biggest failure and the lessons learned from it, as I referenced in the Foreword.

As a novice project manager, I too have made my share of mistakes in addressing Risk Management. After enduring the tongue-lashing I received at the hands of a client, and the personal embarrassment of the incident, I quickly took Risk Management seriously as a core element within any initiative. With that said, let's review the next case study:

Case Study #6: Risk Management. Almost.

A newly minted project manager and a veteran administrator of an obsolete mid-range Document Processing platform embarked on one work-stream of a project that required choosing a method for the capture and retention of legacy documents. Since the system had suffered under a lack of maintenance for some time, and the vendor/manufacturer was slowly closing down their business operations, the project manager's company had chartered him to convert the operation to a PC-based solution using Word Processing and Desktop Publishing packages, as well as overseeing the conversion of functions previously done on the legacy platform.

To convert the existing documents, a major upgrade was required to the legacy Document Processing Platform to a newer version so that PCs on the network could directly retrieve legacy documents. Both the vendor and the platform administrator felt that the upgrade was a low-risk event. As a contingency, another conversion facility was put in place that required a dedicated PC and a cabled connection to the legacy platform, and could archive directly on a document-by-document basis. While a slower process, it required no system upgrades and was even lower-risk than a complete system rebuild. The system upgrade would continue as a parallel track.

The system upgrade was disastrous, and required a full 1.5 days to recover from the prior system backup. While it was one of the last work streams in the project, it was a black eye in the face of the project manager, and provoked anger from the client due to the work hours entailed and loss of productivity of users for the period.

As usual, there are some lessons to be learned from this case study, so let's walk through them.

1. There was a contingency plan. This was a positive and successful piece of risk planning for this event, and it averted a worse potential outcome.

2. There was a backup taken of the system before its upgrade. This partially mitigated the impact of the failure, since the environment could be recovered if it failed. Had this not been in place, the failure would have been catastrophic and document loss nearly complete.

3. Serious analysis was not given to the potential for upgrade failure. Note that I mentioned that this was a legacy platform, and that the vendor was winding down their operations in support since they had been overtaken by other, newer technologies. It would be possible that the vendor may have also forgotten issues with upgrading their older platforms. That occurred in this case.

4. Communication had broken down across the board. I'll talk about this using the case example, but I mentioned that the project manager got a strict dressing-down from the client. This suggests that the overall risk planning had been poorly socialized, and expectations were not properly set with the client. The client might not have been involved in the decision-making, or did not understand the potential ramifications.

5. Outside parties were not engaged. Such an effort is not likely unique and conferring with outside parties to share knowledge is a practice that is often overlooked. The knowledge may not exist within your own organization.

In using these case studies, I pull points from all so that the experience gained from each can provide value to others as they consider the importance of each topic.   This is a case study taken from my personal archive of failures, and was one I made early in my career as a first-year project manager. I'm thankful for that early learning experience, as I learned numerous key concepts. Failure can be a very enduring teacher.

One was risk planning and risk mitigation. In the case I cited above, I had a somewhat painful way of mitigating the overall impact of the risks that we'd undertaken and underestimated. Unfortunately, there was no mitigation plan for the dressing-down I received from the client.

The other great lesson taught was humility. Everyone is going to make some error of judgment during his or her career. This was one I felt was worth sharing to underscore that point. No one is perfect, no matter how much they try to convince you. You may often come across situations where there are few good options, and let's begin with that premise.

Risk Identification

Foremost, it is important to assemble your project team to identify and discuss risks. If the work is generally understood and within the core competencies of your organization, there may little discussion other than listing the known risks. However remote they may be, I strongly suggest that no risk be excluded from consideration or underestimated – quite often those that are overlooked will be more probable since they are more likely to be overlooked.

While important for the project team to identify risks, the Case Study demonstrates that the knowledge required to qualify and quantify those risks may not always exist within the project team. When faced with that challenge, I propose a method known as either "Delphi Technique" or "Wideband Delphi Technique" – the process is simply to assemble panels of experts both internal and external to the project team, and rather than outlining effort estimations as is done in a normal Delphi group, they review the nature of the project work and outline risk estimations based on the description of the project. A facilitator then socializes the inputs, develops a Risk Matrix that addresses these for ranking, and assigns actions and ownership.

This is a more qualitative risk analysis exercise, and quantitative measures can be assigned once each risk is rated and ranked, and risk response planning is performed.

Risk Response Planning

There are 3 general options for addressing risk responses, plus one that is not as commonly used or considered:

- Accept – acknowledging that the risk can occur, and that measures to address it are either limited or not feasible. Usually, a contingency is developed around the risk to address the ramifications of occurrence.

- Avoidance – acknowledging the risk with a plan outlining specific steps that will be taken to minimize the risk's impact to the effort. Any deviations from the planned activities to manage the avoidance are also documented.

- Mitigate – taking measures to lessen the severity of impact of an identified project risk. For instance, in the event that power might go down due to frequent thunderstorms at a critical time during the project at a location, the location may be moved or a backup power source (generator) be procured to provide continual power.

- Transfer – assigning the risk to a third-party owner who is qualified to accept it, or coverage using insurance to help offset the risk's impact.

In practice, only the first 3 responses are commonly used.

Transference of a risk is limited to contracting a third party for work, generally a contractor willing to accept a high level of risk (which is viewed by most as a mitigating action), or taking out some level of insurance against the anticipated loss. The latter option is not common and seldom referenced. Most risk plans focus on the first 3 options.

Once risks are identified, a response action should be assigned to an accountable party (i.e. "owner"). This is important to mention, since the risk owner needs to clearly understand their responsibilities and actively track the status of that risk on a routine basis. The Initiative Manager owns the overall Risk Response Plan; if a risk owner should change as a result of later discoveries during the project's lifespan, the risk owner cannot simply reassign it without the consent of the Initiative Manager.

Risk Communication

I make specific mention of this for a few reasons:

1. I mention the Response Plan and ownership. It's important that the plan be circulated periodically and that all owners report on the status of their individual items to ensure that proactive focus continues on managing risks versus reacting at their realization.

2. Reviews of the risk plan need not be lengthy, but do need to be periodically scheduled to set a leadership example to the team. For instance, if there is a weekly meeting that involves status and communication to the initiative team, alternate weeks provide a good forum to set an expectation for timing and to place the right degree of emphasis on review – neither overemphasizing nor demonstrating panic.

Risks Becoming Issues

Despite all our best efforts, accidents will inevitably happen and risks will be realized. Once realized, the risk becomes an issue for the project team and a source of stress for the initiative manager and risk owner until resolved.

As risks become issues, the timing toward resolution becomes more critical as those issues can impede progress on subsequent work packages in the Initiative. It becomes just as important to manage the issue to gain appropriate traction and support as it does to socialize the realization of the risk with all appropriate stakeholders.

Risk and Issue Owners can exhibit stress about risk realization, and it can be a natural human tendency to freeze and turn that focus only inward, thereby becoming stuck versus admitting there is a problem when help is needed.

> *Case Study #7: Risk Realization and distributed organizations.*
>
> *During the execution of a major infrastructure project, a risk that had been accepted by the project team – purely because nothing else could be done other than socializing its existence and communicating the risk across business lines – had been realized when a migration failed due to functionality that interconnected the new infrastructure and different infrastructure owned by another business group.*
>
> *Despite the best efforts of the project manager, the priorities of the other business group had been set and were difficult to change without heroic efforts.*
>
> *By all accounts, the right communication had gone forward and the right resources were on hand to handle the change, While the failure was socialized, it received little attention or trac-*

*tion with the other group since they had their own initiatives to progress; initiatives under-
taken by outside groups, while also important, took a back seat in priority.*

In this case, the solution was more of political priority than the ability of one or two key resources to
devote a couple of hours to investigate and solve the issue, which was relatively minor. As I explain
the eventual outcome of the case study, I'll tap onto a key issue within any project: Value Proposition.

It's also referred to by its common acronym: WIIFM. This is not a soft-rock radio station east of the
Mississippi River, but an abbreviation of the words "What's In It For Me?" A clever initiative manager, when given lemons, will learn quickly how to make lemonade. That's a kind way of saying that
there isn't always a good response to make a value proposition resonate with another party because,
candidly, there may be no value whatsoever to them. Dale Carnegie has written books[3] and developed
research focused around influencing skills, which you might not have realized that you need as an initiative manager. It's one of the core skills of such a role.

An effective project, program, portfolio or initiative manager needs a few key skills to address such a
situation, along with strong influential skills.

1. An ability to understand the problem and the impacts to all parties.

2. Ability to foster collaborative relationships that focus on an overall positive outcome.

3. A strong sense of the organization's strategies.

4. The options available.

5. The political facilities at his disposal that could be leveraged if needed.

6. Strong negotiation skills.

It sounds like a job description, and a couple of those lines were lifted directly from Project Manager
job specifications. As an initiative manager, you are not often given functional responsibility over
your team, but as a leader you do have access to certain types of power. The general 5 types of power
as defined by social psychologists French and Raven[4] are:

1. **Coercive power.** This means the power to punish.

2. **Reward power.** As there are many kinds of rewards, this power can be used in a variety of
    ways, ranging from an affirmation to a privilege to financial reward.

3. **Positional power.** This is the power granted by some kind of authority. This is usually func-
    tional authority over a specific resource.

4. **Expert power.** This generally comes from experience or education, or recognition as an ex-
    pert. People perceived to be experts are likely to be followed based on their knowledge and
    experience.

5. **Referent power.** Referent power comes from admiration or respect, and is generally consid-
    ered the most collaborative and influential. This power comes from character, influence, val-
    ues and integrity more than the power derived form other sources.

---

3 Dale Carnegie's "How to Win Friends and Influence People", originally published Simon & Schuster, 1936,
ISBN-13: 978-0671723651
4 French, J.R.P., & Raven, B. (1959). 'The bases of social power,' in D. Cartwright (ed.) Studies in Social Power.
Ann Arbor, MI: University of Michigan Press

In the above case study, the initiative manager may have perhaps 3 of the 5 types of power, perhaps a fourth if he has some authority to coerce or punish. However, it's far more likely that the initiative manager has purely referent power with not much else to influence the process. In a purely political sense, some combination of the above in most organizations is more likely to yield the desired result, as not all players within an organization operate on the same tactical agendas.

As we return to the Case Study, I'll introduce another key concept, which is stakeholder involvement and stakeholder communication, and while introducing some aspect of it now, I'll review more of its detail as we progress.

> *The Project Manager, unable to progress further, escalated the issue to his Program Manager, who had stronger referential power with stakeholders and other involved parties and could outline the value proposition quickly and concisely. By diligently using that power, along with some coercive power introduced by potential escalation through senior management channels, the issue was assigned a much higher priority and fixed with minor impact to the project timeline.*

In this example, 3 types of power were required: Referential, Coercive, and Positional. Referential, based on relationships, was able to get the Program Manager through the doors to the next level for quick decisions. The Program Manager used Positional power influence along with Coercive power, which influenced successive levels to collaborate toward a resolution. The senior levels of management also used positional power during the escalation process by directing their subordinates to focus on a resolution.

Ideally, use of power in all situations would be purely referential. Reality recognizes a variety of agendas, and some use of all 5 sources of power may be necessary to achieve the desired outcomes.

In the next chapter, we'll discuss the importance of Communication in the Initiative Process.

Q&A

The following was another publicly posed question related to the subject of Stakeholder Engagement, which we'll also cover in subsequent chapters.

Question: What are the 5 most valuable things a project manager can do to maximize stakeholder commitment to a project?

Answer:
1. Create a communication plan that focuses their attention to the projects in a clear, concise, and value-oriented fashion. Do not over-communicate -- ever. People will try to convince you that it's better to communicate more than less, but it only creates more noise and confusion, and diminishes the value of all communication.
2. Ensure that the stakeholder/sponsor understands the value objectives, the structure you are establishing to achieve those outcomes, and agrees by providing you the proper charter to make decisions that help realize that end goal.
3. Establish a variance threshold, or a level of tolerance at which the stakeholder feels they need to be advised (i.e. a cost variance of X%, a time-delay or change due to external forces, competing priorities) versus decisions with which they're comfortable in delegating authority.
4. Present options and solutions. Too many PM's believe it's only their responsibility to present information, rather than providing options and solutions that help achieve end goals. A sponsor will respond better to a series of recommended options, even if they do not al-

ways agree with your recommendation. At least they'll understand the thought process you gave.

5. Be the voice of the customer! Too many project managers only manage by the numbers versus taking a personal and professional/organizational/team interest in the project. Don't be a hands-off PM, but act as if you were the stakeholder yourself since you are the voice of the customer/sponsor/stakeholder. When you establish the relationship with the sponsor, ensure that they understand that you are there to be their voice; in return, you expect and require their engagement to ensure that all participating understand the Project Manager's leadership role, and provide requisite support. When a sponsor sees you sticking your neck out, they're generally more inclined to put their skin in the game too.

A real-world view suggests that a very busy sponsor of a project may for various reasons -- geography, time-differences, and over commitment of time -- be too busy to address every issue of a project. This happens very often, and you might notice my pragmatic view above that suggests (rather than throwing our hands up in surrender) checking items 2, 3 and 4. At the beginning of the effort, if you have a very busy sponsor, be realistic and have them provide either delegation authority to you or to a key member of their team. It's especially important to consider if your key sponsor is 6 time zones away, and a pragmatic solution is needed.

It's my view that the above shows more leadership and engagement with the organization's strategy than simple acquiescence.

Chapter 3:
Communication Management
(Including Project Teams and Stakeholders/Sponsors)

Let's start with talking – to define part of what will be discussed in this chapter – about communication. During this chapter, we'll discuss levels of communication, importance, frequency, content and organization. I'll begin with some anecdotes that explain the importance of the right communication at the right time. I'll also explain a few pointers about substantiating the communication with objective fact rather than subjective opinion.

People love to talk. It's part of most human nature, and only the most introverted and reclusive among us reject interaction among others. The Kiersey and Myers-Briggs Temperament Indicators[5] define each one of us into 16 fairly scalable categories, one of which is our own "introversion" or "extroversion" behavior. When managing a team, it's important to understand the wallflowers from the bumblebees – the wallflowers will blend into the wallpaper, and the bumblebees will be busily chattering and going from person-to-person. Those are the extremes of the spectrum, with most of us falling somewhere between the two.

A quick trip to http://www.keirsey.com/sorter/register.aspx will bring you to a page where you can test your own temperament.

We've also known people in our lives who believe that more communication equals better communication, and those who prefer to talk and direct rather than actively listen. During this chapter, I'll touch on many of those traits and offer pragmatic advice that I hope will help address communication problems that exist in every organization.

Globalization and Communication Challenges

Globalization has increasingly brought challenges to the initiative management for many organizations. Diverse working shifts, methods of working that follow local time zones, and a culturally diverse workforce have injected a wide set of challenges to anyone managing an initiative that crosses geographic boundaries or using a distributed working team.

In the prior chapter, I responded to a question on Stakeholder Management that was asked in a public forum. My response was taken from my own earlier experiences in managing initiatives with

---

5 Myers, Isabel Briggs with Peter B. Myers (1980, 1995). Gifts Differing: Understanding Personality Type. Mountain View, CA: Davies-Black Publishing. ISBN: 0-89106-074-X

stakeholders that were several time zones removed, as well as somewhat disengaged from the day-to-day workings of the project. My approach considered this very critical yet somewhat difficult stakeholder. By determining that his involvement would be by proxy only, we had a very candid conversation that started with my listening to his expectations and responding with my expectations to meet his requirements.

While not an easy conversation, the stakeholder in question understood my mission and provided great leeway in carrying out that charter. A few things enhanced that conversation:

1. While understanding he absolutely would not attend meetings, but would assign a proxy, it left the decision-making process with a designate who (by that statement) was given the authority to act on the sponsor's behalf.

2. We established a variance between budget and costs that was tolerable to all. We would not breach that threshold but would convene a meeting with all parties for any changes that created such a breach.

3. We agreed on the goals and success criteria for the project. I reminded him that the success criteria requires that the product launch, so it was in our mutual interest to meet that objective rather than continually delay.

4. I underscored my role in acting as the voice of the customer. Without understanding his needs, I could not be an effective advocate for him, and he'd not be satisfied with his end product. Again, because of his schedule, he deferred all voice-of-the-customer concerns to his proxy.

5. I clarified that he would receive communications from me as the initiative manager, like it or not, because he had a right to oversee and not encounter surprises. This was a method designed to keep everyone honest. He decided it wasn't a point worth arguing, and acquiesced.

So when I mentioned in my response "Do not over-communicate – ever", I truly believe that. I'll cite the literary prowess of Aesop in "The Boy Who Cried Wolf" in that the value of communication is in its purpose, audience, relevance and brevity.

- **Purpose** underscores why you're communicating with them, beginning the value proposition to the recipient. This is part of the "WIIFM" dialogue we began in the last chapter. It's critical to ensure that any communication is fulfilling that mission; if not, regroup and assess that mission to determine if the communication fulfills that mission, or if revision is necessary.

- **Audience** underscores the specific people who need information, when, and why. In a moment, we'll discuss how we can keep this organized. It's of noteworthy mention that we should not extend or remove members of the audience randomly, so that all communications are ensured of reaching their intended recipient.

- **Relevance** underscores the need for the communication to be relevant to the audience. If you are communicating a general status, a wider audience will have interest versus communicating interim fixes on an iterative development deliverable.

- **Brevity** denotes the requirement that communications have a standard format and address their points concisely. A summary should focus on key points of an initiative or status; a memorandum citing a specific issue should focus concisely on its message and consider the value to the reader, as well as predict and answer key questions. Simply put, make the information useful. "Brevity is the soul of wit." – Wm. Shakespeare.

Removing Chatter: The Communication Channel Conundrum

Communication channels expand as your initiative expands; therefore, it's important that the initiative manager sets the correct tone for how information should be organized, disseminated, and treated. Consider the following equation:

$$Y = n*(n-1)/2$$

Where Y equals the eventual number of communication channels, and n equals the number of people within the communication chain. Anyone sitting for the PMP exam can rest assured this question will be presented in some format. Therefore, if your initiative includes 20 members, $20*(20-1)/2 = 190$ potential communication channels. You can begin to see where management of this can lose control. Thus, a major reason why I've dedicated a section of this book to speak specifically about the subject.

> *Case Study #8: Controlling the message, controlling the project.*
>
> *A Director of Program Management, new to an organization, quickly learns that the discipline leads within the organization interact in a very dysfunctional manner. While they all are friendly with each other in person, meeting environments were hostile affairs, and each felt they were acting as the leader. Meanwhile, key decisions that would ordinarily take mere minutes to make – right, wrong, or in between – would tie up hours of time. When the subject of a short meeting chaired by someone else was suggested, no one wanted to invest the time, indicating that all they did was sit in meetings.*
>
> *No one dared to depict that they rarely emerged from a meeting with consensus, much less direction or decisions. The leadership of the organization was ill equipped and unprepared to manage his new direct reports, and the new Director of Program Management on board was thrust into the instant role of meeting facilitator without understanding the full background of the dysfunction, which was largely a result of their own culture.*
>
> *The impact of this dysfunction manifested itself in emotionally immature behavior in the office, and eventually client satisfaction issues with the results. It was at this point that the Director assumed the leadership role that his manager should have taken to bring order to the chaos.*

Before we discuss the case study, some of the underlying issues become clear in the description. Namely, that the leadership was ill prepared for its role in managing direct reports. Meeting facilitation was lacking – meetings were held without agendas and without a tangible goal for the meeting, as well as clear hard-stops. The emotional immaturity is also depicted in the case study. All contributed to the end problem.

The breaking point in this case occurs when the new Director "assumes" his manager's role in the absence of other leadership. Let's start from that point and work our way back through the problem.

The underlying issue is lack of supportive leadership, as well as the lack of a common charter and strategic goal. Had the organization's leadership established and enforced the expected behaviors, we could chip away at the underlying issues. If that changed, the next issues could be more readily addressed.

Issue #1 is meeting behavior: Establish the agenda, goals and objectives, and tenor of each meeting.

Issue #2 is command and control of each meeting. The meeting should have a single facilitator or leader, and several participants.

Issue #3 is meeting outputs. Since nothing was accomplished within each meeting, a template for documenting the results of each meeting would help to make each event more tangible; actions and expectations could be assigned and status given.

Issue #4 is one of resourcing. A Project Manager could have been facilitating these tasks. Notice that is not mentioned in the case study, and this is not an omission.

Normally after dissecting the Case Study, I'd cite the outcomes or end result, or perhaps what should have taken place. For this case study, let's address this issue by issue, with the final outcome at the end.

> *The assumption of the leadership role by the Director was not viewed positively by the re-maining staff, and was less-than-fully supported by his boss despite the evident need for lead-ership. Once leadership behavior and command/control issues were addressed, and docu-mentation of meetings routinely occurred, conditions improved briefly. But without continued and engaged leadership support, they digressed just as quickly.*

> *The Director of Program Management left on medical leave 5 months later with a shoulder injury. Coupled with a lack of change in organizational culture and inadequate leadership, as well as other business missteps, the organization shut its doors for good 2 days after the Director left.*

There is no happy ending here, although one could have been achieved through leadership. Without leadership and direct charter in support of the Program Management function, success is a difficult charge. We'll discuss the leadership aspects of this case study later; for now, let's restrict the case study to communication and control. This study outlines that a communication plan cannot be unilat-eral and must have the correct support and charter. Without supportive messages being conveyed, ini-tiative delivery is hampered significantly, if not completely.

I cite this example so that Initiative Managers understand the ramifications of acting without proper charter. The initiative manager must be supported with proper leadership backing.

Over-Communication: What's the Right Amount?
The answer to this question reverts quickly to the 4 characteristics defined above: Purpose, Audience, Relevance, and Brevity.

Ask yourself the following questions:

- How much communication do you receive in a single day?
- How much of it is relevant to you?
- How do you really tell the difference?

There are some simple facts around how much information the average person retains through the course of any dialogue. The maximum is about 25%. In rare cases, it exceeds that, but what anyone retains relates directly to the value we assign to that information and our frame of mind in receiving the communication. Through my career, I've encountered people who only assign a value to positive rein-forcement, and retain nothing about corrective, constructive, or potentially negative commentary. This makes the communication process even more challenging as the listener clearly is only retaining those aspects that focus on positive self-image.

So before we truly begin to answer this question, let's talk about the elements to effective communica-tion:

The "Sender-Receiver" Model

It is the responsibility of an initiative manager to ensure that communication is both receiv
derstood. The sender is the active participant in such a model, and receiver is less actively participating. While there are ways of changing or bolstering the model, let's talk about some of the challenges.

Foremost, one party is responsible for communication being understood. This places greater pressure on the sender to adhere to the 4 principles above to ensure the message is clear, concise, and relevant. If you've ever had a neurological test, an IQ test, or perhaps a test for Alzheimer's, the person administering the test may have asked you to remember a sequence of items: For example, a shoe, the number 7, ice cream and a table. They'll return to asking you to recall those items after a certain period has passed to determine if you can clearly remember those items. If you think about it, we do a similar but much more complex test everyday by providing instructions and information to our work teams. We expect they'll remember the information they've been told verbally, or ask them to recite it back.

I recall a job that my father had for several years in Appliance Repair where his assignments were dispatched via two-way radio. He would call in for his assignments, and the dispatcher would tell him "Who, where, what, and any other descriptive information," much like a police dispatcher. My father would respond back with an acknowledgement of the assignment and location, and the numbers 10-4 – in radio-jargon, this meant "OK" or message understood. But while he was listening to that information from the dispatcher, he'd be writing the details on his clipboard to keep a clear schedule of his day's work in view. I know this because my father did a "take your child to work day" long before any such formal tradition was created, and I tagged along a few times.

In both of those illustrations, I outline some key points: Feedback and acknowledgment.

Feedback gives the receiver a chance to respond with their recollection of the message sent; in other words, what was "effectively received". It helps define any gaps in understanding or any missing parts of the message that require clarification or reinforcement.

Acknowledgment occurs when the message was received, understood, and correctly interpreted back to the sender. It tells the sender that the message was delivered and clear. Let's call this the "Return Receipt" that we normally request when we send important mail and want evidence that it was received at the address based on their signature.

Both of these must occur within the Sender-Receiver Model for it to be effective. This is an often-overlooked element to the communication process. Dog-ear this page in the book if you would like to refer back, as it's critical to understanding the next topics in this chapter.

Myth #1: Over-Communication = Good Communication

False. Over-communication is a clear indicator of ineffective communication. Over-communication quickly equals chatter. The more chatter, the less information is retained. In a society where people are quickly overloaded with information, 50 emails in one day about your initiative will render any one of those emails as less-than-meaningful. Several issues could be lurking beneath the surface to cause the need for this:

- Lack of team engagement or support
- Lack of communication clarity
- Lack of credibility
- Cultural issues (whether corporate or geographic)
- Lack of a defined communication plan

- Competing agendas
- Personality conflicts

Through this book, there are a few that I'll discuss in greater detail. I've listed some specific bullet points that hopefully open a more productive dialogue about team-building, interaction, and something I'll kindly refer to as "leaving your ego at the door".

Despite the contention that some people would rather be over-informed, it becomes clear that information can create a swirl of responses that can become uncontrolled within minutes if not hours in an age of electronic email.

Case Study #9: Roles and Expectations

The new Project Management Lead at one of the practices of a Web Development Consultancy noticed one of his Project Managers struggling with deliverables, deadlines, and overall engagement. He observed several meetings, and had discussions with others in the firm. When he asked each of them their view of the underlying problems, the answers ranged from "(person) should know this already" to "I don't have time to repeat information" to "I can't attend everything" or "we don't accomplish anything through meetings". The Lead then asked one more important question: Did anyone sit with the Project Manager one-on-one and discuss any of this.

The answer was always "no".

When I began outlining this case study, my goal was to demonstrate some of the issues listed within the bullets. Everyone had a reason to blame the Project Manager for some failure to get traction on delivery, yet no one was taking action to support the project manager's efforts in attempting to do so. Each of team members had their assigned project accountabilities, yet placed no importance on team engagement or support. Let's continue.

When the Lead asked to see the Communication Plan for the troubled projects, he was greeted with a blank stare. "This is not something we've done before." At the heart of the problem was a lack of clear definition around how communication should be facilitated. This contributed to a loss of credibility for the Project Manager. Further along, competing agendas and personality conflicts were the outcomes of those interactions.

There was no positive outcome other than starting anew with a Communication Plan governing project engagement, and setting clear responsibilities and expectations going forward. Such a plan needs clear support from management and sponsors to be successful. Implementing such a plan is not a panacea for addressing competing agendas or personality conflicts, nor did it affect those in this case study since the damage was already done.

Further on in this Chapter, we'll discuss the extension of this point to setting the correct expectations from inception, and how that should be most effectively accomplished.

Myth #2: Communicating Extends Value to Everyone

False. I wish I had a nickel for everyone who genuinely thinks this adage is true. This comes under the heading of "Audience" out of the 4 qualities of communication. Having managed large global teams, I made it clear to my surrounding contacts that I need not know about everything, but rather only those areas that directly concerned me, my staff, my functions, and the clients I served, or anything that would affect those. It restricted a lot of noise.

During my career, I worked for one large organization that had someone we'll call a Lead Implementation Manager. Although that was his title, and he was viewed as an expert within the organization, a view of his overall day revealed that the following were his responsibilities:

- Attending Conference Calls
- Redistributing emails
- Reviewing status reports

Very simply, he was viewed as an expert purely based on the chatter he created using the "Forward" and "Reply to All" buttons on his email client. He was a pure fountain of information, none of which he created. I learned to quickly dispatch his emails into a separate folder, which during one day collected over 80 separate emails, making the volume impossible to manage. This was an organization that consisted of 31,000 employees, so you can imagine the result if everyone subscribed to the same method of communication.

Many of us were relived when his email system was migrated to one with restrictive limits on how much mail he could keep. Our share of his mail decreased dramatically. Of course, that's not always an answer, though the anecdote underscores how information turns quickly into chatter.

More About Globalization...

I started this discussion mentioning the impact of Globalization on communication, as well as the impact of having distributed teams. While it opens up great possibilities for how organizations can now leverage staffing across geographies, it also creates a series of challenges to effective communication. Let's explore some of those in more detail:

Teaming. In a Globalized effort, it's very likely that teams will not meet one-another on a face-to-face basis, but the work will be divided into parts that can be managed across distributed teams. It is naïve to think the story simply ends there. Very often, teams are cobbled together using people across the world that must interact and exchange both their ideas and deliverables. When a project is formed and communication plan drafted, it's important to describe and outline a chart of the team so that team members can understand their interactions and responsibilities. I highly recommend an intended kick-off between members of the team within a global effort once they have been given their roles, so they have a chance to interact through video or teleconference. This sets the foundation to normalize quickly and helps improve performance.

In addition, it's human nature to interact much differently in email than by voice or when you can see the other person. The investment in orderly team forming will pay benefits as the initiative progresses.

Process. It's important that you define a process that governs communication, written interaction, reporting, and workflows across the project. Quickly standardizing communications between teams, as well as setting processes for capturing documentation, quality control, change requests, and all matters related to the project will set the correct methods of working for the entire team, avoiding later confusion. Cultural differences can also be overcome by having a defined process for interaction and clear templates that remove ambiguity.

I once worked for a manager who described a specific culture as simply relying on constant direction, or mapping out step-by-step how something should be completed, using a repeatable process. They would follow directions well, but would be stuck on the thought process when asked to explain or create a process. His actual insight was stated a bit more colorfully and not suitable for printing. However stated, many cultures are far more comfortable in following a very tightly controlled and defined process than in working without constraints. Clear step-by-step outlines of actions can produce better results.

Cultural understanding. Please keep in mind that this book is being written from the point of view of an American. In a global perspective, most cultures find Americans to be very direct people. This can be good or bad, and can affect communication unless this is explained when working in geographic regions whose communication style and culture is much less direct. For instance, in some cultures it is considered rude to ever say "no"; nodding one's head up and down means only a polite acknowledgment; and saying "I don't understand" is thought to be inconsiderate. Americans are often viewed by other cultures as confrontational. Before beginning any effort in a global setting, it is important to understand the following

- Local customs and culture. This can frame how you should expect to interact for optimal success in your effort.

- Mutual expectations. This frames how you should communicate with one another, and set the expectations around deliverables, deadlines, and overall accountability. While it's helpful for Americans to understand other cultures in our interactions, it's equally helpful for us to educate on our culture and expectations, and how our words and actions should be interpreted.

Accountability. I mentioned expectations in the previous point for a reason. While it's part of understanding the culture, it helps to frame the criteria for managing the initiative, raising issues, and handling open communication. A deadline remains a deadline, and if missed can result in problems for other tracks of work within the initiative. Throughout this book, we'll often mention establishing *success criteria*. This should be discussed with your global teams in complete candor, letting them know that they have a responsibility to the team, culture notwithstanding, to interact as the project defines.

I mention this for a reason, as I've seen globalized initiatives fail due to a lack of understanding of cultures and expectations. The results included disjointed and dysfunctional communication, missed deadlines, and flawed deliverables to name a few. Many organizations continue to struggle with this, even those that have established presence around the globe. Understanding this can mean the difference between initiative success and catastrophic failure.

Defining the Communication Plan

The answer to this question is not "the plan that defines how we'll communicate", but goes into somewhat more detail than a simple answer.

A solid Communication Plan need not be burdensome or pages long, but should define the methods, frequency, and audience of communication. The initiative sponsor and Initiative/Project Manager are defined in the overall Charter and Project Plan Document, which we'll talk about shortly.

Specific items defined in a comprehensive communication plan should include:

- **Change Log** – retains historical tracking of changes to the document

- **Project Identification Section** – captures any unique identifying information about the project (project number, tracking data for any Project Portfolio Management System), document ownership, Business Unit, Start/End Dates

- **Personnel Inventory** – captures the roles and contact information for each member of the project team, stakeholders, project manager, program/portfolio managers, PMO, and sponsor

- **Role Inventory** – defines the responsibilities for each member of the project/initiative defined above

- **Documents & Reports** – contains a listing of individual documents, including status updates/reports/artifacts associated to the project, and key communication deliverables; explains the definition and purpose of each; identifies the audience for each; identifies the specific target date or recurring dates/times for each; defines the method of distribution and/or define a location where the information can be obtained (Web URL, Server, PPM System, etc.)

- **Meetings/Presentations/Conferences** – as with the above, contains the purpose for the meeting and a general/high-level agenda; the audience for the meeting; the dates & times or occurrences if ongoing; the meeting method or logistics (i.e. video conference, conference call, face-to-face meeting, etc.)

The initiative manager, who will update this as needed, owns this document. As a project/initiative progresses, it is possible that some entries in the communication plan may become less frequent and some may increase in frequency. Any changes need to be communicated to the affected parties, and be captured as artifacts within the Communication Plan.

Every project team member must see this, without exception. I've witnessed instances where the person responsible for leading a particular track of work will dictate how the team receives communication; when that person suddenly becomes unavailable, chaos and an information void ensues. In sending this to everyone, be friendly but firm in expressing the need for this and the benefits derived from everyone's understanding.

Now that we've discussed communication theory, I'll provide some thoughts behind mediums for ensuring good team communication practices.

Instant Messaging (IM). Organizations have varied views on the permission of Instant Messaging (IM) protocols within their environments, and with good reason. While the underlying technology improves and allows people to be in constant and free contact around the globe, it is not a completely secure technology (for that matter, neither is email) and for some organizations under regulatory supervision, it may provide an opportunity to leak confidential information quickly. I've seen IM work very well in organizations, and become a distraction to productivity and attention. While it contains its drawbacks and isn't for every organization, for those with fewer restrictions or a more relaxed atmosphere it can offer productivity benefits. (I'll speak about meeting behaviors later)

Video Messaging Services. There are a number of services that offer the ability to use even a simple Webcam connected to a computer to broadcast good quality video across broadband connections. I'll refrain from naming or endorsing products within this book, but a Web Search will quickly disclose a number of utilities that will fill this requirement adequately. For remote teaming, it also helps bridge the divide created by distance, and creates a friendlier and more collaborative atmosphere largely because interactions are more face-to-face. Some similar concerns from my discussion of IM services also apply here, so you should consult your technology organization's policies and procedures on use. Also, many of these services will require access to specific Internet Protocol (IP) ports that your technology group may have blocked to traffic to help secure their environment. Discuss your requirements to help ensure that your use of such a tool does not place your company at security risk.

Teleconferencing/Video Conferencing Services. Perhaps the widest used of any of the tools, and the most basic since it requires minimal setup for a wide audience. You should check with your company's purchasing managers or appropriate personnel (IT group, Administrative personnel, phone personnel) to discuss use of such a service. Most services in their host country provide a local or toll-free (free phone in the UK) access number, as well as a code to access your particular conference if it is unattended (self-hosted). Make absolutely certain that the service you are using provides for a local access number for remote teams, or determine what options are available from the service provider.

Online Presentation Tools. Without naming names, there are many good tools that support demonstrations or presentations for a remote audience. A search of the Web will reveal many of these products. Many also allow remote collaboration or transferring control from one user to another for longer presentations involving a dispersed audience. Anything from PowerPoint or Keynote presentations to product demonstrations to Web walkthroughs are possible using combinations of these tools, and many will accommodate all the needs you require. Before selecting, see what is currently available through your organization and what can be supported within your infrastructure. Many of these tools may also be used as a Hosted Service/Software-as-a-Service where none of the content or maintenance resides with your internal IT staff, and are a good option if cost control and overhead are important. Most providers will also furnish functional demonstrations for prospective customers to become familiar or acquainted before a purchase or hosting decision. This should absolutely be considered if multiple locations are being leveraged in a globalized initiative.

Good Meeting Behaviors

A few bullet basics surrounding Teleconferences/Video Conference good behaviors:

- Agenda mandatory. Make sure that you are following an agenda and that all participants are kept apprised from time to time via a verbal prompt ("Next agenda item is…") or some other queue that will keep the meeting on track.

- Ensure there is one chairperson who will run the meeting and document any issues or summarizing points (preferably, delegate a scribe so that meeting progress isn't slowed by note-taking).

- Be clear but succinct. Phone lines often prevent the speaker from hearing others contribute when needed or interrupt when appropriate. Be conscious of that while speaking, and do so succinctly allowing time between speech bursts for others to comment. This trait is a little more pronounced over Voice over IP (VOIP) networks that may delay transmission briefly due to routing and packet switching.

- Remove distractions. Unless the meeting involves a live presentation (next topic), the meeting chair should insist that laptops be closed so that they don't detract from the flow of the meeting. In addition, it can be perceived as rude.

- Provide for wrap-up and summary. In the second bullet, I suggested that someone scribe the meeting – at this point, he or she should read back the items discussed, actions, ownership, and status or timeframes involved. A five-minute wrap-up is customary, and should be included in the agenda (an AOB or Q&A item is sufficient).

- Timing. If the meeting is about to run over, quickly poll the room to determine if further discussion is needed or if others have commitments immediately afterward.

- Make sure that your agenda is not "hijacked" or you've unwittingly ceded control of the meeting to someone else's agenda, by politely but firmly reminding that the agenda of the meeting has been established, and the procedure for adding agenda items before the meeting. For those wondering why that was my first point, this is one example.

- Squelch side conversations that may occur in the meeting. A diplomatic way of doing this is either to point out that multiple conversations are distracting attention away from the speaker's point, or more to the point asking the other party if their sidebar can wait until the conclusion of the meeting. If those don't work, interrupt the speaker and stop the conversation to bring attention to the bad behavior. Supplemented by a comment such as "Pardon me, are you finished?" or "If your conversation is critical, please take it outside the room", the sidebars from will generally cease allowing the chairperson to assert control of the meeting.

- Ensure that progress is being made against the agenda by holding to times. This means that when conversation topics are getting sidetracked, action the participants with a follow-up shortly after the meeting to resolve.

- Summarize all meetings with a written follow-up based on the Communications Plan as quickly as possible following the meeting. If there is an area of dispute, ask that someone "respond directly to the author" to clarify – thereby avoiding any confusion that a mass reply might trigger.

Bad Meeting Behaviors

Now that I've covered Good Meeting Behaviors, let's also focus on behaviors that should be discouraged.

- Distraction behavior. If you noted my fourth bullet point above, you'll understand why I've placed this first. A mobile workforce with portable devices and wireless networking has enabled us to instant message, web surf, and use meetings as time to do other tasks that detract from the purpose of the meeting. A former colleague of mine found a subordinate checking Cricket scores on the Web during a very useful presentation. It became a career-limiting move for the offender. Answering IM's or email during important discussions is also a distraction – believe it or not, most humans cannot multitask.

- Late and lax meeting start times. This is rewarding the behavior of showing up late versus promptness. It likely takes two meetings before the reality of on-time arrival becomes habit. Make sure you start no more than a minute behind schedule as a grace period; you're otherwise eating into important time.

- Sidetracking. I've worked with some masters of the art of confusion who use any opportunity to spin a meeting or subject out of control until the original topic has been forgotten. Set the rule that if it wasn't on the agenda, it isn't being discussed. Be friendly but firm about that, reminding them of the procedure for updating the agenda.

- Interrupting the speaker. Briefly interjecting on the interrupter to suggest that they hold their thought until the person speaking finishes generally works in most cases. If the behavior continues, be more candid and direct by sidetracking the interrupter, admonishing, "In order for the meeting to progress orderly, I really need you to hang tight until the current speaker finishes, and I'll be happy to recognize you afterward."

- Mobile Device abuse. We've all seen the person who constantly pulls out a mobile device to check on anything more urgent (or interesting) than the meeting at hand. If you have not otherwise set a rule about this during important meetings, a suggestion to break people of the habit is to suddenly refer to them during the discussion -- it will get their attention, although it won't engender you to them. Otherwise, if the individual is truly ancillary to the meeting, concede that you understand his tight schedule and if something else seems pressing, he can certainly be excused and informed of the outcomes later.

- The control freak. I've been witness to some embarrassing situations when such a person has been publicly admonished, or clearly directed to "sit down and shut up" by a superior. The control freak is another version of the 'hijacker' I mentioned a few bullets back, and must be reminded of their role and position in the project. Politely but firmly assert that you'll keep to the standing agenda of the meeting; if that presents an issue, arrange to speak privately after the meeting. Then follow-up by approaching them with the reminder that you've scheduled and are responsible for chairing a productive meeting. Remind them also that they probably wouldn't care for their own meetings being taken-over in such a manner, and ask that they extend you the same courtesy. It's a firm but friendly way of emphasizing the behavior and tone that needs to be established.

- The meeting windbag. We've all encountered them – he or she is the individual whose car doesn't need airbags because he or she comes equipped with their own. Simply put, the windbag will say in 10 minutes what could have been said in 10 words. This is where you can take a bit of creative license in keeping a meeting on track. Given my personal flair for sarcasm, which may not go over well but will certainly drive a point, I've listed some clever (or sarcastic) options below:

  o "I'm sorry (name), you've probably lost us on the way there. Is there a 25-words-or-less version of that?"

'That's 10 minutes I'll never get back, can you shorten that so everyone gets the essence of the point?"

"If there was a point to be made there, I'm not sure I heard it. Can you summarize that in response to the meeting minutes we'll be issuing as a clarification?"

o   "Can you condense that into a Cliff's Notes version, please?"

…and while I could suggest even more sarcastic responses, I'm sure we can think of our own. The point simply is to change the behavior of the more long-winded speaker to come to a more concise distillation of their point. In a friendly manner, have a sidebar with the individual, invite him/her for coffee, and start by explaining how valuable his/her input really is, but that his/her points would be much better adopted if expressed concisely. Don't shut him or her down, but you do need to keep meetings on track.

- Lack of summary/lack of clear conclusion. When scheduling any meeting, the value proposition for the meeting should be clear to everyone. If the participants leave and have neither a sense of accomplishment or decision, nor any tangible reference that outlines and captures the discussions and decisions, it undermines the value of future meetings. Again, this underscores the importance of post-meeting recap, actions, and outcomes.

Some Additional Points

I've outlined the meeting behaviors to be encouraged and discouraged. Let's also reinforce behaviors to manage initiatives in line with good communication and example setting.

In my role with a prior organization, I suggested that my direct reports use the "Two Foot Rule" for any meeting that did not include an agenda. Very simply, they had two feet they could use to leave; it helped reinforce the behavior that I instilled that every meeting have a discussion agenda of what was expected.

How many of us have attended meetings where we said to ourselves at its conclusion, "That's an hour of my life I'll never have back"? Even one is too many. As leaders, it's up to us to set the standard for ensuring that our communications, including meetings, are productive events and not merely excuses for avoiding actual work.

Expectations

In the beginning of this Chapter, I began with the premise of defining the value of communication in the right amount, format, and structure to provide value to its intended recipient.

There is no single stylistic formula that works universally in all situations, so that segues into establishing expectations and goals with the project teams, the Initiative Sponsor and key stakeholders. There are many ways to accomplish this.

1. **Ask**. It's very simple, but your sponsor or stakeholder may take a more hands-on or less hands-on approach to the initiative. They may simply request status reports and escalation only, or be too busy to accommodate routine meetings. The question needs to be asked and a reasonable and workable solution is required from your Initiative Sponsor. As mentioned previously, ensure they understand that success requires their tangible and visible support, whether by chartering you to act on their behalf, or delegation to another member of their staff.

2. **Offer**. As an experienced initiative manager, you'll have constructive feedback to offer on best approaches. Consider that the sponsor will more likely appreciate having a cafeteria list of options presented for their review versus being asked for a decision without the benefit of

informed guidance. Most sponsors appreciate someone presenting an issue with a choice of solutions in hand.

3. **Listen**. Presuming that most people are basically honest, and that all desire success, listening actively to the areas about which they care most and understanding their motivations will reveal much about their concerns. Some sponsors may express concern over team morale, others strict cost control and transparency, and still others potential risks, to name just a few. When discussing these, understanding the key motivations and business conditions driving the initiative (i.e. what is the business case?) is important. It's even more important to actively listen to and understand their response – both what is said and inferred from the conversation.

It's been stated that nearly 90% of a project manager's time is spent in communication. For that 90% to be productive, much of it will be listening to and processing information, and engaging in "active listening".

Active listening provides a structured way in which undivided attention is focused on the speaker, and listening is accompanied by clarifying and processing – often by recapping or rephrasing the speaker's words or expressing questions directly related to the speaker's specific topics or key points.

Active listening is not simple acknowledgment or placating the speaker. It requires the listener suspend his or her own opinions to understand the speaker, and thereby process that information in a non-judgmental manner. My experience has suggested that too many people are simply awaiting their time to speak or ask predetermined questions they feel are important – though they may be, by placing the wrong emphasis on the conversation, the listener will likely miss an important piece of information. Often the buried treasure in the conversation will provide valuable clues toward how to approach the project.

I've spent significant time and verbiage discussing the importance of communication to reinforce the concept that effective communication is neither easy nor always controlled. If approached with an open mind and the correct tools, it can be the difference between a dysfunctional project and one where customer and project team satisfaction are paramount. Much of this has been background intended to provide the foundation for the remaining tools to further an initiative. I'll also provide some suggestions that should be considered to foster initiative success.

Responsibility Assignment Matrix (RAM): You may hear this term associated with a Communication Plan. It neatly identifies several items for both the Initiative Manager and his or her team:

1. It defines the initiative/project roles to a level where each person understands their specific responsibilities and accountabilities.

2. It defines Problem/Issue behavior, and how it should be effectively handled, by whom, and when.

3. It should define the escalation paths. For instance, if an issue is stalling project/initiative progress or priority calls are needed, it defines the parties for immediate escalations. Another example, all software developers might have an escalation to a software development lead/manager/director who has the authority or autonomy to make decisions that help initiative progress.

The concept is simple even if the name is confusing. It's often a component of a Comprehensive Communication Plan. If you've chosen to contain this information within a spreadsheet format, individual tabs may contain the RAM data.

RACI Charts: This is often also referred to as a RAM, though with a twist. RACI is an acronym defined from the four letters that identify the level of an individual's involvement with the initiative. As follows:

- **Responsible**. Normally, the person(s) assigned or charged with a task, deliverable, or work package.

- **Accountable**. Generally, the person who is accountable for completing a work package, task, or deliverable. He/she may also be referred to as an **Approver** since the role includes some element of sign-off on the deliverable to ensure it meets defined criteria. There is one person assigned as **accountable** to avoid confusion among multiple parties.

- **Consulted**. Someone whose opinion might be sought as an expert, or who is asked about a deliverable or work-package. Some tangible examples of these include:
   o   Subject Matter Experts
   o   Industry Experts
   o   Legal Advice not known by the Initiative Team
   o   Technical Experts/Technical Consultants with specific knowledge
   o   Others with experience in the type of initiative being undertaken.

- **Informed**. Someone who is advised on progress. Unlike the **consulted** role above, there generally exists only a status or reporting communication with that individual, whereas the **consulted** party would actively be engaged in dialogue.

A common misconception is for **Responsible** and **Accountable** to be confused as identical. For clarity, they are not. A more tangible example cites project sponsorship – the initiative sponsor may be responsible for the business requirements behind an initiative, while business analysts are accountable for completing the work defined by that business requirement and/or elaborating it toward further clarifications by the sponsor. In a smaller initiative, the sponsor may hold both roles, though this is uncommon.

Remember that a RACI Chart is designed for consumption by the entire Initiative Team, and helps them to understand their individual roles within the initiative. Some Initiative Managers believe that RACI Diagrams or RACI charts are a "must-have" item for any project. This is debatable and dependent on the overall maturity of your organization. Consider the following when deciding if a RACI Diagram is needed:

- Size of the initiative – if this is a smaller initiative than standard, it could be considered overkill; if it is larger, more complex, and has more moving parts, it might be found as helpful.

- Audience – your audience should understand it without extensive explanation. If this is something that makes logical sense and demystifies the responsibilities of an initiative, it could be worthwhile; if it confuses people and requires constant education, it quickly hinders progress and should be excluded from consideration.

- Maturity of your organization – if your organization is unaccustomed to seeing multiple charts, diagrams, or mountains of documents, they may be slow to adopt or not understand the benefits. If your organization's maturity is improving, this might help in continuing overall process maturity.

These decisions will be subjective, so I encourage caution in considering the communication method. The responsibilities for each team member need to be clear and understood, whether by RACI, RAM, or other means. Make certain the communication does not undermine or confuse the message.

What's In a Name?

"What project are we talking about?" Ever heard this complaint? "Several people referring to the same project being called several different things." Welcome to the world of communication, where language may be used to describe the same thing in different ways. It happens very often with projects, and multiple people can find themselves further confusing the matter when they believe they're referring to the same project under different names, or different initiatives entirely.

It's human nature to require a common point of reference – a number (especially if the project is part of a Portfolio Management System that treats each project with an account number) or a commonly known name. It reduces confusion, and makes the performing organization and sponsor more cognizant of the initiative's importance. As a result, they pay greater attention to communication.

Formatting Consistency

"What type of document is this?" It's a common complaint that someone should understand what they're reading before they read it. For example, this book references a Strategic Approach to Initiative Management, so the reader understands that by reading it, they should be able to learn something about how to effectively manage an organization's initiatives. Not to be confused with a recipe book, or a reference manual on repairing home plumbing disasters.

Documents will not always look exactly the same based on their content. Many organizations have adopted templates or a "style guide" – something in the creative professions that has been used for years to help define the general look and feel of a document, Web Page, or other organization literature to carry forward the specific branding of that organization (be it use of logos, use of typefaces, and so forth). Ensure that you do not vary so much from that convention that people look at your initiative documentation and discount it as not something of organizational importance.

Also ensure that the purpose of the document is clear in its opening. For instance, a Change Management document should be clearly identifiable. A Weekly Initiative Report should be recognizable. If your organization has a division that handles corporate communications, ask them for a copy of their style guide and any templates that may be useful for this process; otherwise, ensure that the style you select is consistent enough that it engages the reader to understand quickly the type of document they are reading and it's importance.

Kickoff Meeting

Normally, in a book that describes how to effectively manage an initiative or project, this would lead the discussion. However, I've placed this last since a thorough understanding of the tools, approaches, and issues is necessary to understand the keys to creating a successful Initiative Kickoff. There was a reason I had you read through all the information first, then understand how it should be applied.

The Kickoff serves a number of key purposes for the initiative, along with setting the tone, leadership, and official naming. It identifies the team, roles, strategic objectives, and the criteria for success. It outlines why the initiative is being performed; the importance to the organization; the organization's commitment to the initiative (usually as part of the alignment with larger strategy); the expected timeline and deliverables; the team membership; the key stakeholders and sponsors; and the general communication surrounding the initiative.

It gathers everyone involved aligning them to the common goal. It's also a good opportunity for everyone to get acquainted with one another, the sponsor of the project, and with the initiative manager. A well-organized Kickoff sets the right tone for the remainder of the initiative, and emphasizes the importance of the Initiative Manager as leader of the working group. Now why does that need to be emphasized?

Everything we've said until now serves to establish the Initiative Manager's authority and role in fostering productive communication. A Kickoff meeting with the initiative sponsor in attendance to reinforce that message – that the initiative manager is the "voice of the sponsor" – is crucial to framing that the leadership role has been decided. It is important to differentiate how the contributions of the initiative members differ from the accountability to deliver results applied to the Initiative Manager. This is the most opportune time for the Initiative Sponsor to help in establishing that authority, and often quells disputes on the subject at later stages.

It also sets the foundations for familiarity and respect of others by establishing the importance of the initiative members' contributions while not coming across as a Pep Rally.

In decades of managing initiatives, I'll close this Chapter on Communication with the following thoughts:

1. Too many Initiative Managers view the Kickoff as superfluous and optional, assuming everyone understands the nature of the initiative and its importance to the organization. Don't make that assumption.

2. Too many Initiative Managers don't recognize this as a time to organize people around a common goal by missing that opportunity. Don't fall into this trap.

3. Too many Initiative Managers miss the opportunity to fully address and promote the initiative, and are later asked questions by key stakeholders of "when did this start", or "why should I devote time to this", questions that would have been answered had they held a Kickoff Meeting to impart a common understanding. An hour of time invested in conveying the message will resolve untold communication conflicts later.

4. Initiatives that have visibility and a clear consensus are far less likely to be cancelled or postponed due to the visibility given them. A Kickoff develops support for the initiative versus ambivalence to it.

Those are 4 important reasons to ensure the opportunity to set the correct foundation isn't ignored.

E-Mail

I've covered an entire chapter on communication, but reserved e-mail for last because it could comprise a chapter of its own, in much the same way that email can get a life of its own.

When companies began to take note of email systems and implement them in their enterprises, little did they study or understand the ramifications of what it would or could do, positively or negatively. I've watched organizations squander time on email banter between people who sit no further than an arm's reach away. Consider also that the average typing speed of a nonprofessional typist is likely between 20-30 words per minute – usually higher for transcription and lower for composition. My father, while a 24-year computer user, never types more than about 8 words per minute since he doesn't know or recognize the layout of the keyboard.

By comparison, people speak at somewhere above 120 words per minute. Joie Chen, the former CNN Anchor and CBS News Correspondent, was clocked normally speaking at above 200 words per minute, very clearly. If you use those examples, we communicate between 5 to 8 times faster by interpersonal communication than writing. While it's not always efficient to convey a message verbally to each person, there are certain appropriate places and practices behind email use.

Organizations have extensive policies governing the types of information that may or may not be communicated via email, retention policies, and storage limits enforcement. While they clearly speak to the logistical types of "do's and don'ts", they're usually silent on how each person should to use email in their own organization.

Case Study #10: "Just the facts, ma'am, and just to the people that need them."

Imagine managing a Program Management group in an organization that has quite a dysfunctional culture. Now add to the noise and confusion a veteran of the organization brought in to assist an inexperienced Senior Manager, a dysfunctional team, and a Program Management Group trying to deliver against those challenges. Already, this is a challenging environment in which to manage communications.

Two people are charged with submitting a status report every two weeks: The organization veteran and the struggling Senior Manager. They submit a combined status report to their management to outline progress and shed insight on those areas that need attention. It's within one of those reports that the organization veteran writes some subjective and unprofessional commentary about struggles with the Program Management team. The company had tailored communication lists, each containing members – Company – Executive; Company – All; Company – Location, etc. Whether it was accidental or not, that e-mail is sent to the "Company – ALL" distribution list for consumption by the entire company.

Uh oh. Already this isn't good because it's an email coming from a Senior Manager that will get very close and immediate attention. It did. Especially when reviewed by both the right and wrong people.

The Manager of the Program Management group, whose entire group had been maligned by the actions of this note, quickly saw and complained about the contents and audience. The individual criticized the content to both individuals, as well as the unprofessional handling, and demanded damage control. What came next was even more shockingly bad.

The original note was sent as a Reply-to-All with a covering note stating, "As tempted as you may be to read the earlier captioned note that was sent, please do not."

Obviously, everyone went back and read the note. The attempt at damage control further reinforced the original damage.

Yes, this really happened. We'll never truly know whether the actions were intentional, but it outlined the careless and improper use of a broad communication medium and its inherent flaws. It also presented an opportunity for damage control that focused on how to correct the problems and issues rather than increasing the impact. Instead, it exacerbated an already poor situation making it even worse, demotivating the team. It also forced the executive management of the company to take a serious look at this division of the company. The organization veteran was returned to the home office in a much different role. The senior manager of that division was moved to a role in business development before being moved out of the organization altogether.

There are quite a few morals behind the story.

1. Never say something in an email that you wouldn't discuss with the people being referenced in that message. It's known as "open-and-honest communication". If you believe a problem exists, email is not the forum to address the problem as it creates a tête-à-tête atmosphere between the parties. If need be, bring in an impartial third-party to mediate the dispute.

2. Email responses cannot be "quick". How often has someone sent something and wished they could rescind it? You cannot UN-ring a bell once rung, and words in any format have impact. Be mindful not only of "what" you say but "how" you say it. I'll cover this topic momentarily.

3. Email is an impersonal medium. It conveys only written facts. It poorly conveys sarcasm or comments that would be best discussed verbally. Although informally we've introduced the existence of "emoticons" – for the uninitiated, they're those little smileys, winks or frowns that can be included to help the reader distinguish tone – these don't translate well to formal writing. They do not belong in any business communication.

4. Audience. When a distribution list is constructed, you are trusting that the members of that list are truly representative of the audience you wish to reach. In the case of "Company – ALL", clearly everyone in the organization will see that communication, relevant or not, provocative or not, intended or not. Email also has a tendency to be public. Not everyone can be trusted with confidential news about an impending merger, or troublesome earnings report, or some factor of a major initiative that needs reconsideration given market conditions. People can print emails and leave them on an unintended recipient's desk; they can be forwarded; they can be misaddressed.

Clearly, I'm depicting the hazards and flaws of email. By no means am I suggesting that we return to the Stone Age where memos are typed and take days to wend their way through internal mail. There are very appropriate uses for the medium, and I'm encouraging its use with proper cautions and caveats.

I'll introduce the following Q&A on which I'll base the rest of the discussion:

Q: Do you find yourself immersed in your email replying after each alert? Or do you wait for some time to pass before responding to questions?

A: The best way I have to answer this is simple: Negotiate expectations. People tend to be lousy multi-taskers when their attention is divided between their actual work and responding to email as if there's nothing more important, and I've seen organizations operate in this manner (it's not pretty).

1. If something is truly urgent, pick up the phone and call. If it's less urgent, email. Setting that expectation will remove content from your box that serves only to create clutter.

2. Set fixed times and block them out so that you can address each piece of mail. I like the notion someone mentioned of RAFT (Read, Act, File, Trash), I've also heard of the 4-D's (Do, Defer, Delegate, Delete) for the disposition of mail.

3. Quick responses are often not "correct" responses. Set an example that unless it's a truly simple answer, it may take a bit of fact checking to ensure you're providing accurate information; otherwise, you'll be perpetuating misinformation like wildfire. Don't fan the flames.

4. Turn your alerting OFF. Both audible and visible alike. I watched the embarrassing experience of someone who had theirs on during a presentation, and the first line was none too flattering of a person in the room.

5. Watch your audience, make sure it's relevant. Having been on the wrong side of an email someone addressed about me to an entire office, damage control to that sort of thing is difficult.

I recently read a newsletter where the question was asked if your organization has an open communications policy. The answer was that if the person's attention was diverted by email, Blackberry and the like, you don't have such a policy or aren't upholding it well. Email has a place, but it needs to be prioritized below personal and telephone communications accordingly to be effective.

Email has a time and place. If your initiative is global, you cannot always expect that your team can fully assemble at one common time – for instance, 10:00 AM in New York is generally 10:00 PM in Singapore, or either 6:30 or 7:30PM in India. Conversely, 3:00PM in Singapore means 3:00AM in New York; even in "the city that never sleeps", I'd challenge you to find anyone awake and on a conference call at that hour.

I started the response to this question with the answer of "set expectations". This is truly important since setting the right boundaries with people will do more to build good will in the initiative than leaving this open-ended. It's simple, but it's missed much of the time. If you're inclined to always respond quickly to any question, 3 things will happen:

- You'll set the expectation that all such questions, regardless of complexity, will be answered as quickly.

- You'll spend most of your day and attention on email rather than your actual tasks.

- You'll likely drop in on a question and give the wrong answer in an effort to be proactive.

People will use email like a bridal bouquet – throw it back to see who catches it. If you're insecure in leaving the question unanswered versus letting your team handle the Q&A discussion, then you should reconsider your role as a leader versus an individual contributor.

I mentioned inside of the response that we aren't good multi-taskers by nature. Once we derail our train of thought to address another issue, it takes us some time to get back on the rails and continue down our previous track. Imagine doing this all day long as some people actually do: it reduces our overall productivity (although some are inclined to think just the opposite is the case). If we leave people alone to complete their tasks without superfluous interruptions, they'll complete work in shorter periods and with better accuracy.

I mentioned controlling communications at an earlier point in this chapter, and this is where you can provide value to the initiative team in helping to do that.

Avoid the temptation to be constantly alerted to e-mails or Instant Messages when you're deep in thought or concentrating on an issue -- you'll be far more inclined to respond than essential. That applies to both audible and visual alerting. I referred to a situation where an email alert was left on during a presentation, and some unflattering comments were made about a specific member of the audience in the room within the first few words of the e-mail. It was a very uncomfortable moment then; it was far less comfortable when the sender learned later what had occurred. While alerting is a nice feature, it's also one that has its place.

Avoid the fault – I've been guilty of this as well – of using your Inbox as an organizational tool. It's not a good one. To be efficient, the answer I've quoted uses 2 different philosophies. The first is a less "empowered" philosophy called "RAFT" (Read, Act, File, Trash), which insists that you should touch your email once. In some ways, it falls a slight bit short of the mark as an Initiative Leadership role, since it is silent on the issue of delegation. The second and more empowered approach is the "4-D" approach (Decide, Defer, Delegate, Delete).

- If you're empowered to make the **decision**, do so.

- If the issue is not critical for the moment or phase, **defer** the action with a clear expectation of follow-up.

- If you aren't the person best placed to take action, **delegate** it (both higher and lower than you, depending on the nature of the mail).

- If it's irrelevant, **delete** it.

By the way, don't file everything away for a later date, because it's too common that a critical issue will pass without being recognized as such. Make an effort to take the other 3 actions before deferring action, and set a time when appropriate to return to it.

Block out times in your calendar during the day when your sole tasks are responding to email and voice messages/voicemail left for you. I recently had dealings with an individual who set this type of service expectation with her customers of responding within that business day or early on the following day, since most of her dealings involved processing paperwork or discussions over the phone. It was helpful to understand that, and she largely met or exceeded that expectation.

Consider the relevance of the audience. I mention this as a closing point only to underscore the opening part of this chapter – more communication does not mean better communication. I've seen a few haphazard incidences where audiences for email were completely irrelevant, and audiences escalated issues unnecessarily under the premise that they were not previously informed. Here's a couple more amusing anecdotes:

- Misuse of the Reply-to-All function to remove yourself from an irrelevant mailing. While working in an organization all too tied to email, someone sent an email to the "Company-All" list, over 4,000 recipients. One simply pressed the Reply All button and said "Please remove me from this distribution." This was followed by dozens of "Me too" responses until someone finally said "Please use the 'Reply' button and notify the sender who did this, not all 4,000 recipients who cannot help you." (Unfortunately, he also used a Return-Receipt, and received receipts for all 4,000 recipients too)

- During a merger, several email address books were being combined. So the audience originally targeted in a email distribution had grown sevenfold overnight, unknown to everyone. As a result, people from around the country were panicking in response to a message that their PCs were about to get a system upgrade. That evening. Traffic went from zero to infinity in mere seconds.

Things can go haywire quickly.

Your audience must be appropriate – no more, no less than what is required for your particular email. I am not a fan of wide-distribution emails because they're subject to raise more questions than they answer unless the subject and content are exceptionally short and clear (e.g. "e-mail services will be unavailable from 6PM to 9PM on Sunday for routine maintenance").

I'm also not clearly a fan of a "Reply to All" function, and I wish most organizations would restrict its use as it invites counterproductive behavior to the initiative. Let's talk about managing the message first.

Some elements to consider in managing the message:

1. More information is not good information. I keep repeating this mantra, but the context this time is somewhat different. If your message must be succinct, do not offer information that will confuse or incite reactions unnecessarily. If the information is not relevant, leave it out. Stay on topic.

2. Stay tuned to your audience. If your audience includes nonprofessional level workers, keep the message oriented at that level. Where explanation is required (e.g. "What does this mean for me?"), explain that clearly.

3. People generally do not want very long messages. Throughout this book, you'll note that I've positioned lists and bullets appropriately, and divided topic areas where possible. If you begin to get wordy in your message, stop, look at ways to shorten the message, and incorporate those. If the message becomes pages and pages, the content will be lost.

4. If you know your message will be longer than normal in opening, a good way of handling this is to help organize the content at the top so that the reader can see the organization of content and understand what will be discussed, guiding them accordingly.

I'll show an example of how we might start such a communication to a recipient audience, outlined below and following:

To: Claims-ALL
From: Initiative Manager
Subject: Information about your New Claims Processing System

The date is getting close, and the much-anticipated New Claims System will finally go live on (Date). This message contains helpful information about the transition from the existing system to the new system, and is divided into sections for ease of reference:

1. What you need to do before the transition?
    a. Take the Computer Based Training.
    b. Dispositions on existing Claims
    c. Locking your PC the night before the conversion.
2. What to expect after the transition?
    a. Support personnel the first day of live work
    b. Support hotline for issues
3. Frequently Asked Questions (FAQ's)

What to do before the transition:
First, make sure you have logged on to the Computer Based Training before (date) to learn about the features…

There's a lot of information to introduce to the audience, so at the beginning of the message, this example sets the structure and organization of that information to set the reader's expectations.

It also structures the value proposition for the reader so that they do not immediately dismiss the message. Rather, they get the answer to "What's in it for me" at the very beginning of the message – they understand what they will expect, receive valuable information, and perhaps get answers to some important questions. This is a great example of a long-form message that divides itself and considers what the reader wants or needs to know from their perspective. It sets their expectations.

Final Words on Audience and Message

You already know that you're busy. Expect that your recipient is as well. Make your points sincerely and succinctly. Be considerate of their time, and expect they're considerate of yours as well. To expect a behavior, exhibit that behavior by demonstrating a leadership example.

I mentioned earlier why I'm not a fan of a "Reply to All" function, since it is so frequently used for the wrong reasons. It adds to a cacophony of noise and simply amps it beyond the reach of anyone's control unless draconian steps are taken to control this. It's very important to set the right views and expectations around email behavior.

For instance, the person hitting "Reply All" to highlight a missing point with meeting minutes is doing so either out of ignorance or arrogance. In fact, if I send a draft of meeting minutes out for review, I'll generally end the summary with the words "Issues/Questions/Corrections, please reply to the author." This lets your team know you're open to constructive comments and input before sending a final version.

I mentioned good and bad meeting behaviors in the prior section. Much of that addresses the email behaviors that should be part of a productive initiative environment that focuses the team's energy toward accomplishing the initiative's objectives. In that spirit, I'll offer some suggestions on what to avoid given the uniqueness of email as a medium:

- Avoid replying to any email when angered, whether by the situation or by another influence. Cool off first, draft the message, then let it sit for a bit before coming back and pressing send. If you think you'll regret sending it, you're probably correct. The same applies to negative comments.

    o In fact, if you're angered by the above situation, e-mail is not an appropriate forum for venting that anger. Arrange to voice your concerns by phone or in-person.

- Do not conduct an argument via e-mail. This is especially true if others are included in the dialogue. A better way to address this is to stop the conversation by indicating, "Email isn't the appropriate forum for what we need to discuss, let's get together 1:1."

- Avoid inflammatory messages, otherwise known as "flaming". Abuse whether by email or in person isn't warranted (See Information Case Study #10).

- Typing in all CAPITAL LETTERS GIVES THE APPEARANCE OF SHOUTING. Avoid this.

- Avoid sending one-line responses to lengthy emails while quoting the entire message back. It's wasteful and serves no purpose.

- Not spell-checking. There is nothing more embarrassing than sending an email out that reflects poorly on your capabilities simply because you've made a typographic error. It looks careless.

- While we're on the topic of spellchecking, grammar-check yourself. There is nothing worse than seeing a supposedly college educated person not know the correct usage of the words "your" and "you're", or the differences between "their", "there", and "they're". Spell-check will **not** catch that.

- Send to the correct recipient. (Again, see Case Study #10 above).

- Internal communication should not be sent externally. Remember that email is not a private medium.

Underscoring that last bullet, a major marketing and media company in 2008 was about to announce layoffs that would affect a sizable portion of their staff. An email was sent around from a senior executive on how to discuss the impending reductions in staffing and the phrasing to be used when discussing the situation. However, the email itself was also sent to several people who should not have received it, and subsequently leaked to the media. Many of those who were about to lose their jobs were reading the speech before it was released. It was a public relations nightmare, a very severe black eye to the firm, and an embarrassment all around that could have been avoided.

I'll close this point by saying that the written word is subject to an amazing degree of interpretation. It's as much interpreted by the reader as the author. Just as you are interpreting this book for its content – which hopefully I've clearly articulated – any area of the written word should focus on a neutral statement of the facts. Be respectful, be culturally sensitive, but still convey candor in the right manner.

Chapter 4:
Constraints, Perceptions, Conventional Wisdom and Misconceptions

My Own Experience as the Example

I mentioned in a prior chapter the issue of "PMO relevance" and how the notion of a "Project Management Office" has gained a poor reputation in many organizations, some for whom I've worked have been included in that number. One of my cited case examples was directed at the core issue of why PMOs tend to fail: Irrelevance. This is otherwise known as the lack of the proper charter. As a former Director of a PMO and having managed Program Management functions several times over, forming a Project/Program Management Organization should be rooted in one fundamental question:

"Why?"

Therein lies the key question that begins opening doors to understand the motivations for creating, improving, or reorganizing this function. It quickly cuts to the perceptions held by the key stakeholders seeking project success. Where do they feel that projects are failing? Why do they believe they're failing? What are their success criteria? Why do they believe a PMO is the answer? Asking those questions will reveal more information than uninformed speculation, or continuing without the proper consensus.

Remember this statistic from Chapter One: 68% of projects fail. It's an abysmal statistic. It reflects poorly on the profession, and where the buck really stops or accountability ultimately lies: The Project Manager.

If I were a baseball player, a .320 batting average wouldn't be too shabby. If that was a career average, I'd probably be among the highest paid players in the game. It's also much too easy an analogy to make, and if we're viewing that average as one of "process", we're also heading down the wrong road toward a solution.

So this chapter will take a short breather from Case Studies (mostly) and textbook information to shed some light on some potential issues that act as inhibitors to project/initiative management success at the root cause level. In short, giving thought more to the factors that inhibit the success of projects versus the extraneous factors that create noise. If we remove the chatter and ambient noise, we can consider what exists beneath the surface.

Focusing on Process and Not Results

A process simply means that you have a repeatable method of performing repeatable work. While admirable for ongoing endeavors, the temporary nature of projects puts this immediately at odds with accomplishing an objective in the most pragmatic way possible. While a workflow might be consistent through an organization – for instance, an Accounts Payable Department may have a specific process of checks and procedures before a bill or vendor is rendered payment – the defined nature of projects demands a level of flexibility not usually attributable to exact process driven steps versus general guidelines.

The process does not guarantee the result. Organizations talk about adherence to process guidelines as a way of preventing project failures; when those process guidelines fail them, the first inclination is to refer to what did not work in the process, not whether the process was suited to purpose.

Process is a Buzzword Rather Than Having Value

Let's examine this point carefully, and in doing so, question organizations that extol their adherence to process. Several are external vendors seeking to manage projects for organizations, announcing that they have achieved CMMI Level 5 certification. This indicates that they have a process that is standard, quantified, and continually reviewed for improvement (note: For a complete definition, please see http://www.sei.cmu.edu which outlines the entire CMMI process, the properties of each level are defined later in this book). It presumes that from the process, improved productivity and quality are the result. CMMI only defines that a controlled process exists, the level and existence of quantitative management and process improvement. It is silent on the overall effectiveness of that process.

I once worked for an organization that in theory qualified under all aspects of CMMI Level 5 Certification. Did it mean that we delivered all projects on time and had practiced all of those aspects always in an efficient manner? Frankly, no.

So we must be careful about equating a process with effective project delivery. While an understanding of process can be useful to achieving successful delivery of initiatives, I would caution the tendency of many organizations to blame a failure in the process for a failure in delivery versus taking full accountability to address the issue more fundamentally. And pragmatically.

Process doesn't guarantee results. Simply focusing on the process deflects the emphasis from accountability of those involved, but results in no further emphasis into root cause analysis.

The Methodology Question

Organizations will often focus on standardizing with a single development or delivery methodology as best fits the focus of that organization, and establishing standards and rigors associated to the delivery of products, services, or new introductions. The range of possibilities can be endless, and each is tailored to a specific approach to delivery. This presents a conundrum to the variability of projects; for instance, a mainframe-based system development project will resemble few of the issues encountered in a Website development effort. However, when asked of their methodology approach to systems and application development, most IT managers will frame their answer into only one box, such as:

- "We're an agile shop"
- "We're using Unified Process"
- "Strictly SDLC or Waterfall"

Let's understand why this is done:

- It provides a clear guideline for how development efforts should be managed.

- It sets expectations on how deliverables are provided or demonstrated.

- It provides a metric against which process maturity can be based – CMMI, for instance.

It also introduces inherent issues, as I mentioned in the previous paragraph. Different technology solutions might require different approaches to the methodology lifecycle, and a lack of flexibility – while potentially confusing and daunting to the individual performing the work – might result in poor product quality, rework, or project abandonment in a worst case.

I mention CMMI in the prior example since it can be interpreted to presume that only a single process can be in place, and then construed to infer that only a single methodology solution must be defined. Let's debunk that rumor now: CMMI in any of its certification levels is silent on the use of a "single process" or "single method"; it stipulates only that they exist formally to control a managed set of activities.

"What's the Point?"

Process is neither the baby nor the bathwater that should be thrown out when something fails, nor should it become a panacea for resolving any failures that may exist.

I described in an earlier chapter the experience of sitting through a meeting originally designed to discuss technology failures and seek a solution for later implementation. I jokingly referred to this as the Monday Afternoon Blame-Storming Session because the focus became less on how to resolve the issue than whom to hold responsible. Had the sessions truly done more about resolving the root cause, they could have been far more productive, and the process been much more successful.

It may seem as if I've contradicted myself in this section. In a moment, I'll explain why I've not.

Projects are learning experiences for all engaged, and faults and failures can occur each time. We can use those experiences as teaching tools for future endeavors by capturing that information to optimize controls that will impact the eventual outcome of the project. Proper root cause analysis plays into this perfectly so that we can learn more pragmatically what occurred and ensure that it isn't repeated.

As we progress, we'll discuss the capturing of artifacts, project history, business requirements, lessons learned, and other material that will build upon project management competency.

Constraints

We're taught from a very young age about "constraints". How many of us were given a coloring book and crayons (or colored-pencils if you were really lucky) when you were a child so you could draw green dogs and blue-colored cats? Many of us have this memory. My own background was perhaps different in that I was fortunate enough to have colored pencils, but I was given the back side of 8 ½" x 11" paper that was used for computer generated reports from my Aunt's work – I viewed it like manna from Heaven since I could make use of the non-printed side of the paper.

I cite this example for a reason. Let's assume that you were groomed like most children with a coloring book. The phrase you likely heard was "color within the lines". It's the first way we were taught how to constrain our activity. Nobody bothered to dictate colors, but hoped that a dog would be a normal color, a tree usually green, and the rest left to chance. It's the first good example of how we're taught about constraints, and you probably didn't realize it until you noticed your own children wanting to color outside the lines.

If we were really creative, we probably would have given our kids a lesson in how to do something slightly more creative by describing what we wanted them to draw as an assignment – for instance, the example that child psychology uses in asking a child to draw a picture of their family – and observe what emerges from the process. The results can be an interesting insight.

The underlying point is that often we create our own constraints where perhaps none should exist, or we shun new ideas because we've assumed an artificial constraint that does not or should not exist. Excellent initiative teams and some very accomplished initiative managers can easily fall victim to this trap rather than questioning the relevance of the constraint or challenging the stakeholders to help determine better alternatives. Often, they may be adding complexities that are counterproductive to progress.

Every initiative is an opportunity to look at the example of the coloring book, except that we first need to define the outline of the picture to be colored as part of the background business requirements defined in the scope of work, and then we can dispatch the work to be colored, further developed or given further dimension. Those working in interactive or Website development might recognize this process under a different name: Wire-framing. It's a great example of our showing the stakeholders and sponsors the idea so that the constraints (or lines we'll eventually fill with color) are validated or changed. Once the outline is correct, then we pull out the crayons and the next stage of work begins.

> *Exercise 4-1:*
>
> *Assemble a team of say 5 or 6 people, along with a canister of tennis balls. Give them the following assignment:*
>
> *"Everyone in the group must touch each of the balls at least once in the shortest possible amount of time." Have a stopwatch ready to time 2 things (one won't really require a stopwatch, the other might). The first is how long it takes them to reach the solution with which they're satisfied. The second is how long it takes to execute the solution from start to finish.*

Later in the book, I'll explain the exercise again, but think also about how you might envision the mechanics of such an assignment and consider whether you've placed artificial constraints around the exercise.

Perceptions and "Perception vs. Reality"

How many times have you heard the phrase that "perception is reality"? How many times have you grown tired of hearing it?

Perception is simply the way in which we interpret something as opposed to the properties of that object. It can apply to situations, people, objects, or even ideas. Perception becomes reality because that reality has not been communicated or reinforced to counter the influence of the perception. The influencer may have strong and believable arguments, although they may be completely inaccurate and unfounded.

Example #1: The Salem Witch Trials of 1691: We recognize in retrospect that there really were no witches other than some mischievous children with a vindictive streak. But it didn't stop an entire village from challenging innocent people as accused until the prank was later uncovered.

Example #2: You cannot UN-ring a bell: Heaven forbid this happen, but it often does and destroys lives and careers. Suppose someone tasked with child development (a priest, a pastor, a teacher, a Scout Master) is accused of actions with that child so unspeakable that their life is turned upside down to prove or disprove the allegation. There are countless cases where this may have happened, but perhaps countless more where a person's reputation, once damaged, cannot be repaired if the allegation is later proven false. Regardless of being found innocent, suspicion will usually follow the individual.

I list those as examples where perceptions can over-influence the reality of a situation. I've spent much of the previous chapter discussing communication, but the need to dispel inaccurate information is just as crucial in influencing perception as it is to defining the overall tone and success of an initiative.

It's also important to recognize this trait with individuals on an initiative team.

Case Study #11: Project Team perceptions

Stan was a brilliant UNIX Engineer with a wide range of technical knowledge that was a value to any project team he served. He had a keen understanding of potential issues, and could easily resolve problems very quickly. Those who knew this found his knowledge a benefit. He was rarely engaged on projects, however, because his overall attitude was "doom and gloom". Most of the team members found him to be negative, or suffering excessively from viewing the glass as always "half-empty". He was never elevated to be a project manager and suffered in his role for years on end, despite his talents.

Here, the perception of Stan being the go-to-guy is overshadowed by the perception of Stan viewing everything as a negative. For anyone who has read A.A. Milne's "Winnie the Pooh", you could liken Stan to Eeyore, the overburdened and dour donkey in the book. Can you recast a perception? The answer is "yes", if you can reset the stage with the reality – in the continuation of this example, we'll show how this could happen and how it serves managers to focus and build their teams in a well-rounded manner.

A turning point for Stan was a very critical project to re-platform major technology for the organization. A critical piece of the project required some very detailed knowledge and expertise shared by 2 people – one of whom was the project manager, the other was Stan. Both spent weeks, both in person and over phone conversations, in debugging and testing various scenarios to make the proposed changes work on the new platform. Though the teams knew that Stan was not the project manager, the project manager ceded much of his communication to Stan for status meetings and deferred much of the credit for the work to him. The PM also shared some advice that was often difficult for Stan to accept, though after some influencing he did. With some minor changes and informal coaching, plus a situation that provided an opportunity to be seen as an expert with strong skills, Stan's profile changed to one that was often demanded by teams who needed both a leader and an expert.

So a few things helped change Stan's profile and perception among teams:

1. Stan being seen as a helpful and positive contributor.

2. Stan being seen as the key to resolving problems.

3. Stan being viewed as a proactive leader.

4. Stan's collaboration skills becoming known.

5. Coaching that helped Stan focus on keeping to the facts and de-emphasizing any negative phrasing.

Changing a perception to a "new" reality takes an investment in time, effort, and building on key successes. It's not a job for the faint of heart, because once a perception is viewed as negative, changing it to a positive one is generally an uphill battle.

Case Study #12: When perceptions cannot be overcome despite effort.

Tom was a Senior Project Manager hired in by a multinational corporation to perform work with which he had familiarity and key knowledge. Tom's understanding of technical issues was very clear; his ability to handle typical project management scenarios was lacking, and Tom's lack of effective organization skills, proactive communication, and follow-through on any more than one item became clear to his manager and his customers, some of whom expressed concern to Tom's manager about competency. As part of the Development and Cor-

rective Action process, Tom's manager began to challenge him further on key points, targeted deliverables, and took a higher than normal interest in Tom's work versus all of his other staff to turn-around performance and perception.

A few points are key to the situation:

1. Poor communication skills – noted by lack of proactive communication.

2. Poor expectation setting – it's important for the Project Manager at any level to set the correct expectation and follow through by delivering against that.

3. Lack of organizational skills – Tom struggled with handling more than one focus at a time, something needed by any successful project manager.

Key to note in this case is that the project manager has already set a poor reputation with a key customer, something that is difficult to overcome. Let's continue with the case.

Tom's manager met with Tom in a semiweekly basis for 1 hour at a time and reviewed all work, spoke about customer interactions, and often sat in and observed behavior within meetings. It was here that Tom identified critical flaws with Tom's understanding of issues, and his propensity to set unrealistic expectations to please the customer when delivering against them would prove challenging. Tom and his manager met after each of these interactions to debrief and review the steps. Tom would take detailed notes, and his manager would evaluate progress during their one-on-one sessions.

Tom was also given very clear delivery goals and actions to meet to demonstrate success and competency. Progress against these was also slow. In addition, Tom's manager sat down periodically with Tom's customers and charted their experiences, as well as the level of change being evidenced. The results were less than convincing.

Key to the resolution of this problem included some of the following actions:

1. Defining clear deliverables within an action plan.

2. Observing Tom's interaction and follow-through on tasks and commitments.

3. Meeting with the customer for their input.

4. Continuing coaching on a one-on-one level.

Tom's manager took many of the right actions; the results of those actions remained less than persuading to the end customer, who saw insufficient improvement. Not every chance to change perception is followed by a positive outcome, and several factors – customer experience, customer satisfaction, improvement in organizational skills, and follow-through on commitments – must improve to ensure success.

Eventually, Tom was made redundant by the organization. (A nicer way of saying "terminated")

Clearly, there are times when you can manage performance toward improvement and change perceptions, and times when it won't happen. Once a perception turns negative, it is difficult to change it.

Setting the correct expectations is key to handling any perception issues. Delivering against those expectations is even more important. The Case Study I just outlined demonstrates this very clearly – once someone has adopted a negative view of an individual, it's difficult to change that. However, it's not impossible, and there are many occasions when a person's errors in judgment and individual mistakes can be overlooked – former President Clinton's dalliance with a White House Intern demonstrates a good example of a President who remains popular in the eyes of many, despite making a very grave error in judgment and then obscuring the truth behind the situation. This is where I introduce the word "contrition", coupled with the concept of "sincerity".

Everyone gets to make a few honest mistakes in their lifetime. Everyone has likely felt the pressure – personally and professionally – when those mistakes happen. As human beings, we're not perfect. Part of influencing others' perceptions about those errors is to simply "fess up": acknowledge that the mistake happened, demonstrate that you understand why it happened and know how to resolve it, take immediate action, and show sincerity. It demonstrates that you are contrite in admitting the mistake, and most people view it as sincerity and honesty rather than weakness.

The power of most people to forgive when they denote sincerity and contrition cannot be underestimated. Jimmy Swaggart, Bill Clinton, Former NY Governor Eliot Spitzer and former NJ Governor Jim McGreevey have all admitted their faults. For it, they may be briefly maligned but forgiven as human in the longer span.

Conventional Wisdom
"Common sense ain't common." – Will Rogers

Will had it right. Common sense isn't as common as you might believe, and the same holds true for conventional wisdom.

"If you always do what you've always done, you'll always get what you've always gotten." – attributed to Anthony Robbins among others.

Somehow, you might have expected that I would sideswipe the notion of conventional wisdom in making this statement, and you'd be correct. When one idea doesn't work, try another; then a third or fourth. If we never experiment and challenge the conventional wisdom, the pace at which progress would occur would be remarkably slow. We learn through our attempts at improvement.

Project management has been a recognized profession for years. During the decades since its inception, our base of knowledge has expanded and improved, as have the tools and techniques for more effectively managing complex efforts. More proof that if we simply accepted the conventional wisdom and stopped there, we'd never progress or innovate beyond that. Another quote from Thomas Edison underscores the learning behind developing the incandescent light:

"We now know a thousand ways not to build a light bulb." – Thomas Alva Edison.

To reach a conclusion, you need to begin viewing the issue in different ways. Organizations that are classically known as "Learning organizations" build on the knowledge gained from previous exercises and understand the outcomes and metrics behind their success and failures. See the next quote.

"Failure is not an option." – phrase popularized by the movie Apollo XIII

Sometimes, as we observed in the Thomas Edison example, failure provides us with valuable information that guides us closer to a correct path. In manufacturing, the first built prototype isn't always going to be perfect, or flaws will be detected that will require correction. Failure is a tough taskmaster and a great teacher, and if we never fail, we'll never truly appreciate the meaning of success.

Everything we do is a learning experience upon which we build our base of knowledge. Out of failures in other processes, we've developed successes. In Chapter Two, I mentioned the cases of Aspartame ("Equal") and Minoxidil ("Rogaine") – two inventions created for completely different purposes, both of which are now household names.

Imagine for a moment that the time is near the close of the Fifteenth Century, AD, and a trade explorer believes there is a more efficient trade route to India and the Far East that does not entail the perilous trip around the tip of South Africa and weeks at sea. Convinced of his theory, he seeks sponsorship for his exploratory journey from the Queen of Spain, who devotes enough resources to send 3 ships to embark on this new route. He clearly believes in the recent theories that the earth is round, and he can take a short cut.

He doesn't discover a trade route to India, sadly. He discovers the Americas and what will later be referred to as the West Indies, as well as the natives (which for years were referred to as "Indians", though we now consider that as culturally incorrect). So be the judge – was Columbus' journey a failure or a success? Or both?

Presuming you're sitting in the Western Hemisphere, you'd likely feel it was successful, though for much different reasons than originally imagined.

While not maligning conventional wisdom, it represents a comfort zone that may inhibit innovation and creative thinking among project teams. If you suspected a rationale behind mentioning this within the same chapter as "Constraints", you were correct. Making the leap between the two isn't as difficult as you would think, as the idea of constraints is often inherited out of conventional wisdom, which in turn places artificial limitations on the manner in which something can be done.

Let's view some common quotes that relate well to the topic:

"We've always done it this way." Anyone working on a process redesign project, as I have a number of times, has probably heard these words uttered often. I've asked such irreverent questions as "why" or "do you like it" or "does it work well, because someone else doesn't think so". Incidentally, watch carefully how you ask those questions so as not to alienate the responder.

"That isn't the process we follow." See the above answers for my views on this topic. Processes normally should contain exception handling; those that don't haven't considered that exceptions will happen. For instance, the reason that most of us carry an insurance policy of some sort (life, health, homeowners, auto) is to protect against unexpected events. No one expects his or her car will be stolen in the shopping center parking lot, but it happens. Consider this in terms of both planning and risk.

"I'm not empowered" or *"That's above my pay-grade"*. Both suggest rigidity and lack of empowerment, resistance to change, or lack of collaboration. Instead of suggesting how you can accomplish your goals or guiding you to someone more appropriate in completing your task, they create a barrier toward further progress. The classic example of this is the telephone customer service representative who is a gatekeeper and handles no exceptions – once the customer becomes tired of hearing the script, they'll either demand to speak to their superiors, or quickly take their business elsewhere. Who loses? Usually, it's the worker who isn't empowered.

"This goes against procedure." I'll relate a story that harkens back to the earlier days of Health Maintenance Organizations. I worked for one. That same organization provided my health-coverage, which wasn't a bottom-of-the-barrel policy. My doctor at that time wanted to see me frequently; I'd continued to encounter communication issues with his administrative staff. I finally stood there and demanded to know why they could only schedule me once every month when the doctor wanted me back in 2 weeks. The reply I received was "Because that's how the insurance company pays us." It was unethical, it was wrong and I knew it, and it forced my hand. Laying my company badge on the counter I suggested 2 ways of settling the dispute – either schedule me as the doctor directed, or I'll tell my company that you are not acting in the patient's interest and we'll see what they do.

Suffice it to say that I never had a problem getting an appointment whenever the doctor wanted in the future. But it did little to engender me to his office staff.

The real question here was "whose procedure", then whether it was right or wrong, or potentially harmful. Conventional wisdom might not have challenged some of these statements. I also never said that conventional wisdom was wrong, but it presents a fertile field for us to review whether it makes sense in a situation. It also generally inhibits creativity because it presents constraints, real or imagined.

Misconceptions

Much of what we've known or believed has been formed by misconceptions, often convincing enough to make us believe they're universal truths. If we never challenge the misconception, it too becomes a constraint to progress. Our job is to not only seek out the truth but to dispel misconceptions. If something is reinforced often enough, people will likely continue to believe it without disproving evidence. Consider the number of erroneous emails distributed each year warning of a false virus that continue their redistribution in various forms because the story is plausible enough to believe.

In one of the previous Case Studies, I depicted Stan and how the misconception that he was difficult held him and the organization back from using his talents more effectively.

Here are some other common misconceptions:

- "George Washington's Teeth were made of wood." No wood was ever an element of George's dentures, though many other things were.

- "Tomatoes were once thought to be poisonous plants." We all know this now to be false.

- "Chewing Gum takes 7 years to pass through the human digestive system if swallowed." If this were true, there would have been no room in my stomach – I often swallowed mine as a child.

We could go on, but while entertaining, misconceptions are simply that. This is why countless scientists have done research to debunk rumors – such as the earth being flat. Some are silly; some are scary, most do nothing but hold us back and are also ripe for challenge.

By the way, http://www.snopes.com (from where some of these examples were cited) is an excellent source for information on the veracity of rumors. Before you simply forward information about that next virus or email, do the rest of us a favor and verify first before blindly accepting data on good faith.

It can be very easy for a misconception to become something big and ugly. As with the Stan example, we form misconceptions based on a lack of verified information or personal experience; as a result, we perpetuate those misconceptions. None of us are immune. I'll cite my own example about misconceptions; beginning with the house I live in now.

When I bought the property, the former owner and I spoke. Being an attorney in his late 50's, he felt more loyalty to his elder neighbor just to the south of our property than the large family with 3 or 4 girls to our north. I trusted his views until I began to develop my own experiences. I quickly found out that the elder neighbor to my south was the most irritable and obnoxious neighbor one could find, and my neighbors to the North have been the sweetest people with well-behaved children (who shriek a bit as young girls often do). It didn't take me long to dispel the misconceptions that had been planted by the former owner once I'd had developed my own experience with the elder neighbor. Unfortunately, well into his 80's, it seems as if God doesn't want him just yet so I likely have more experiences to develop with him.

Summary

Part of the objective of this Chapter was to discuss our human thought process, and the constraints that we place around it. This is far from being a scientific discussion of human thought (I'm not a psychologist or sociologist), but rather intended to promote a pragmatic view of the realities that can be faced with implementing any initiative.

The goal of keeping any initiative on track is to dispel myth and illusion, focus on facts and evidence, and develop an environment where creatively thinking through a problem results in developing solutions. I'll end this chapter with one last Case Study.

Case Study #13: "Nobody told you that you couldn't."

A management-training course given by a facilitator was scheduled for about 20 managers at an offsite conference center. On the first afternoon, the entire room of 20 people was divided into 4 equal teams of 5 people a piece. Their task was to develop an Informational Presentation that included agendas, maps to the conference center, listings for activities in the surrounding area, and a flip-board designed with information on the activities. They were told to use all the resources at their disposal.

On Team D, one of the team members on the team noted that there was an open business center in the facility that had a PC and printer, and suggested that all the written package materials be the task given to him and another team member. The team leader approved the request, while she set her remaining team to fill out the other parts of the assignment in the 90 minutes allotted. The team divided and began completing their tasks.

The other teams in the room stayed close by their grouped tables and began creating diagrams of what their presentation package would roughly look like. Some were cruder than others; those with artistic talents were chosen to do rough-out drawings, others were writing out the information on pages of loose-leaf paper or blank white copier paper.

The Team D leader began getting a little concerned as an hour ticked off and she'd not heard from the missing team members, though she focused on the remaining work. The missing team members reappeared with 30 minutes to spare and the main parts of their assignment completed and printed. Time enough to spare to help the other members of the team complete their tasks, and relax with a few minutes before the deadline. They all looked calm in the face of pressure. Eventually the 90 minutes elapsed, and the teams were called to present their work one by one in team letter order.

They were surprisingly rated on the professionalism of the work, and when Teams A through C approached to give their presentations, there were many gaps and missing pieces. It was finally Team D's turn, and they revealed a completed presentation, with well-thought whiteboards, drawn out activities, and a professionally printed packet for each attendee. They'd scored perfectly on the presentation and given high marks for innovation.

What did they do differently?

First, the team became comfortable with assigning roles, and despite nervousness around completion of the tasks, everything came together with time to spare because of the ideas and resourcefulness of the team. They also recognized opportunities in the Conference Center by leveraging the available facilities. They did not constrain their activities to working as a group that could not work individually, so the tasks were completed easily because there was a division of talents and labor to do so.

What did they lack? Nothing the other teams didn't otherwise have, other than constrained thought. Let's conclude this with the comments that were levied by the other teams at Team D's presentation.

One member of Team B spoke up and said, "Hey, that isn't fair, they went up and used the copy center and business center. We didn't know we couldn't do that."

The member of Team D that thought of the idea spoke up and reminded them that they had use of all the resources at their disposal. Nowhere did the facilitator say that those were all located within that conference room.

All the other teams looked around at one another and said, "Geez, we could have done that too, now look at us." The facilitator reminded them of the rules, and the first lesson that was taught – the one that Team D perceived quickly – was not to create constraints where none exist. It was a valuable lesson learned for a few people, including the leader of Team D who had to trust giving control of a task to another team member without constantly understanding the status.

Moral of the story: Shackling your mind as you would your hands and feet will only restrain you in the same way. Think about whether the constraints are real and challenge them when necessary.

Chapter 5:
PMOs, Fact and Fiction

In Chapter 1, I introduced various anecdotes about PMOs and how each presented a learning experience to their respective organizations. Since I've covered a Chapter on Perceptions and Misconceptions, and I'm usually prone to a good debate, let's discuss the subject by providing some background on a few topics.

In this Chapter, we will cover:

- Organization types

- Project Management Organizations

- Metrics (Baseline and Reporting)

- Governance Organizations

- Reporting, Monitoring and Controls

Organization Types

Organizations generally fall into a series of categories, ranging from those most aligned by projects to those most aligned toward functional groups. Various texts on organizational design and various Project Management texts and organizations define these categories very well. For a quick review, I'll give credit to Kim Heldman for the reference to the 3 major types in her book entitled "PMP Project Management Professional Exam Study Guide":[6]

- Strong Matrix – designed and focused largely around projects, where the balance of power rests largely with the project manager. Otherwise called a "Projectized" organization.

- Weak Matrix – a more functional organization, with the balance of power resting largely with the individual functional managers; the project manager is largely of a coordinative level and has very little authority. Usually referred to as "Functional" organizations.

- Balanced Matrix – the balance of authority is leveled between functional managers and the project manager, and the functional manager assigns resources to projects.

---

6 (ISBN: 978-0470152515)

It's important to understand the type of organization in which you're operating to understand your level of authority in progressing an initiative. In Chapter Two, I also mentioned the 5 types of power that can be leveraged, including those that have the greatest impact.

Project Management Organizations

The question least asked about any Project Management Organization (PMO) concerns its charter. The two examples in Chapter 2 illustrate keys to making a specific PMO structure successful in any organization, as well as key questions to be asked both when entering an organization that has/is starting a PMO, and when working within that PMO.

"What is Our Charter?"

It's common to think that one PMO is exactly like another and that they all do the same thing. Nothing could be further from the truth. Case Study #2 and 2a speak specifically to those points. More misconceptions have risen about what a PMO is or does, and I've had ample experience speaking with people who have had poor PMO interactions (myself included). Most of them involve a lack of understanding of PMOs Charter.

It's also often a lack of outreach and communication, or a charter that lacks relevance to the stakeholders who should derive value from the PMO. Everyone espouses a theory behind how to create a successful Project Management Oversight group or Project Management Office, so one would presume by now that this is more science than black art. Despite the best efforts of the profession, we've yet to reach that point.

So the first question addresses "what" we should ask ourselves about any existing PMO, or what we should ask when creating it based on the culture and structure of the organization it serves. Although I could have entitled this book "PMO in a Box", and it would likely sell quite a few copies because people want an instant solution, (1) it won't work for everyone, and (2), it's completely disingenuous. My profession would likely hold me as an example for ridicule, despite my challenging conventional thought in this writing. (Note: I've added the (Not) before my title to ensure the differentiation.)

There are questions to be asked in forming a "PMO" – and because that term has garnered such a poor reputation, I'll align it with a new term that I'll call "Initiative Management Group" or IMG for short. Since this book specifically discusses managing initiatives, let's begin referencing that.

Let's begin with the fundamentals of establishing an IMG within an organization, using questions I've posed to various stakeholders:

1. *What are your expectations from the IMG? Specifically, with what responsibilities do you want to empower them, versus the responsibilities that are to be retained outside the group?* Notice that I ask this question openly to help determine the type of organizational model being employed. If the goal is to align the initiatives with the initiative managers responsible to the business, the goals are different than making the initiative managers a functional part of the IMG.

2. *What issues are prompting the decision?* Here, I've asked for the motivations behind an oversight function. Answers may range from "transparency" to "active management" to "initiative performance" to "reporting and communication" or even "all of the above" and others not mentioned. It's important to note that you need to ask a variety of stakeholders the same sets of questions, and then actively delve into the responses to justify examples – requesting stakeholders to cite examples will reveal details that might not be revealed in a short-answer, or that might highlight a much different problem or behavior.

3. *What is it you're doing now? What about it do you like or dislike?* Do not discount that the person to whom you're speaking may think that nothing is wrong, and likes things just the way that they are; nonetheless, listen to them to determine their motivations, and review the answer carefully. Do not

discount that the motivation toward establishing an Initiative Management Function is to help circumvent barriers to success – they can be process or people, though many result from a lack of transparency in both. Be mindful when asking, and listen carefully to the responses; ask to cite examples when necessary.

4. *What would you like to see change?* This is a deliberately open question that will provide a variety of motivations and responses. Be prepared for some venting, but strive to keep the answers on track. It's a question that will provide information about the responder as well as the organization. It may also hold useful keys as to what has not worked in the past – recall, you could be entering a brownfield situation where a PMO-type organization was established, lacked traction, and was abandoned. So listen carefully, focus on tone, inflection, and overall mood along with the words in the response – what is being said may indicate something different from the other nonverbal cues you're being given.

5. *What are your priorities? What are your pain points?* Every organization charges its managers with the achievement of objectives that are passed along to their teams. Perhaps the pain point is "doing more with less" or "sourcing issues" or "prioritization of shifting workloads". Whatever these are, note the responses since they're important and may be a good indicator of the changes that could be productive, or help gain support for the function.

6. *What are the criteria for success for you? How would you define success for this role?* By human nature, it will take several passes of the working group to gain a singular consensus, or a workable plan to achieve the success desired. The criteria for success must be measurable, realistic, achievable within a defined timeframe, and both specific and sustainable. In the first Chapter, I've outlined four goals that I used successfully to get a Project Management function up and running in short order based on individual meetings and building consensus around the main issues.

Once you have this information, you'll have immense data to digest. I've done this intentionally since the process is not simply a multiple-choice questionnaire. The data will require analysis and presentation to a working group to discuss the information gathered, find common concerns, and arrive at the criteria on which the IMG should be based. There is one more important area that I've not mentioned as of yet, since for many organizations it may be information that is not available or measured.

Metrics (Baseline and Reporting)

This is a difficult topic, especially if your agreed success criteria includes reducing overall project delivery timeframes on an average basis by X percentage, or to reducing costs by $XXX,XXX. Some of this data may be available from past initiatives undertaken by the organization; conversely, it may not have been adequately captured.

The underlying point is that achievement of any goals involving savings needs to be compared to a baseline measurement. Otherwise, you will be unable to measure trending or success until the practice has been in place for some time. A couple of useful hints might be employed in the absence of other statistics:

- Speak with your Finance Department, since most costs associated with project purchases will be assigned to a cost-center or a particular code; this will normally permit you a look at the overall budget for the initiative and whether that was breached.

- Speak with your timekeeping people, especially if any granular effort is made at tracking time spent on projects versus overall work. Otherwise, this will not be a factor on which you can create a baseline until you evaluate the third criteria.

- Review the project history and overall reports on previous efforts to determine how far projects strayed over their expected delivery or expected timings. Microsoft Project has a baseline function; if the prior project manager used this correctly, it will reveal the established baseline for variances to be calculated. It will also create a lot of data to review to build the baseline.

In short, an initial baseline is preferable but not always possible. Your key stakeholders may so desire a baseline that you might find information and figures to support it in other places than those listed above. It's advisable to be identifying explicitly how to demonstrate the value behind this function and the need for starting details for the information and metrics to be valuable.

As we discuss metrics, let's do so on 2 fronts:

- Initiative related metrics

- Post-implementation metrics

Initiative Related Metrics are those designed to show the underlying value behind a project/initiative. Earned Value Management is one method to base the planned work against the overall schedule and cost on a point-in-time and trending basis. If at any point, the Earned Value (EV) divided by the Planned Value (PV) yields a value at 1 or above, you are on or potentially ahead of schedule. Otherwise, the inverse is true.

Cost Variances can be achieved by subtracting Actual Cost (AC), which includes all costs to the project, from the Earned Value (EV). If EV-AC yields a number above 0, you are within your cost targets.

These are simple metrics. Your organization may want to use a different or more detailed set of overall metrics, or wish to extrapolate those metrics to develop trending and analysis, as well as project variances and potential increases of cost to the project. I won't replay the statistics and calculations for each, as they're explained in much greater detail in other texts[7]. However, there are metrics with which it's reasonable to be concerned and highlight during an initiative:

- Cost – planned versus actual; trending both as a general trend and/or under or over-estimations of the overall initiative.

- Resource – planned utilization versus actual tracking against submitted time, and compared to the planned work completed. The comparison of the three figures will reveal trending that may suggest that date and dependency planning for the initiative may not be following an accurate model. If these are greatly over or under, review the issue to determine root cause and corrective methods.

- Schedule – planned versus actual, as well as whether tasks are being done as agreed with the project, and as represented in the actual project plan. Any large variances from the planned dates or tasks performed out of order should signal that resources are incorrectly estimated (note that I did not say "over" or "under" as both can occur at the same time). Example: A team member estimates that his work will require 40 hours of effort, yet marks it as 100% complete after 10 hours of effort, would create a legitimate reason to question the estimate.

- Estimation processes – as part of the metrics captured, variances in tasks that breach an agreed-upon tolerance or variance (i.e. +/- 10%) should be captured as inputs to the overall process and questioned as future projects are estimated. There may be legitimate reasons, or tendencies to "pad" estimates with time that is used to support unforeseen circumstances. As you begin to capture and see trending, use that to support future estimates based on Parametric Estimation (estimation based on historical data and scaling).

---

[7] "Earned Value Project Management, 3rd Edition" by Quentin Fleming and Joel Koppelman, ISBN-978-1930699892 is a typically recommended reading for all aspects of Earned Value Management.

It's important to review and report these metrics to stakeholders as early as variances are noted – both positive and negative. More important is to develop solutions for corrective action where possible. Presenting a problem with no solution is a disempowering experience that reduces confidence in the Initiative Manager's capability; coming equipped with an understanding of the root causes first (note my choice of words – to fully understand any corrections, you need to understand what first caused the problem) as well as suggestions and recommendations for corrective action will generally be better received and demonstrate thought, understanding and leadership.

I've given a small sampling of the types of metrics that are important during the initiative. Your organization may want to rank and rate the initiative based on other internal metrics and specific methods. It is important to understand that items such as a "customer satisfaction index" is not a figure quantifiable by a specific metric, nor is it objectively measurable. Any metric requested must therefore be a measurable indicator of the initiative. The example of a "customer satisfaction index" is something that is more quality driven and depends on a slightly more fuzzy logic. While there may be methods of measuring – surveys, questionnaires, etc. – such undertakings are generally less frequent.

Remember that most customers will be quite vocal when they're unsatisfied; if the initiative is progressing within the approved variances, continued discussion is not a considerate use of their time.

Post-Implementation Metrics are those that can only be measured after the initiative has been completed. Most initiatives have a business justification that can be quantified in some respect – as we mentioned before, all metrics are quantifiable items. Therefore, at the beginning of any initiative, it is important to capture a baseline of the areas to be measured at future points in time.

Example: *An initiative is being undertaken to implement a back-office processing and workflow solution designed to (1) reduce processing time by 40%, (2) reduce headcount by 20% overall within a 2 year timeframe, and (3) permit a 20% year-over-year growth in processing capability.*

In the above example, only one of those metrics is measurable – the second one provides a baseline to be achieved that can be measured against since it declares when the goal should be achieved. Both 1 and 3 are lacking that detail, and while both are reasonable goals, they cannot be accurately measured without a timeframe for achievement, A minor change to the objective of the initiative will make all 3 measurable, so note the rewrite below.

Example: *An initiative is being undertaken to implement a back-office processing and workflow solution that within 2 years should achieve a goal of (1) reducing processing time by 40% from its current average, (2) reducing headcount by 20%, and (3) permitting a 20% year-over-year growth in processing capability based on the figures from the prior year.*

All three are now measurable and can be charted.

Let's discuss the business case behind such an initiative. Suppose that this particular business represents $250M to the organization. A 20% increase in business would represent $50M more in the first year, and $60M in the second. Supposing that headcount costs represent $24M based on 600 people at a total cost of $40,000 (including benefits and overhead). Savings here would represent $4.8M. As we don't know the costs of reducing processing time, other than the ability of a person to do work 40% faster, let's assume that represents an additional $9.6M in savings that could be claimed by the business using the prior personnel costs.

This opportunity represents a potential income of $110M and potential savings of $24M based on the 2 years of headcount costs and productivity improvements.

The initiative would need to return the investment of the $24M and reveal the capability to have written $110M in new business during that period. This represents the investment.

Our obligation to the business, and their obligation to the initiative manager post-implementation, is to track those savings and revenues to determine if the initiative has met its goals and achieved Return on Investment (ROI). You should also factor the overall costs of building and implementing the solution, along with the operational costs of keeping it running and serving the customer, which will also be detailed in a later chapter.

As you might suspect, there's more than meets the eye with the ROI for this initiative, especially since we have only spoken about one portion of the equation – the amount needed to represent the system meeting the goals set for it. We've yet to outline the costs of developing the system, as well as the ongoing operational costs. This is a picture that should be discussed carefully with the sponsor to set their expectations of delivery and overall costs – too often, the part removed from an ROI equation is the ongoing cost of maintenance (software licenses, hardware maintenance, real-estate and power costs, networking costs and the like).

To return to our original point, measuring the post-implementation metrics involves reviewing all costs and whether the initiative is meeting those projections or falling short. This helps provide some level of historical data, and whether the Return on Investment can even be met. It's also important to understand the effectiveness of the overall investment in making future decisions and in adding value to the strategy of the organization.

This segues nicely to the next logical section.

Governance Organizations

Depending on the organization, "governance" can refer to a process, a specific organizational group, or sometimes both. I'll briefly cover one, and will speak more in detail about the other.

Many organizations have developed "Governance Committees" that are used for reviewing the investments being made by the organization to ensure they're cost-justified and align with the core goals and strategic direction. They provide an important check and balance to "sign the check" funding the initiative. Governance can be handled in a number of ways. I'll outline one example:

Example: An organization sets up a Governance Office that has a matrix relationship to several other individuals that represent constituencies throughout that organization. Their charter is to review any expenditure that breaches a specific dollar-cost threshold, and ensure that a reasonable business-case justifies the request for funding. Ultimately, they review upcoming projects and determine how a central pool of resources will be divided among several competing initiatives when all require central funding.

In the above example, a matrix organization provides review of a central approval process. This may not be the case in other organizations where the individual business units or lines-of-business may control their budget and have reasonable discretion over their spending once that budget has been approved. However, even that type of process requires planning, overall justification of a reasonable business case, and demonstration of benefit before the line item can be added to the budget.

Incidentally, adding a line item to a budget does not guarantee that an initiative will be undertaken, but merely provides the funding if and when needed. Many organizations will present a wish list of items to be completed within a budget year; in reality a fraction of those will see implementation, and funding from others potentially redistributed to support more strategic goals. During the course of a year, it is not uncommon to see organizations review their budgets and address the likelihood of a particular initiative being undertaken. If likely, the funding may stay intact; if unlikely, that funding may be reallocated to another initiative.

The short lesson is that budget approval is not a guarantee of either prioritization or undertaking of an initiative; simply, that it may be voted as strategic versus other initiatives competing for the same funding.

Having described organization around governance and how this is accomplished in various organization types, let's now discuss the concept of governance in general.

Governance is a controlling process providing guidelines, regulation, processes and policies to ensure that the direction and administration of any process or effort remains in a controlled state and delivers the desired and expected result. It provides a framework under which an initiative should be controlled to help achieve (note: not ensure) successful selection and potentially successful outcome.

Let's focus more on **financial governance**. In the examples cited in the prior section, I noted a desired initiative that had clear and measurable goals and a solid business case – namely, deliver a capability to reduce headcount, increase productivity, and increase business processing capacity. It's the duty of people surrounding the Initiative Manager or the Initiative Management Group to help the business parties support the business-case as reasonable, achievable, and the outcomes reasonable to expect given the scope and objectives.

Starting with the business case, we've outlined that the objectives are both cost-savings and revenue growth. For other initiatives, it may be addressing a new market opportunity. It is the responsibility of the initiative sponsor to provide a solid business case that will withstand scrutiny and that can be financially tested. The organization's financial wizards (usually a comptroller's department or the finance representative for the business division) can assist with validating the business case on financial grounds.

In the event that this is a new market opportunity, the initiative sponsor will be responsible for establishing the opportunity's potential and pursuing the funding to complete the initiative.

Myth: *It is the responsibility of the Project/Initiative Manager to justify an initiative, or to support its background details.* False. It's the responsibility of the Initiative Sponsor and his supporting staff to make the business case behind it, and to ensure that the information can be supported with reasonable financial, marketing, or technical detail. The Initiative Manager, once the business case has been approved and funded, then becomes the voice of the Initiative Sponsor in carrying out the initiative to successful completion. Too many people believe it's their responsibility to justify something that hasn't been supported with proper research.

In Chapter One, I mentioned my experience with establishing a financial governance process to create transparency around project investments. As these were examined, very few of the projects that were proposed and reviewed by a larger committee (after my own review of the details) could be supported by the data or argued by the sponsor for approval or continuance. As a result, we influenced an overall cut of 75% in project spending for that year, and it taught the business unit some valuable lessons around creating a solid business case before presenting a project concept.

To summarize, the process of governance is designed to ensure that initiative investments are properly managed and correctly aligned with strategic goals and objectives. Our role as Initiative Managers should consider a healthy dose of skepticism about those goals and understand enough about the organizations we support so that we provide guidance and expertise as a trusted partner in that process.

Reporting, Monitoring and Controls

Part of our Initiative Management role falls within 2 general categories:

- Reporting – providing accurate information about the status of an initiative, including metrics, resource utilization, activity, milestone achievements, measurement of planned activity versus actual activity, and the overall financial health of the initiative. Simply, where does the initiative stand at a specific point, and are there issues that should be escalated for awareness and action.

- Monitoring and Controls – Control implies monitoring to ensure that all the individual tasks and accountabilities are progressing per plan, and that any adjustments to plan are approved by the Initiative Manager.

Reporting. During the prior chapters on Communication, we discussed status of the initiative itself, and providing concise and meaningful information targeted to the correct audience. Thought must be given to the formation and communication of initiative metrics to the appropriate audience based on the factors we discussed above.

Your audience may want an exceptional amount of financial detail; they may also wish to see only high-level detail and expect to be informed of the more granular information when necessary. You will need to gain consensus with your sponsor and stakeholders on the reporting content to ensure relevance to all parties, and to avoid creating work that detracts from monitoring the project. As mentioned previously, I recommend graphing/charting the overall initiative trending for schedule and financial delivery against expectations, as information presented in a graphic format tends to resonate with its audience.

Monitoring/Control. The central theme within these points is that control cannot exist without a proactive monitoring mechanism for ensuring and validating information. Monitoring begets control, and provides a proactive means to pre-empt issues before they impede active progress.

"What Do I Monitor?"
Every element of the initiative from the following perspectives:

- Risk – proactively assess each risk; review and update an active register minimally on a bi-weekly basis.

- Issues – anything that has emerged threatening overall progress to the project, or requiring corrective action.

- Schedule progress – does the work match or vary from the schedule? Are there issues on activities that form a critical path and threaten a date? Do the initiative tasks require resource augmentation to complete deliverables within schedule? Where can tasks be reassigned or resources leveled to reduce team stress and bring tasks in on time (or preferably ahead of schedule, especially for those with an impact on the critical path of the initiative)?

- External/Third-party/Vendor deliverables – this is a concern with any initiative, since the priority you have placed on your critical initiative may not match your vendor's expectation. There are ways of mitigating these as risks. It's advisable to maintain engagement with your vendors so that they feel a part of the team, and understand the importance of their deliverable – this will help drive their behavior, and empower them to address items that may hinder progress. In fact, you should treat anyone contributing to the initiative as a valued member of the team; consultants, vendors, and third parties are increasingly important. Viewing them as "hired help" will decrease their compliance and willingness to meet exceptional requests and demands.

- Financial progress and financial demands – presuming you have control over the budget of the initiative, it's your job to ensure that funding is spent in a prudent manner, particularly if the result may breach the funding variances and further money is required to meet either a quality or date-driven deliverable. For instance, hiring a contractor to meet a date along the critical path could achieve the initiative objectives, but require additional funding. Your organization should provide guidelines on how this situation should be managed, but it should also be discussed candidly with your sponsor. I've mentioned variance thresholds previously, so these should also be discussed and agreed.

- Morale – it seems obvious when listed here, but it's the most neglected aspect of an initiative. So let's spend a few moments discussing this.

Why is morale important? If you need to ask this question, think back on past initiatives in which you've been involved where people are engaged, functioning as a team, working at their peak efficiency, and feeling that their role was important to the organization. Compare that to an experience where no one was engaging with you, your role was viewed as a miniscule part of an effort, and team members really didn't care about the quality of their output. Chances are you've encountered both experiences.

The difference I noted between the two related directly to morale. Team morale can make or break an effort, and the Initiative Manager should be viewed as someone who understands the roles of his contributors and takes an active interest in their work. While I wish I could quote a study on the success ratio of projects with strong morale versus those with weak morale to underscore its importance, the underlying point is that most people would rather work for someone who genuinely appreciates their contributions than someone who is aloof and uninvolved.

It's important for the initiative manager to be open and receptive to comments and questions, and approachable when a team member wants to discuss options that haven't been considered. Open-communication should be a core value of the initiative, and comments or suggestions welcomed. Some of the best ideas on completing an initiative come from those closest to the work, and brainstorming to offer feedback can overcome issues and avert future problems.

This is especially important when you consider geographically dispersed teams and the impact that distance can have on a relationship. The person most distant from the Initiative Lead can often feel the most neglected or "least loved". It's important to recognize that perception and use it as an opportunity to periodically reach out and form relationships with those people. I'd worked for a number of months with one developer whom I'd met only once in person for a few minutes. When I spoke with him long after the initiative was completed, I asked how he felt the interaction worked between us. He noted that since I routinely communicated with him, he felt as if he was a part of the team despite being remote and having met just that one time.

Summary and Upcoming Points

The most complex problems are often solved with the simplest solutions. I'll underscore this point with a personal experience some years ago. At a breakfast meeting in London with my British colleagues, everyone around the table had small teapots, each holding about 2 cups of tea. The British suffered and complained that their teapots always dribbled tea onto the tablecloth. I revealed a trick I'd learned by spreading a little butter on the lower lip of the spout. Lo-and-behold, I could pour a perfect cup of tea without spilling a drop. The British at my table – feeling somewhat slighted since they viewed tea as a national pastime – were left scratching their heads about how an American figured out this as a solution.

But I'll guarantee they remembered it.

We've discussed the framework around organization types, specific to Initiative Management Groups (however phrased), metrics and their importance, the meaning and importance of governance, and the reporting and monitoring/control process. While not an in-depth discussion of all the possible aspects of these, the objective behind their mention relates directly to the case for understanding the development of an Initiative Management Group and how that can be most effective for an organization. We'll begin our next Chapter discussing that point.

Chapter 6:
The Relevance of Initiative Management

Background

Thus far, I've presented information to consider in the development of an Initiative Management Organization. In Chapter One, I referred to the alignment of the Project/Program/Portfolio Management profession more strategically against the values and objectives of the organizations they serve, as well as providing inherent value by structuring their interactions for success.

In my original case for why I've referenced this as "Initiative Management" versus the variety of terms that fall within the Project Management lexicon, I outlined the staggering project failure rates and overall loss of confidence by numerous people both within and external to the Project Management profession.

Over the previous chapters, I suggested that rather than meeting the goals of achieving strategic progress for a business or organization, we seemed to have become entrenched in the rules and fraternity of our own profession by creating our own bureaucracies. Many organizations have questioned the value of a "PMO" and either abandoned it or marginalized its role; others have a mixed or amorphous view of what a PMO is or does. For those believing they need one, the logic varies widely if present at all, resulting in an unclear charter and lack of adoption. All of these confound and continue this vicious cycle versus making the necessary corrections.

For those who have adopted processes surrounding the PMO and methodology implementation, the answers can be equally unclear – either a one-size fits all process that works for some initiatives and not for others, or an unclear process that defines no useful methods of working. If we begin to understand these as the perceptions from the current state of project management, we can modify the behavior to represent the changes needed in the profession.

Sometimes, this will be called "Project Management 2.0", which implies more of a "social networking approach to project management", but doesn't address the underlying foundations necessary for success (simply adding a spanner to the toolbox when a hammer is needed won't work here). I've also seen and read reference to "Smart Project Management", inferring that Project Management principles are somehow "not smart"; here again, I question the nomenclature and motive.

For every problem, someone will offer a quick fix solution that masks and never effectively addresses the underlying symptoms. While I'm not suggesting an approach that tosses out both the baby and bathwater, I suggest taking a more holistic view at the entire process and extracting the parts that can be reused effectively into a comparable set of ideas and pragmatic approaches that focus on overall leadership and processes best suited to the sponsoring organization's requirements.

It requires using our knowledge in a much different way; and explains why I've surrounded this under the banner of "Strategic Initiative Management" to overcome the perception of and objection to the words "Project Management" (or more specifically "PMO").

As you'll see, the approach is not cleverly word-smithing a new name to an old product.

In Part Two, I'll begin discussing the underlying methods, procedures, overall roles and accountabilities for successful initiatives to occur. The background of the first few sections has served as education to understand where we have been as a profession, and the areas that require focus and specific attention. As we further define Initiative Management, we'll discuss additional elements that build on that foundation.

Before we do so, let's review where the existing processes have failed to meet the desired objectives more than 68% of the time by detailing more of the information reviewed in the first chapter.

- ***Failure to provide agreed deliverables on time or within budget/approved variances.*** Central to the argument of how and what to deliver is a clear negotiation of expectations. Many organizations have a high threshold of demands without recognizing their impact, cost, resource implications, or factors that pose threats to delivery. Others create a culture where negotiation is not possible, or where simply saying, "Ok" without a dialog on the ability to deliver against the expectations. I'll later discuss setting appropriate expectations.

- ***Failure to address quality standards.*** Most methodology approaches include some passing mention of "quality" as a component. However, in most cases, it is not a core component, nor is it part of the design or business requirements process. As a result, when the product is finally turned over for quality checks and validation against requirements, time has usually been pulled from a later point in the schedule; usually it will come from the Quality Assurance and Validation processes. In addition, a change to meet one standard of quality can have residual impacts on other components, something usually not considered based by assuming that "we'll just do things correctly" (generally, a naïve assumption).

    The approaches to address this have included "Test-Driven Development" which bases itself on the theory that all development will follow the expected test pattern. However, it risks neglecting the user specification and results in a core focus of passing the subsequent QA checks as a litmus standard of success. The elements of Test-Driven development are needed along with a complete understanding of how the product will be used, with thought given to that inclusion into the design and specification – generally the items that will break and result in finger-pointing are the ones not questioned or actively considered (read: ignored), which begins an unproductive cycle that could/should have been avoided.

- ***Inability to address scope.*** This reflects on our first point, but also requires that we consider the potential for change. Therefore, a thorough understanding of scope, the necessity for iterative changes, and the ability to moderate and control the discussion provide keys to successfully managing an initiative. In a rational approach to completing an initiative, some items must be considered:

    o ***Phasing*** – Is the feature or Change to Scope essential to first-day operation and how will that affect the overall initiative? See the section on Change Management in Chapter Two.

- o *Change Management* – the purpose of a scope discussion is not to deny that change will occur, but to focus around its necessity and priority. Can version 1.0 be released without the feature or change until it can be later implemented and funded in 1.1? Is it superfluous? An open and candid dialogue is essential to success in this aspect.

- o *Scope Control* – this does not suggest that Scope cannot change, but the sponsor must understand scope definition, his or her options, and how this will affect their satisfaction and project outcomes. Common to all of these is a review of whether features can be introduced iteratively. If reasonable discussion is not possible on those points, success is jeopardized.

- ▪ *Inability to deliver value for money (financial governance, ROI) or escalating costs due to artificial deflation and invalid financial models.* This was discussed in Chapter Five (Governance). In summary, many organizations will inflate the expectations of future returns to focus attention to their initiative and obtain requisite funding. An astute Initiative Manager should question whether the fundamental details behind those estimates are correct or inflated, or if poor assumptions (too optimistic, not reflective of actual market or actual market conditions, etc.) are being used to drive the initiative.

- ▪ *Ineffective or inadequate communications, or poorly structured communications.* Chapter Three – yes, all of it -- discussed the importance, structure, and parameters around ensuring productive and meaningful communications. An effective Initiative Manager's role is to communicate in **ALL** directions. I've seen too many would-be Project and Program Managers believe they were highly effective based solely on their ability to manage and communicate upwards, then use that influence downwards. Positive impact includes the ability to influence all stakeholders and members of the initiative team, not simply one constituency, and communicate in all directions. The world could use fewer people who can only speak glowingly to management and in a condescending tone to all others. Communication is a 360 degree art and science.

- ▪ *Inadequate stakeholder/sponsor/executive support.* Your initiative will fail if your key stakeholders have no interest or investment. If the sponsor doesn't care, why should the team completing the work? It's important for everyone to feel that the investment of their time and effort is recognized and appreciated by senior-level involvement, whether that is appearance at status meetings, or short responses to indicate their concerns or pleasure with progress. Engaged sponsors and stakeholders will quickly observe changes in the level of engagement of the initiative team. Anyone who has managed a project with weak sponsor support will relate how it feels to be left with your tail exposed and hanging in the breeze. In gaining agreement on the importance of the initiative, it is imperative that the Initiative Manager expresses the need to see support from the sponsors to help assure successful outcomes. If their answer is "I'm too busy", that's the wrong way to start and sends the wrong message – counteract this immediately through mitigation. It's an opportunity to show leadership.

- ▪ *Poor management, implementation, and leadership.* While this seems like a restatement of the prior point, this isn't. As an Initiative Manager, this is "you". Projects fail due to lack of strong leadership and poor management practices – these range from being too far from the details; failure to see the big picture; failure to take the efforts necessary to bring things back on track; failure to take proactive measures when needed; complacency; failure to act to avoid escalation of problems; failure to exercise controls, and the list goes on.

Too often, I've watched as Project and Program Managers have stood aloof and aside as events happened to adversely impact their initiative because they've lacked the right sense of ownership. An Initiative Manager owns the execution of the work, and is the accountable party to see that issues are being raised and controlled, as well as arbitrating disputes and finding resolution to apparent crises. Acting helpless – part of the culture of many organizations – is an aspect of Project Management (and often many candidates out of PMO-type environments) where the Project Manager feels no ownership stake in success or failure; only a duty to report status as Red, Amber, or Green yet take no action to change it. Look no further to find where some of the negative feedback about PMOs originates. It's within our power to change that perception.

- *Incomplete success criteria.* How many projects have you managed where the definition of success is amorphous at best? Can you even define whether the project was successful? How would it be measured? Success needs to be a measured and quantified standard such as "Release of Project X successfully before time and within budget or variance, including all agreed-upon features or approved variances." We can baseline against those and determine that Project X was successfully implemented. We can later check the assumptions about ROI and determine if those are being met. But a big mistake behind defining any initiative is poorly defining how success will be measured. The criteria need not be complex, though it must be quantifiable.

- *Poor understanding of organizational intersects and how to manage within the organization.* Each organization is different, culturally, structurally, geographically and politically. In a very large organization, there is not one person who knows every employee or every intersect. Getting to know these people helps to properly structure the initiative -- finding the subject matter experts and stakeholders, as well as those people who will help you get things done. It will also help you find ways to hindrances to your efforts, and every organization has a few of those as well. Everyone was new at one point in their life, and should understand that a new Initiative Manager (especially if they are new to the organization or division, or a consultant brought in for purpose) will have questions. Organizational charts will help, as will asking for the key individuals to help in directing traffic.

- *Early abandonment, or cancellation before completion.* This typifies a key reason why many projects are cancelled, and when a project is stopped, it strands resources (sunk costs) that must be understood. When abandonment or cancellation happens, there is often little understanding of the events leading to cancellation or contributing root causes. Some may have been within the control of the Initiative Manager, and others outside their control or influence. In fact, postmortems are routinely overlooked resulting in valuable learning experiences being lost and never recalled until someone remembers (generally when it happens again the second or third time around).

- *Poor sense of charter (i.e. What is the success criteria?).* Here is a question – when do you establish the business case for an Initiative to the Project/Initiative Team? Answer: At your Initiative Kickoff presentation. In fact, it should be among the leading topics to set the stage and common understanding of the initiative. Moreover, it's the Initiative Sponsor's chance to pitch why the initiative is important to the organization and underscore his/her support and backing for the Initiative Manager to be voice of the sponsor. If you suspect this is done less often than it should, you'd likely be correct. It provides the initiative with proper visibility, and reduces the chances that a highly visible effort would be cancelled.

Before I began the background detail of Part One, I began outlining the case for Strategic Initiative Management. As the structure and complexity of projects evolve, as our workforce diversifies globally, and as the lines between technology and business solutions continue to blur so that the utilization of technology is more ubiquitous, there are clear arguments that a new approach to how we view "projects", then "programs" then "Portfolios" must also reasonably evolve.

If you've inferred that I believe the structure and wisdom of our Project Management learnings to date have no place in the future of managing initiatives, you would be incorrect. Rather, we need to incorporate these with less focus on the result of Project Management being "process" and place more attention on an outcome-based philosophy.

Project Management cannot exist without Initiatives to manage. Project Management needs to evolve beyond the insular view that many in our profession have taken. Our profession, often maligned, has not been recognized for being a contributor to progress in the way it should. Rather than calling this "Project Management 2.0" – a term already coined, but in my view lacking clear definition, seemingly applying nothing more than a "New & Improved" label to something existing -- I'd like to begin now discussing the case for why we need to view all work as initiatives.

In Part Two, I'll begin outlining the thought process behind this and outline the framework toward achieving pragmatism and strategic alignment.

Part Two:
Strategic Initiative Management Demystified

Chapter 7:
An Introduction

If your answer to 'a failure in process is corrected by implementing more processes', you now have a good opportunity to rethink that answer.

With that thought to ponder, I'll begin with the core of the approach to Strategic Initiative Management. The goal is not to simply layer one process upon another, or implement more complex processes that create a shackling and helpless influence to initiatives. The goal is to create the right atmosphere for change, and the correct processes and exception handling to counteract failures when these occur.

We can walk as straight a line as reasonable possible from Point A to Point Z. Or we can create such a circuitous route for ourselves that we never reach the Point Z objective.

As we talk more through the overall elements of Strategic Initiative Management (SIM), we'll discover more of the intent of this as a practice.

Lexicon
In beginning this section, let's also begin with a clean lexicon of terms that will be used to help set the stage on where Pragmatism takes hold and Strategic Initiative Management begins to propel the results-driven approach.

IMO/IMG – Initiative Management Organization/Initiative Management Group. The oversight group responsible for alignment of all work, vertically, strategically, and organization-wide, and charged with the fulfillment of the charter of managing the paths of initiatives, including relative dependencies.

Initiative Manager. The person ultimately responsible for the delivery of approved initiative work within the organization; ultimately, he/she provides a validation point to ensure that a collaborative atmosphere conducive to success is fostered and that initiatives are monitored through their lifecycle, including post-completion work and validation of subsequent operational life cycle costs.

SIM – Strategic Initiative Management. The methods, procedures, and specific processes that help expedite strategic change for an organization, as well as create an environment of collaboration in which a greater focus is placed on quality of results than on any specific element of the overall process.

ROI – Return on Investment - Signifies the expected return on the investment in a quantifiable format that is measured over an agreed period.

TCO – Total Cost of Ownership. The total of all fixed costs of an effort, as well as the continued costs of ensuring operational function over a project life span (Variable and Recurring costs)

Introduction and Background

I recently watched a story on the local television news about an organization that builds homes for disabled Iraq and Afghanistan War Veterans. In the story, an Army Sergeant lost both of his legs when a roadside bomb hit his convoy. He survived, but is now confined to a wheelchair. In the meantime, in the midst of 90+ degree summer heat in New York State (and tropical humidity), an organization that builds homes for disabled veterans of these conflicts found a building lot a few towns over – the organization gets the donated materials, has a basic floor plan for the house, and recruits volunteers from within the neighborhood that care enough about the cause to donate their hard work and sweat equity to the construction of the home. This was not a small undertaking, but a fully handicapped accessible home that would suit both him and his family's new requirements.

I cite this type of story for a couple of reasons that we'll find germane to the tenor of this book.

1. A clear strategic goal and a clear equity proposition coming from the effort. The mission was clear: Build a home for someone who served our Armed Forces courageously.

2. A clear but minimal process. Basic plans, little variation, and a home well-suited to its planned purpose.

3. Collaboration all around. The resources were donated at little or no cost, and the group works from voluntary donations as a charitable organization for anything not donated. The rest relies on neighbors doing the tasks they can by using any free time available. Quite a few sacrificed their vacations in order help complete a home in August heat.

A goal. A process. Collaboration. A strategy. It's said at times that a house is among one of the most complex things to build because amidst the process there are code and quality checks, there are local requirements, and there are structural requirements. This project was not only heartfelt by its participants, it also had some added wrinkles in that it needed to be fully accessible – that means wheelchair accessible showers, bathrooms, kitchens, and egress. This is more complex than a standard wood-frame Habitat for Humanity Home, yet more than 40 of these projects have been completed for disabled vets across the country.

I'll never know who the Initiative Manager was that led this, though the recipient will – they'll be neighbors.

I cite this as an ideal situation. Keeping this simple and lean, having collaboration, and maintaining concise planning kept this effort on track. Pragmatically.

As a Project and Program Manager, I've raised some eyebrows with colleagues in the types of individuals I would select for my team – especially given that I was usually the last kid picked for dodge ball, let alone any sport. While many in my profession will always seek out the "A" players – the "rock stars", or those who are standouts from the crowd as individual contributors – I've sought people a little lower down the ladder that show great collaboration skills and demonstrate that they're team players. There's a difference between the 2 psychologies.

People who are great individual contributors often have egos that match their talents. While they'll score high marks for their achievements, they're also most often resented because they are among the first chosen for leadership roles where they carry the same approach. That approach is not conducive to effectively managing others, so they often become inferior managers and really belong in their original comfort zone until they've demonstrated the right collaboration skills.

People who are good team players are humble enough to know their strengths and weaknesses, and smart enough to know when and where to seek help or advice on improvement. They quickly learn how to work effectively with others because they don't let their ego take center-stage. If you assemble that type of team, you'll have the collaboration necessary to achieve greater things, versus the attention-hoarding individual contributor.

I once had an argument with a colleague who insisted that I needed a specific resource on my initiative, and should delay the project to secure that person, who was described as "the Eric Clapton of his trade". I responded that I didn't need Eric Clapton to get things done, when a bright, enthusiastic, capable pair of hands (Eddie Van Halen or Bo Diddley would have been fine) was required. It taught the individual an important lesson that while having a known entity on an initiative is nice, it's not always guaranteed and quite often not the best answer.

Provide me with a solid team of good solid players that can work together without letting egos get in the way, and I'll deliver a solid result. Deliver a team of individual contributors, and watch the battles begin.

Case in Point: The 1997 Major League Baseball Season

The New York Yankees have traditionally been a team that has lured high-priced and talented individual contributors who have demonstrated success on other teams. They have the highest payroll in Major League baseball. Rarely have they taken the time or effort to groom a player on their own and congeal as a cohesive team on the field. No one can dispute that they play well, but finishing second place in the American League East that year was a disappointment to their fans.

The Florida Marlins were among the newest teams in the league. Through some acquisition of talent during the season, and constant coaching between some "A" players and a roster mostly of "B" players, they managed to finish second in the National League East and entered the championships as a Wild Card. No one expected them to handily beat the San Francisco Giants in 3 games, nor were they expected to beat the Atlanta Braves to win the National League Pennant in 6 games. The last thing anyone expected was for the lowest paid team in baseball to advance to the World Series and win in 7 games, beating the Cleveland Indians.

It isn't what you pay, or how great an individual contributor may be; it's how you work as a team. The Marlins that year were a great example of that sort of teamwork.

Core Goals

It's important to recognize the core goals within an Initiative and begin with those plus our Project Management Knowledge to set the baseline for achieving overall quality, compliance and successful delivery. Some Core Rules underscore this:

Core Rules

1. Process is not the output of an effort. While process acts as a guide, it does not represent the end goal of an effort other than one geared toward a process design for project/initiative management functionality.

2. Process is not the excuse. Again, it is a guideline. If an initiative manager adds no value to the strategic goals other than following a set script, he/she will be paralyzed by events falling outside that script.

3. Pragmatism is the keyword in the governance of activities.

4. Collaboration is core to the value behind Initiative Management; without it, no reasonable framework will deliver, much less this one.

5. Promotion of value in all activities is paramount. If we are doing something that has no quantifiable value to either the initiative or its stakeholders, we should not do it.

6. Communication is 360. We promote and encourage interaction and managed communication, but we also promote the management of information in an organized fashion. If it's not relevant to the audience, see Rule 3.

7. Options, decisions and consensus lead to actions. Discussions, while important, should focus on precise issues and result in options, decisions and consensus.

8. Act ethically.

This likely sounds somewhat like "Agile" or "Lean" principles, and perhaps there are traits borrowed from it. But the difference with SIM is not defining that an effort must be iterative or defined by sprints. While they may, an effort may also be defined via a waterfall process or via a traditional SDLC system of development. The framework is neutral to product development style, as this is an area best left to the organization's preferences and working methods.

Later in this section, I'll define some breakpoints where Strategic Initiative Management clearly breaks with a traditional rigid approach that typifies the definition of other frameworks. As you review this, allow some leeway in avoiding a rigid categorization under one size.

That said, let's begin walking through SIM and sorting through the points referenced above.

1. *Process is not the output of an effort. While process acts as a guide, it does not represent the end goal of an effort other than one geared toward a process design for project/initiative management functionality.*

Process is not a goal. While constructive and fundamental rigors can and should be used to command and control initiatives, the end goal should be process neutral. Although I dislike the overuse of this phrase because it loses its relevance, the fundamental thought behind it should be part of the initiative guidelines: **Process does not exist to hinder progress; it exists to facilitate progress**. When process stops meeting that criteria, it's time review the relevance of that process and make adjustments.

This becomes a thorny and misinterpreted issue among Project Managers. Notice that I did not state, "Process is not required" but that "Process is not the output of an effort." There is a distinct difference. The process needs to be appropriate and aligned with the overall size, scope, and complexity of the effort, and defined for clarity.

Process is not the objective. Process is not the strategic goal unless the charter of the initiative is to create a process. There are far too many within the profession who believe that the magic formula for success is to simply follow a tightly scripted process, and when the effort fails, point back to a failure of the process versus the accountability that rests with the Initiative Manager and his team. Process is not the rock we hide behind when under heavy fire. It's a poor answer to a question that centers on competency.

Process is a guide. Expect to come across exceptions in every process. This doesn't require that we invent an entirely new process, or add existing weight to an otherwise acceptable process that is pragmatic and makes sense. Just as when an automobile develops a flat tire, the solution is not to replace the engine but to fix the tire or install the spare tire in the trunk.

I recognize that this could create a freeze point in certain cultures where working without a very specific script creates a state of inertia for those members of a team. We'll discuss the advice around this as a separate topic.

2. ***Process is not the excuse. It is a guideline. If an initiative manager adds no value to the strategic goals other than following a set script, he/she will be paralyzed by events falling outside that goal.***

This is a pet peeve with me and managers and clients with whom I've worked in the past. Process revolves around scripted events – after each event, there should be a response, set of responses, or even a response branching that includes available options. A script will not adequately replace intuitive thought, especially when events occur outside the parameters of the script.

As I've watched the prevalence of "process-focused Project Management" – meaning individuals or organizations who operate within a very rigid set of processes – I also witness denigration of project management capability to a very secretarial level: Capturing notes, taking minutes, assigning actions, and demonstrating competence in executing the process script.

You cannot process-legislate leadership characteristics. To my knowledge, there isn't a run-book or script that explains the steps and branches of leadership. I mention this to differentiate "process excellence" – which is a good and worthy accomplishment – from the achievements of "Project Excellence", and subsequently, Initiative Excellence.

This is a good segue to discuss process versus project in terms of the confusion between methodology and practices. In the current business climate, there are organizations that represent their credentials as being "CMMI^{TM} Level 3 or Level 5 Certified". This indicates that the organization has mastered a level of documented and repeatable processes that in and of themselves are admirable accomplishments. They provide no assurance of results, however, or that an organization can capably handle project-related activities, even though they may be adequate in managing application support functions or data center activities.

The information below relates specifically to CMMI^{TM} Maturity Levels and their associated competencies for depiction and example purposes:

Maturity Level	Competencies and Artifacts
Maturity Level 1	Initial - Competent people and heroics
Maturity Level 2 - Managed	• CM - Configuration Management • MA - Measurement and Analysis • PMC - Project Monitoring and Control • PP - Project Planning • PPQA - Process and Product Quality Assurance • REQM - Requirements Management • SAM - Supplier Agreement Management

Maturity Level	Competencies and Artifacts
Maturity Level 3 - Defined	• DAR - Decision Analysis and Resolution • IPM - Integrated Project Management +IPPD • OPD - Organizational Process Definition +IPPD • OPF - Organizational Process Focus • OT - Organizational Training • PI - Product Integration • RD - Requirements Development • RSKM - Risk Management • TS - Technical Solution • VAL - Validation • VER - Verification
Maturity Level 4 - Quantitatively Managed	• QPM - Quantitative Project Management • OPP - Organizational Process Performance
Maturity Level 5 - Optimizing	• CAR - Causal Analysis and Resolution • OID - Organizational Innovation and Deployment

Notice that 3 areas of CMMI refer to Project Management within the process – the rudimentary application in Level 2 (the fact that a plan exists, is monitored and controlled); Integrated Project Management in Level 3; and a more quantitative view in Level 4 (Quantitative Project Management, where individual efforts are viewed with metrics). CMMI may provide a base to begin a review of your project processes, and determine assessment on end-to-end process data. But while useful, it does not offer a path to "project excellence", nor any core guarantees of success; it simply espouses that a process exists, regardless of its effectiveness.

Many organizations will cite their CMMI Level of Certification. Two points to be reinforced in this regard:

(a) Understand how the organization has been certified, as well as the artifacts related to projects.

(b) Ask the organization to provide a reasonable explanation of how CMMI compliance has enhanced execution excellence for initiatives.

This is not intended to malign CMMI as a process, though I reference it as an example of a process-centric approach that contains minimal guidance specific to the discipline.

As another example, I'll cite the Swedish retailer IKEA for a moment. For anyone not familiar, IKEA sells unassembled furniture and small house wares that are ideal for furnishing a small apartment. My wife and I both furnished a small one-bedroom apartment in "early-IKEA" some years ago and we managed to squeeze most of a 2-story town-home into 680 square feet.

IKEA's products come with sets of Allen Wrenches, pictorial instructions, and usually a few extra parts that make you wonder after the product is assembled what you may have missed, even though it resembles the showroom floor model. Some things are so simple that a 6-year-old child could construct them (unfortunately, the 6 year old child was not included), and others that will have you looking at the pictures wondering about the PhD that created the schematics. My wife and I have been on both ends of the spectrum, but still managed to assemble by assigning some logic to what we were doing. If it was assembling a wardrobe, I could understand the outcome and enough about the pieces to form an understanding around putting the pieces in their correct place. At times the schematics helped greatly; other times, they became confusing.

The schematics to the IKEA furniture in this example are what I'll liken to a process. If we so relied on the schematics versus using some degree of independent thought within the defined boundaries, we'd have thrown our hands up in resignation and been left with a pile of wood and particleboard rubble on the floor. Blaming the schematic or process was not an option, nor should it be a hindrance to progress. I alluded to this in the prior section that some cultures would simply stop and not continue further, nor would they raise awareness of their challenges or request help since their particular culture might consider this as rude. In the same way we discussed Communication and Culture in Chapter 3, also consider this when selecting your team, as well as selecting the geo-diversity of your initiative.

Ergo, if you think your team will simply stop when there is a problem rather than reason it out, you have the wrong team for success. Fix it quickly, or your initiative will be hampered.

3. *Pragmatism is the keyword in the governance of activities.*

Not everything will conform to the process script. Although as project/initiative managers we try hard to define and mitigate risks, some will never be foreseen nor is it possible to completely mitigate. And customer decisions to change project direction midstream based on changes in strategy, marketplace dynamics, regulatory issues, and other decisions are ones that usually defy any scripted response.

So why do I say "pragmatism"? Why didn't I simply focus on process in addressing this guideline?

Concisely put, the dynamics between people – stakeholders and sponsors, initiative team members with each other, third-party vendors and initiative objectives, as well as many other intersections – will require some level of leadership and pragmatism to resolve, negotiate, or render decisions based on changing events.

It's unlikely that the sponsor of an initiative will make a judgment based on interpretation of PRINCE2, APM, Rational Unified Process, PMI or other guidelines. He or she will likely look at the background of the issue, and try to find collaborative ground, concede an argument, force a position, or use some other mechanism to achieve resolution. If a strong initiative manager is the voice of the sponsor, they'll use the same pragmatic approach to achieve a similar outcome. While it may not always conform to ideal circumstances, it can help break a stalemate on an issue.

It's thinking with an eye toward achieving the objective, not simply following set rules. It's creating an atmosphere in which all team members embrace that type of approach. I paraphrase this by saying, "Do what is essential, and only what is essential." Supposing that you have a very extensive initiative, examine it closely to ensure that the effort exerted is critical to initiative success.

Do not read this as slave driving. Team-forming activities, collaboration, necessary meetings and statuses, and appropriate forms of team communication are things that are essential to initiative success. I am not suggesting taking such a lean approach that we preclude such activities from consideration.

To underscore an example of this point, a former employee (someone with whom I maintain an informal mentoring relationship) expressed their frustrations with her recent initiative work. Over-and-above the work in managing the progress and organization around a very large and global piece of work, they were also arranging travel for team members coming in and out of various locations. Knowing the organization, as well as the availability of spare time in the schedules of most personal assistants (PAs), I immediately asked why they were performing a task that should be given to a PA to handle more capably and easily. I chided their normally keen judgment in not delegating such a task rather than compounding their stress, In this case, travel arrangements were "noise" that detracted from the realization of initiative goals. A very senior professional shouldn't be scouring the region for an available business-class hotel and coach fares when someone better suited could do so.

Below listed is an example bullet list of other time-wasters:

- Meetings without agendas

- Meetings where the audience is not germane to you.

- Immediate response to e-mails/Instant messages.

- Minute-by-minute accounting of time – I'll cite this as an example momentarily.

- Multiple meetings to provide equivalent status to several individuals (consolidate these where possible, or delegate upward to your functional or initiative manager)

I promised I'd elaborate the fourth bullet on minute-by-minute time accounting. I once worked for an organization and micro-manager who wanted to dissect time into 15-minute intervals, and in one week spent we 8 full hours doting over a 30-minute discrepancy in hours between 2 conflicting reports that were never designed to match accurately. So the result was no longer a 30-minute discrepancy.

It was a 16 hour and 30 minute discrepancy by the time proctology of the situation was complete, a 3200% decrease in efficiency for the team, and time not billable to client work. At our bill-rates, this was a very costly decision to waste time on something that would have had marginal impact, and was ultimately reflected correctly. Sixteen hours that will never be regained. The lesson was less "Keep accurate track of your time" and more "Demand that management not create impositions on it."

In short, pragmatism suggests that we'll do precisely what is essential for success, but avoid any interference to that objective. Any interference should be raised as a blockage, questioned, and addressed once with a firm decision to determine whether or not it enters the scope of the initiative.

4. *Collaboration is core to the value behind Initiative Management; without it, no reasonable framework will deliver, much less this one.*

One of the core philosophies behind Initiative Management is to create an environment that fosters teaming and collaboration.

There are five basic methods applied to conflict resolution:[8]

- **Forcing** – one party pushes its view and position until adopted, often to the detriment of project relationships

- **Withdrawing** – one party simply acquiesces to the will of another party through inaction, concession, or passivity

- **Smoothing** – downplaying the differences to reach a resolution, one which might be somewhat acceptable to either party, or minimally effective in goal achievement

- **Compromising** – both parties agree to a concession of some sort in exchange for their agreement on this particular issue; often each party feels as if they've not quite achieved their main objective

---

[8] "Teamwork and Project Management", Karl Smith, 2005, ISBN - 978-0073103679

- **Problem-Solving/Collaboration (*also referred to as Confrontation in certain texts*)** – both parties work together to focus on the cause of the problem, and without judgment reach a decision on a situation that benefits the objectives of the project or initiative

There are benefits and drawbacks to each, but a collaborative solution in most instances benefits the goals and objectives outlined for the initiative. Team members, stakeholders, and sponsors cannot maintain individual agendas, and must form a cohesive team by focusing on outcomes and delivery.

I call this the "we" orientation, which should be characterized by a value-proposition that positively impacts all team members. When diverse groups are involved in an initiative, addressing the core question that most people will relate to their personal interests is necessary:

"What's In It For Me?"

You'll hear this question, and your response must reflect how the performing organization and individual team member derives a tangible or intangible benefit from their efforts. It's naive and foolish to expect all people to sublimate their own self-interests; as team members see the benefit to the organization, translate that into benefits they should expect (i.e. increased market share, organization growth, more opportunities for advancement, recognition for their contributions, etc.)

I won't condone overstating or misrepresenting the benefits of any initiative. For instance, an initiative could result in employee cutbacks, affecting some team members at the end of the initiative. Keeping a positive view on such an effort isn't easy, but is possible, and many organizations have explained the benefits of the change to employees that are to be severed, resulting in better adoption and a more positive employee outlook.

While not easy, the challenge of thinking through the benefits can reap rewards. As the story below indicates, there's always a positive and negative way of viewing a situation:

> *Two small children were brought out to the farm, and each was put into a horse stall, filled with manure. They were each given a shovel and pitchfork. Their parents left and came back a couple of hours later. The child in the first stall was crying since he'd been left in a stinky, manure-filled stall all alone in a dark barn, screaming at his parents when they returned.*

> *The second child was busily mucking out the stall, moving the manure from one side to another, when his parents asked him what he was doing. So he told them: "Well, with all this horse manure, I figured there had to be a pony in here somewhere."*

There are benefits and drawbacks to many things. Focusing your team on the benefits, or the value-proposition, will be key to gaining their trust and collaboration with one another.

I've had the experience in working within "passive/aggressive"[9] environments where collaboration was a distant myth, and personalities ruled the show. This creative environment – which I'll discuss more as we progress – lacked some of the attributes that helped inspire the practices in this book (among many others). I confirmed knowledge that I'd practiced previously, although it didn't take hold in this environment based on both leadership and tactical/strategic conflicts.

1. Never let your managers speak for you when you can speak more accurately on your own. I often found one manager that would significantly over-inflate efforts that resulted in the firm routinely losing bids. When the same estimates were socialized among his team, different and more concise results appeared.

---

[9] Defined in the most recent edition of the DSM-IV, Appendix B

2. Never permit your managers to answer technical questions when you're more capable of providing the needed detail, or more accurately, when the manager's sole objective is to obscure the detail to protect perceived weakness in his/her position.

3. Communication is "speak for yourself". Be prepared to present alternate views and brainstorm options, and ensure all voices are heard. This is a difficult rule, as some managers may only want their option to be considered despite the experience of their teams. All options need to be considered. For example, I may understand the difference between 2 variant database management systems, but not specific nuances of each that might preclude one from being a reasonable solution for a business problem. Someone with that expertise is better suited to explain and should be given that opportunity.

4. Collaboration of the team outweighs individual contribution or individual achievement. Another way of stating this is simple: "Leave your ego at the door." It's so simple a concept that it amazes me to witness how often it's missed. Collaboration does not equal individual contribution but equates to the power and ideas brought forward by the collective power and focus of the team. I mentioned in Chapter Four an exercise aimed at expanding your boundaries of thought (Exercise 4-1). Have you tried it yet with a team? I did with one team I'm recalling and I witnessed a team so dysfunctional as to give up 2 minutes into the exercise and question the value. It was either a case of Extreme Attention Deficit Disorder, or it truly demonstrated the overall lack of creativity and teamwork that existed.

5. Collaboration comes from mutual respect. An initiative manager does not know enough to "perform" everyone's role, nor is that his or her objective. However, that initiative manager should know enough to understand the contribution of the role. Conversely, the initiative manager shouldn't expect any of the others on his/her team to know the complete details of the initiative manager's role. The underlying point is that each team member plays an important part, outlined by my prior citation of removing the egotistical behavior. Setting an atmosphere of mutual respect will contribute greatly toward overall productivity, as team members will understand their value as part of the initiative. Surprisingly, expect arguments from more "traditional" managers.

6. Collaboration does not mean more meetings. It means more *productive* meetings that end with decisions as their objective. Consensus driven organizations, along with many of those with weak management, will have the most difficulty with the notion of decisions as final.

For Item #6, and as a good idea to understand your team's composition, it's a good idea to ask all the team members to have a Myers-Briggs profile administered, either formally or informally. There are plenty of good free resources on the Internet that provide a short-form Myers-Briggs Type Indicator of 60-70 questions (the fully administered test is 126 questions). This will allow the initiative manager to better understand the personalities and type indicators of his team among 16 possible categories:

- Introversion/Extroversion
- Sensing/iNtuiting
- Thinking/Feeling
- Judging/Perceiving

Every type has different traits, and describes aspects of the individual that foster an understanding of their interaction within a well-formed team. By the way, this is not a test to create the "master race of initiative management" so please view it as a tool to better understand one another.

And for full disclosure, my own MBTI is "ENTJ". I'll leave that as something you can research on your own, but that may also provide understanding why I'm authoring a document and theory on Strategic and Pragmatic Initiative Management.

5. *Promotion of value in all activities is paramount. If we are doing something that has no quantifiable value to either the initiative or its stakeholders, we should not do it.*

Many have heard the term "gold-plating" concerning an initiative: adding excess features or functions that are clearly above and beyond scope and approved requests, but add little value to the initiative objectives. Gold plating is but one example. Let's talk about others. We mentioned meetings in a previous section. Some meetings have value. Many do not. If clearly the value of a meeting no longer exists, rethink that meeting and focus attention on areas that would benefit from the time re-gained.

As an exercise, think back to a recent project or initiative with which you've been involved, and ask yourself these questions about it:

- What was the value in dollar or strategic terms of the activity? (A)

- How much time was spent on that activity? How much was each hour of time worth for each person? Multiply those together. (B)

- How much time could have been saved if it had been done more efficiently? (X)

- What was the result of that activity? (C)

- Did it add the expected value to the initiative? (Yes/No)

Now from those figures, take the value of (A) and subtract the sum of the inputs of (B) once you've figured that out. If the result in (C) was positive, then ultimately the activity did return some value. If it was negative, then it's a candidate for removal or reconsideration using this formula. Now I gave you another figure, which was (X). If you subtract the hours of time in X from B and then multiply by the cost of time, you'll reveal a new (B) based on better work efficiency. If this changes your result from negative to positive, or if it increases the positive result in (C), then you retrospectively understand how you could have been more efficient.

These are not scientific figures to derive X, but a good initiative manager can see how much time was misspent during the activity and will have ideas for how to make that more efficient.

Other considerations include the initiative's expected outcome. If you consider how to realize the initiative's value as quickly as possible – think of how to make the product and process leaner and more efficient to achieve similar results – you can begin to see if adding new features will have a desired impact. For instance, how much time or material cost will be involved, and what is the expected return from its inclusion or exclusion at this phase? Understanding that will unlock a set of decisions that can be informative and useful for your sponsor and stakeholder; it may also create an elongation of the project into iterative phasing – in other words, a stepped approach to feature and function inclusion.

In a perfect world, every feature would be implemented in every initiative and would fall within the allocated budget, no matter what that may be.

We don't live in a perfect world. As a result we make choices that are based on various factors. Budgets, capabilities, market conditions, and comparisons of available choices offer us directions that can be selected. Creativity and ingenuity have intangible costs associated; raw materials, contractor time, facilities, utilities and hardware have very tangible costs. As a result, Initiative Sponsors and Initiative Managers need to make "pragmatic" decisions to justify the additional costs, time, quality, and customer satisfaction factors, as well as weigh the risks behind those decisions.

Notice that I quoted the "iron triangle" within that statement: Cost, Time, and Quality. None of those speak specifically to the value to the customer, nor did those choices alone evaluate or speculate on associated risks.

Within the concept of Strategic initiative Management, all should be considered. So I'll phrase this clarification in a couple of key parts:

- If the decision or activity adds no value to the result of the initiative, question why it is being done and suggest that it be removed. If we don't question the time-wasters, we're not operating as efficiently as we should, and doing less than expected as an initiative manager. (See also "Conventional Wisdom" in Chapter Four).

- The "iron triangle" as a success litmus test is a myth.

Now that I've effectively attacked a sacred cow of traditional project management values, I'll explain my rationale. I mentioned there were 5 decision factors to be considered in a decision: Cost, Time, Quality, Customer Satisfaction, and Risk. That doesn't sound like a triangle to me, but more pentagonal in nature if we accept there are 5 factors. We could adhere blindly to the theory that the 3 factors affecting project outcomes are successful delivery within the approved variances of cost, schedule and quality. Too many project managers view this as the gold standard for delivery. It's mythical at best.

Expectations can change; therefore we have scope and change management practices and procedures. Risks can be introduced or eliminated; therefore we have a Risk Management process to govern control around that. Business conditions can change – for instance, the trend of American automakers to produce larger Sport Utility Vehicles with lower gas mileage in the early part of the 2000s changed toward the end of the decade as fluctuations in world oil prices became more volatile. Many project managers would have been satisfied with producing the next generation of Hummer just as pump prices nudged the $5.00/gallon mark in the US, and sales of gas guzzling SUV's tanked.

Cost, time, and quality might have been achieved. The customer would have been less than thrilled to continue projects that designed that sort of vehicle given the changing market conditions. In short, if we don't consider customer satisfaction with the output, no matter how well it met original specification, we've created a "successful failure": A brilliant product that will never sell. Did we mention risk? Volatility of world commodities markets was probably not considered in the decision.

Our Initiative Management stance must be that Customer Satisfaction is a flexible bubble that surrounds the other attributes of the initiative.

6. *Communication is 360. We promote and encourage interaction and managed communication, but we also promote the management of information in an organized fashion. If it's not relevant to the audience, see Rule 3.*

In an age where transparency and collaboration are the watchwords, we must ensure that we're clear, precise and concise in communication. We need to ensure transparency in our interaction so that our customers, suppliers, teams, sponsors and stakeholders view us credibly. Our messages must reflect the initiative goals and objectives, the collaboration that has been established, and an organized approach to managing both information and the message. Communication in most organizations is fragmented and does not convey a distinct message organizationally across all levels. As we progress, we'll discuss this point in significant detail to ensure that anything undertaken in Initiative Management is not undermined by inconsistency with the message or strategy.

In Rule 8, I'll talk more about an encircling principle of this.

I've met, worked with, and known project managers who can only manage in singular directions – some work extraordinarily well with their project teams; others are very adept in managing a message upward, and using that to create a downward pressure; others can manage well with their Project Management colleagues in promoting cross-communication between projects. A special few have possessed an adaptive communication style that can effectively bring that message to the entire constituency of an initiative.

This is troubling because it represents two failures: Communication and leadership.

The communication failure is obvious in that not all parties are benefitting from the same story. A wise man once said that if you tell the truth, it's easier to keep your story straight when you're asked. Honest communication is usually far more appreciated, especially if it comes as early as possible, and is supplemented with actions or options. How easy our jobs would be if everything went perfectly or according to plan; how astute of many project management methodologies to also incorporate controls around project and delivery lifecycle.

Which brings me to the topic of leadership. Our role is one of managing initiatives, not of being note-takers with a title. To be viewed and respected as a leader, one needs to demonstrate those characteristics, and that includes the ability to communicate news that may not be favorable. In American history, we view political figures such as Franklin Delano Roosevelt, Ronald Reagan, and John F. Kennedy as good leaders. They were not always successful at all they did, but they had a compelling way of communicating their message to a broad audience.

And who among us has not heard Martin Luther King's "I Have a Dream" speech and not felt it to be a powerful message that sought to bring equality to all?

We are here not simply to communicate, but also to lead and embody the message. I mentioned prior failures to effectively communicate, and send a broader message to anyone astute enough to listen. They communicate a failure of the project manager to live up to expectations. It's a message that more organizations are realizing, and still more need to realize, that while upward communication is ear pleasing it's less effective than full-spectrum communication.

Example: I had the unique experience of managing someone who was once a project manager reporting to me, who jumped off the deep end when a project was sliding downhill from his actions and errors. Another team returned him as a face-off to that project by the business group after he suddenly declared he'd become "all better".

During his absence, the entire project (under the direction of someone highly qualified in rescuing troubled programs) had staged a well-structured turnaround. When he returned to the team, I'd recognized what was done wrong in his absence; the most notable was poor, single-direction communication. This Project Manager had set expectations that were communicated upward, and then pushed back to teams without the understanding of how they'd be achieved. Consequently, they weren't, and the project underwent a very comprehensive deep-dive seeking answers. All of them pointed to how the communication pointed in one direction – superiors, myself included – but never downward or across to the many matrixed resources that would help achieve those goals.

I'll never forget the individual – not because of his response to "When the going got tough, the tough got going, far away" – more because of his lack of collaboration skills to convey that common message. It was completely forgotten that in the race to please one's superiors that you need to also make sure those on the front lines are marching in time to the same rhythm. As a result, his style created chasms between people that were legendary.

Communication means that we manage the message appropriately to everyone on the team. Successful managers do manage up. And down. And laterally, so that they form a cohesive and collaborative team around them.

7. *Options, decisions and consensus lead to actions. Discussions, while important, should focus on precise issues and result in options, decisions and consensus.*

Earlier, I mentioned the importance of agendas and decisions within a meeting context, as well as productive and unproductive meeting behaviors. This has a much larger context surrounding it, and meetings aren't the only place where precision and decision should intersect.

Given the often-limited time frames for action and the accelerating pace of change, it benefits the entire initiative team to reach informed conclusions that are followed with specific action and accountability. Items cannot linger when action is needed. Just as we have instincts in a time of crisis, we should use that knowledge, thought, judgment and instinct to reach similar decisions about our initiatives.

Let me be clear that I'm not suggesting that we leap from quick decision to quick decision without first considering the options. Notice my use of the term "informed conclusions" – using the information at our collective disposal to make solid judgments that enable progress. For many consensus-driven organizations, there is a culture where more and more people become involved in the decision-making process; this, in turn, makes both the communication much more complex, and irrationally slows a decision process with limited benefits. In the beginning of the initiative, we defined 3 people who are the voice of the initiative:

- The Sponsor

- The Key Stakeholders

- The Initiative Manager

It's relevant to consider others as subject matter experts, but many organizations tend to broaden the process beyond necessary parties to create comfort with the eventual decision, which will take much longer. If you exist within this culture, and you're an initiative sponsor, consider this scenario when you ask your Initiative Manager about a delay in progress.

Equally relevant, the culture of many organizations negatively influences accountability because a bad decision attributed to one person is considered worse than taking a presumably safer route of abstention. When I mention options, consensus and decisions leading to action, an understanding of that organization's culture should consider whether people are held accountable in a punitive respect, or those who are decisive are punished while indecision is rewarded.

Many organizational cultures have adopted a comfort level with indecision and open-issues – the "open-ended" approach versus the "final decision" quandary. Some personality types feel more comfortable with open-ended discussions, and this will remain a challenge in fostering a decision. Also be conscious that in more assertive environments, those personality types may end up being marginalized and require coaching to increase their comfort with this approach. I tend to use the question "If you had to make a decision now based on what you know, what would it be?" to help drive their input and move toward a response.

Decisions in a pragmatic environment can be very rapid -- mandating that a decision is needed to move forward or avert a crisis. If we thought about the time spent in situations where further analysis revealed no new information, and parlayed that into quicker implementation, marketplace innovation would increase.

It's important to ensure the following is considered:

- People understand urgency

- People understand why decisions are needed

- People comprehend their decisions

- People do not judge an incorrect decision based on the known facts and consensus reached.

The last bullet is important, and I'll return to it momentarily.

How many people have heard the term "**Analysis Paralysis**"? If you've somehow related to that thought, stay with me for a moment; for those who don't recognize the term, it's a state of inertia where comfort is born out of never making a decision because "more time is needed", "more information is needed" or "further study should be done", or "we should have considered another stakeholder". The list is immeasurable. It creates a fine art of overanalyzing beyond a tangible value.

"Not making a decision is making a decision." – Attribution unknown

It's also the **worst** decision that you can make. It's called "inaction where action is required". The following scenario will seem somewhat ridiculous, but it's drawn to prove a point.

Example: *Imagine saying to an office tower of workers that their building is on fire, and then asking, "What should we do?" While the flames are consuming parts of the building, no one has decided to pull the fire alarm, or grab extinguishers, or head to the designated fire towers in the core of the building. No one's picked up the phone and called the Fire Brigade, much less the security team. So while discussing and mulling over the options, several middle managers gather and standard decision avoidance behaviors take over.*

- o *"Have we encountered this before? What did we do then?"*

- o *"Is there a written procedure for this? We should probably assign someone to do that." "Hey, is anyone taking notes on this? Fred, can you make sure we're getting all of this down?"*

- o *"So let's do some brainstorming exercises and see if we can get this down on a whiteboard."*

The building is still burning around them. Does this seem like typical behavior? All too often, it is and it's a clear sign that an organization is not only change resistant, but tries to insulate itself from the risk associated with making a decision. While our ineffective middle managers above are sorting through the options, they're disappearing one by one as the fire takes hold and begins removing them as viable.

Organizations do very similar things each day. My example of a building fire is an absurd extreme to illustrate a point – a fire plan is usually part of the occupancy requirements and security in any building, and no rational person would leave those decisions to chance. But by avoiding making a decision, we lose the competitive edge that comes with pragmatic change and the ability to modify our plans to best leverage the current business conditions.

In Strategic Initiative Management, the goal is not quite to make a lightning fast decision or simply panic and "Break Glass, Pull Lever" each time a new opportunity occurs. We want to consider our decisions and their impact in an organized and efficient manner. The goal is to eliminate the decision-avoidance behavior and create an atmosphere where options are identified, and consensus is built ***quickly*** around decisions.

The following guide-rules help govern the process:

- Meetings with Agendas – clear statement of purpose, clear objectives.

- Call to Action – why the discussion is strategic, why people's input is needed, and the intended use for that information.

- Consensus Development – the objective is not to get unanimous agreement from the group, but a general understanding and majority buy-in against the objective and how it can be achieved.

- Rapid but thorough discussion – make clear that all options should be explored, but the purpose is to reach a decision, not prolong discussion.

- Tight time frames governing actions – if something cannot be decided within the course of the meeting cite a very short and specific time so that information can be researched and informed decisions will result. Think of the phrase "If not now, then when?"

- Clear Decisions – the product of the process is a clear decision on direction, goals, actions, and responsibility, and any next steps.

As we progress, we'll discuss the behaviors we should seek in helping to gain decision and consensus. One side-point is to ensure that the discussion of options gathers the right knowledgeable constituents – I've seen situations where the wallflower in the room will have the best ideas yet be overpowered. As part of your facilitation goals, ensure that you've covered all the important constituents and that everyone has provided their input.

8. *Act ethically.*

In a previous section, I spoke about the importance of honesty and transparency in communication. That extends to all facets of our interaction.

There is a host of good information on Ethical Business Practices, though it seems sometimes that ethical or altruistic interests may not always guide some of our leaders. We build trust with others based on our continued interaction with them. It takes only a single unethical act to unravel that trust, and once lost it's not generally regained; despite our tendency to forgive, we rarely forget and as a result we'll be very reluctant to reestablish a similar level of trust.

Interaction Associates commissioned a study in the spring of 2009[10] demonstrating that organizations where trust had been established across all levels, in conjunction with strong proactive leadership characteristics and a collaborative working environment, outperformed their peers by very wide margins. Those same organizations were more successful at recruitment, retention, and had more confidence in weathering changes in business conditions. Their findings were also important in demonstrating that higher-performing organizations also shared a much greater sense of overall strategic alignment and that employees understood the objectives and goals.

Mentioning this in conjunction with ethics is not a casual reference. The formation of trust starts with leaders who share common ethical views, and a clear sense of the right behaviors that will deliver results. We shouldn't need to teach courses in ethical behavior because it should be a core trait. We should be able to trust one-another, though sadly the agendas of others will cloud and contort that view.

At the time I'm writing this book, the United States is in the midst of a nearly trillion dollar bailout of our nation's banks and financial institutions, and more than a few investment Ponzi schemes have been uncovered resulting in financial losses more than $100 billion to individuals, organizations and charities. There is increasing tendency to resort to desperate over-stretching and misrepresenting their skills to get the coveted few positions being filled. Many recruiters are also endorsing practices that would have been unthinkable a few years ago. Greed is a motivator. Pride, yet another.

---

10 Courtesy Interactive Associates, 2009, "Building Trust in Business, Research Report and Toolkit, Author Linda Dunkel.

As a manager, I've demanded honesty and fairness from my employees. Those who've been candid and honest with me knew where they stood, and could count on my support when they were correct and counseling when not. The few who've violated that trust through unethical behaviors – lies, overt omissions, misrepresentations, and fraud – also knew where they stood very quickly.

And as an employee who had once been asked to take part in an unethical activity, I know the feeling of deciding between your ethics and values, versus taking an action that would destroy your credibility. I resigned on the spot. And I don't regret the decision. While it meant that I went without income until I found my next role, I never regretted making the wrong choice. If I emphasize one point to take away from this book, it's this: Be honest, fair, and transparent in all your dealings. There should be no other consideration. And in case you were wondering, I learned the person asking me to engage in the unethical behavior - a CIO - was terminated with cause within the next month. The reason? Ethical practices.

I had the experience of taking a company-sponsored Ethics Questionnaire in a prior organization. It was a multiple-choice sequence providing a scenario, 4 possible answers, and 2 that could potentially be right. In fact, there were always 2 correct answers: The actual "ethical" answer for those with a decent mind, functional brain cells, and a good ethical compass; and the "ask a company lawyer" answer that was the catchall for those more ethically challenged.

If you ask why I cite the premise of "Act ethically", those reasons in my experience give me some cause to think about that. This is not a book on business ethics (which might seem an oxymoron at times), as plenty is already written on the subject, nor is it the core focus of the framework that emerges. But there are some sub-components that I feel compelled to explore given the business challenges that have emerged in the late 20th and early 21st Century climates.

It's worthy to note that many professional organizations have a code of ethics to which its practitioners must adhere to maintain membership or credentials. It is a minimum standard of conduct versus a more stringent standard, but again provides a baseline on which ethical practices can be built. We can and should aspire to more.

Next Steps...

All of this seems a very tall order, and it requires us to review and perhaps change our thinking. During the next chapter, I'll share some thoughts and anecdotes about this.

Chapter 8:
Changing the thought process

Moving from Tactical to Strategic

I once joined an organization that was small enough that each employee had the opportunity to meet the firm's president for 30 minutes. My own session lasted just a little under an hour, and was held after I'd been with the organization for a month and had the opportunity to review my experiences and observations. I spent part of that hour expressing concern over the lack of actual strategic thought in the organization, and how tactically we were operating. Some of the indicators I'd highlighted:

- Crisis hopping – simply moving from one disaster to the next without understanding how we got there.

- Lack of business development – for a business dependent on obtaining new customers and retaining existing ones, we were doing poorly in the former, and nothing about the latter.

- All our decisions were "in the moment" – we were making decisions without facts, and in isolation. Customer interaction was poor and assumptions were made that "we knew better" about what they wanted; we ended up not knowing what the customer wanted at all.

- The inability to fulfill the strategic business needs of the organization – rather than focusing on results, everyone became a very expensive pair of hired hands, rather than helping deliver results.

The president of the organization, a couple years my junior, appeared to listen. Emphasis on the word appeared. When he heard that our actions were tactical, his response was "well, we need to be tactical for this role, we can't think about strategy."

We can't think about strategy. We need to be tactical. These were the first indications that no one had perceived the problems, and viewed the issues not as a whole, but rather in small parts, each of which should be corrected in isolation. This was their "tactical" view. Except that there were certain parts that culturally they felt should be left alone, and others that were fair game. You can only imagine the results that emerged from this sort of thought process. I'll cite a few outcomes:

- Project Managers were seen as the problem, not the solution. The role of the Project Manager team had gone from facilitator to note-taker; they continually were viewed as adding no value because they were excluded from the conversations, and prevented from asking questions. In short, they couldn't be effective in the role been hired to perform.

- The internal constituents scheduled and held meetings, but these were dysfunctional at best. When the Project Managers pressed to meet to reach a decision, they were quickly drubbed since the constituents were too busy. Having dysfunctional meetings.

- Discussions rather than decisions. Discussions felt comfortable. Decisions felt constraining. The end client – the people who paid the bills – wanted decisions; the internal staff didn't feel the sense of urgency until it was too late. The customer labeled the organization as "slow and not transparent", along with not "providing leadership".

- No one focused on the business alignment, business needs, or business goals.

By the time this organization had heard identical feedback from the customer, it was a "reaction". Had they taken a closer look when the business problems and challenges that were initially highlighted, the actions could have been more "proactive".

Reactive = Tactical. Response and a quick fix to a situation. While this may cover the problem, it still requires that a more thorough response be considered. Tactical responses are generally never durable and are short-lived. Consider the action of adding emergency "flat-fixing foam" to a flat tire. While it may get you to your destination, and perhaps somewhat beyond, the tire will still eventually need to be replaced before it goes flat yet again (the next time for good).

Proactive = Strategic. Recognition of a shortcoming, and an approach to address it as part of continually improving overall competency. It generally happens outside the view of the customer, so the customer sees stability versus constant heroism or an impact to their productivity.

I'm not advocating airing the dirty laundry in view of the customer, but I'm squarely in the corner of seeing or anticipating the issue and proactively addressing issues before they become a problem.

Changing the Thinking Itself

If organizations did not change, did not adopt new technologies, did not invent new products, did not improve upon existing innovations, or did not embark on new fields in which their products or ideas could blossom, they would quickly cease to exist as viable entities. In our own lifetimes, we've seen specific products have their day and then disappear. I'll provide a partial list to jog your memory if the idea doesn't yet resonate with you:

- Manual or Electric Typewriters – these have long since been replaced by the all purpose computer and cheaper printing.

- 8-Track Tapes – later replaced by smaller and less-bulky cassette tapes, which have subsequently been replaced by CD's, then DVD's and ultimately digital download.

- The LP (Long Playing) record – gave way to the CD, though true audiophiles are hoping to stage a comeback based on the smoother and warmer sound of analog technology.

- Landline Rotary Phone – replaced by the touch-tone phone, then the cordless phone, and increasingly by no phone at all with the appearance of wireless/cellular technology, or Voice-Over-IP.

- VCRs and VHS Tapes. Replaced by the DVD and Digital Video Recorders. I'm sure we still have some tapes lying about of the kids playing baseball, so perhaps it's time to transfer those.

- The Walkman or Discman – why carry around a bulky CD or cassette player when you can store the output of 100s of them on a device a fraction of the size?

- Film Cameras – with the appearance of digital technology, the ability to choose what you want to print, and the storage for hundreds of photos on a device now cheaper than the average roll of film, it explains why one-hour photo film processors are disappearing as well. And the only memory you'll soon have of "Kodachrome" is a song by Paul Simon (Kodak stopped manufacturing it in 2009).

The list goes on. Innovation and change are constants. Not every innovation and change will resound with the public; however, the reality of change and innovation is such that we should expect to see more and wider changes in the future. Innovation will drive those changes.

The most successful companies will be those who can adapt and become leaders in creating innovation, and who have a strong sense of the marketplace. Common to all of this is a core value: **Listen to the customer**.

It's true that Project Managers like structure. None of this suggests that the entire thought library behind processes should be eliminated – having a process allows us to put control around the initiative. But I refer to one of the key statements behind the tenets of Strategic Initiative Management: The outcome of the initiative is not process unless the initiative is chartered to create a process. Process provides a guideline from which we base the efforts. Thinking needs to change in both the scripting of that process and any artificial constraints imposed.

Create a Culture of Collaboration

A recent discussion I'd had with a networking colleague asked how one promotes innovation and out-of-the-box thinking.

The obvious answer is to look at the question, and determine the root causes of why the organization lacks collaboration. This is a process that should work from the perimeter into the core by ensuring the core values and strategic goals of the organization and its staff align. I've listed some common steps feeding that process.

- Cultural influence. You need to begin with the top of the culture and gain complete consensus that the C-Levels of the organization support a collaborative environment. Then go back to your lowest levels of the organization and determine if that message of core values resonates and interprets similarly there. Repeat this pattern altered by one level in each direction until you work your way into the middle of the organization, and usually that is where you will find your greatest level of variance. In may organizations, the message and compliance varies slightly at each level (By the way, I'll discuss Bow-Tie Syndrome [TM] later in the book to demonstrate).
- Use validation tools to understand the organization thinking and the alignment of the organization. There are a number of survey tools that will help collect the data and most will have some robust reporting tools to help show the data relationships between levels.
- Study the organization to determine if there is potential for out-of-box thought, and whether the inhibitors are real or imagined, process or rigor, or simply cultural in nature. Then you have a basis to know how and where to begin with the rigidity or pliability of the organization.

Anything being considered and undertaken must begin with consensus, mandate, and business strategy alignment. Otherwise, it will struggle with adoption. Simply put, if the top-of-the-food-chain in an organization doesn't support nontraditional schools of thought, such an effort will not gain traction.

For those that try collaborative management, the results can represent changes in employee satisfaction, productivity, and employee retention that more than outweigh the costs of its implementation.

This isn't always easy or achievable. I once worked in an organization that once struggled to achieve CMM Level 2 compliance as ranked by an independent assessor. They quickly gave up and shelved any plans of CMM compliance until several years later when they've finally reached the next level of compliance. In their case, it took stepping back from the state they were in to evaluate, assess and determine if compliance with CMM standards would yield tangible benefits. When they concluded it would, the effort was far better understood and adopted. The most difficult challenge for many such organizations is stepping back to take that objective view, and then processing that feedback.

So returning to the original question: You begin by creating a culture where each individual's input and perspective is valued, where employees feel challenged, and where they can be proud of their contribution.

It starts with a question. It continues by listening to the answer. It perpetuates by cultivating those organic ideas so that employees see that their input is taken seriously.

As an incidental observation, there is some discussion of the relative height of cubicle walls being a barrier to communication. There's little anecdotal evidence to support this, although some firmly assert that removing walls encourages open communication. My response, having spent time in both types of environments, is simple: It depends on the culture of the organization. To debunk the common theory that "the lower the walls, the better the interaction", here are some examples from the trenches:

- I managed in a high-walled environment for more than 5 years. I encouraged people to walk around, look out windows, and interact as groups. One cube ended up being a centralized point for most of that activity. The walls made little noticeable difference.

- I managed in several organizations that had short-walls and common huddle groups. It did little to foster the communication between team members, since the culture was oriented toward personal achievement rather than teamwork. Very little information and interaction was ever shared.

- I've managed in an organization without walls, and in which you could stand and survey the entire office. In their other locations, they kept to a similar layout, especially in Europe where people were given finite dimensions on a long table. I was surprised to learn in many cases that despite staring across a desk at others all day, most people did not know the people around them, nor did they bother to introduce themselves. Collaboration was tried but failed miserably.

- I've also managed in a virtual organization. No walls, no eye-to-eye contact, and little else other than an occasional visit and routine phone calls, emails, and instant messages. On many days, the walls were that of the 10x12 office on the second floor of my home as I managed several activities from early morning until late into the evening. It would be impossible to say there were any walls whatsoever in this situation. It would be entirely fair to tell you that everyone was encouraged to communicate, and they did so more frequently and with more people than groups led by my peers or others in the organization. We didn't have walls. Or cubes for that matter.

The physical walls matter very little. The intangible walls that are the result of poor behavior matter more. The central issue is breaking through the communication barriers. As we progress, we'll discuss more communication barriers, whether real or perceived.

"I Didn't Know I Could Do That! Then Again, No One Told Me I Couldn't."

Recall toward the beginning of the book where I gave the case study of a group participation activity at a management training and development seminar. I mentioned the story of undertaking an activity that no one else had thought possible because they were still shackled by their own constraints. The facilitator didn't create them. Our team certainly didn't know they existed (though we would have challenged them had we been questioned), and everyone else thought the activity revolved around the information contained within their own group.

Ask yourself whether you've ever operated under a constraint that never existed. Be honest in your own assessment. You more than likely answered yes to that query (we've all done so, it's a typical behavior), because the power and perception of the group is far greater than the individual's ability to persuade in most cases. Often, it's our own professional version of peer pressure that can hold us back because no one wants to appear not to be a "team player". As a result, people within a group will normally tend to conform to the whims of the group.[11]

In the example that I mentioned, the team was acting as a team with individual contributions. The result is that our team completed the task, within deadlines, and no one was viewed as not being a team player because everyone benefitted from the quick win and overall recognition. Each person was given a task and provided their expertise where it was most relevant.

From an early age, in our development of social skills, we're taught how to work together as a team. Either we're given a group science fair project or are chosen to take part in team sports. Neither are activities designed to develop people as strong individual contributors that can think through an issue and emerge with a solution. While team-collaboration is a useful tool, beware that it can also stifle creativity when a very bright individual contributor is introduced, and peer pressure dominates against using that contributor's ideas. As a result, mediocrity can continue to emerge.

So can an *artificial constraint* – something that we think exists or that restricts our decision process, but is disproved after validation. The example I cited above was an artificial constraint – that of not believing that resources outside the immediate room could be pressed into service. Removing the constraint is much like removing the walls and barriers to productivity.

As we begin the discussion of Frameworks and Work streams in a later chapter, we'll discuss the formation and validation of constraints. However, keep in mind the following concepts:

- All constraints should be captured and recorded.

- Once captured, they can be thoroughly investigated, then validated or invalidated.

- Those constraints that are considered valid form the parameters and boundaries of the initiative.

- Breaching the boundary requires Sponsor and Stakeholder consent, and should be recorded within a formal change management process that maintains an audit trail.

- Each change of constraint requires a comparison against the strategic objective of the project.

The last point is based on a topic I covered in Part One: the requirements of formal change control not to prevent changes but to record, evaluate, and assess their alignment with project goals. This is analogous to flying a plane, or at least being a passenger on a flight.

Those of us who've been what I'll call "road warriors" -- frequent business travelers -- have had the experience of circling an airport for one reason or another. It can be especially frustrating if you're booked onto a connecting flight and don't understand why you haven't landed on schedule, and compounded when the pilot doesn't provide updates. Understand that the pilot would prefer to land the plane on the runway sooner versus later, but Air Traffic Control may provide reasons preventing that. In the meantime, you feel the plane banking right or left for what might seem an eternity until you finally hear the announcement from the cockpit that the flight has been cleared to land.

On some of the more raucous flights I've experienced, that announcement is greeted with applause or

---

11 Asch, S. E. (1951). Effects of group pressure upon the modification and distortion of judgment. In H. Guetzkow (ed.) Groups, leadership and men. Pittsburgh, PA: Carnegie Press, was a seminal study of this behavior.

loud cheering that can be heard from the cockpit.

Initiatives can occur in much the same fashion. A sponsor may desire change after change, initially paying no mind to the changes in either the project's costs, scope, alignment with strategic goals, or delivery date. Such an initiative is much like the airplane that circles the tower and never lands. The role of an initiative manager is to perform some level of baseline validation to those factors and convey that affect to the sponsor, who might not initially be mindful, but will likely feel pressure when his customers or his managers aren't seeing the expected returns on their investment.

The goal is to successfully start at point A and end at point Z. Point Z might change location. You may be dodging stormy weather along the flight path. Your pilot might change your altitude to give you a smoother ride above the turbulence. But the plane eventually needs to land – gravity prevails and the plane cannot hold an unlimited amount of fuel. It's not such a complex analogy, but for those of us who've lived through never-ending projects, it's certainly familiar.

Two strategies surmount this:

- Iteration
- Change Control

Not surprisingly, both are customarily needed.

"Where Are The Other Points Surrounding Initiative Management Practices?"

The very fact that you're reading this book indicates that you have some knowledge and understanding of the Project Management discipline. If you recall the introduction of the book, I mentioned that this publication is not intended as a primer on fundamental project management skills.

Therefore, I'll simply state here that your organization likely already follows a methodology as a guideline for activities, and that your individual activities fall within some phase of that. In general, that methodology will follow a series of phases that govern the stages of the project lifecycle -- each methodology will reference these differently. Understand that all have an Inception Point and a Closure point. For more on specific methodologies, I've provided links that outline details in full:

- Rational Unified Process (RUP) - http://www.ibm.com/software/awdtools/rup
- PMI/PMBOK - http://www.pmi.org
- Agile - http://www.agilealliance.org
- PRINCE2 - http://www.prince-officialsite.com/

These are provided only as independent reference, not for endorsement or use purposes. Please assume that the remaining assumptions in this book will largely remain agnostic on the topic of methodology, and the purpose of this publication is not to endorse or evangelize any particular methodology. As you'll note in subsequent pages, I will lay out various stages for pre-and-post-delivery that should be considered. These do not purport to replace an existing methodology as much as their goal is to propose new approaches to the existing challenges.

Chapter 9:
A 12-Step Program for Initiatives

Why initiatives can Fail Before They Start, and How to Correct the Thinking.

This chapter will be notably longer, because I'll begin with an extensive case study that reveals exhaustive information about non-performing and dysfunctional organizations through the initiative challenges encountered. This case study will be followed by 9 questions, some of which you may wish to expand upon based on your review of the material, and some of which you might feel to be subjective.

The objective is to create a judgment based on the information provided. You may use the information to infer other scenarios or behaviors, but the basis of those inferences should draw from clues in the original case study text.

Case Study #14: Frank.

Frank was a manager in a medium sized financial firm. His background was unremarkable, and if you tried to find reference to Frank on the Internet as a subject matter expert -- demonstrating leadership vision, writing productive white papers, or other minor reference to him -- the closest you'd come was a single reference that fell subordinate to a similarly named guitar player in a grunge-rock band.

Most of the firm's software was implemented either by consultants or a "buy" decision. There was minimal technical staff on board to develop or implement custom solutions. There was no development team. Support and business analysis teams did exist.

The challenge of the firm was to implement a Custom Off-The-Shelf solution (COTS) using a major market vendor's document and group collaboration package. Frank kicked off the effort using 2 vendors with split responsibilities, an internal Application Support Manager who was charged with running the program, and another manager who had been pressed into service as a Project Manager. The collaboration package meant significant change for the organization and was to be a standard for all the firm's financial advisors. Because various methods of working existed based on business lines, some customization would be required.

A kickoff meeting was held, and a PowerPoint Deck was produced to outline the goals of the project. The effort was targeted at taking a running leap with a very aggressive target date and expectations of completion by the end of the year.

Within 2 months of the kickoff, things were already in dire shape, and the acting project manager was being criticized for her lack of ability to drive the process. The vendors were not acting together on the effort, and business analysis was running behind schedule. The program manager's views were never really known, but there was little evidence to suggest him jumping in to lend guidance since his role was also an acting role. What should have been a 6-month project was looking to take longer, and this was a high visibility effort for the organization.

Frank decided to call in consultants to take over the effort due to comments such as "the project manager isn't getting along with others", "business analysis deliverables are being missed", and "the project isn't going according to the plan". Frank felt it was time to see consultants who could handle the role. He had interviewed candidates for the position, but had rejected them for being simply "reactive" in nature. He had seen two other candidates and was on the fence. A third-party showed him the resume and background of a third candidate and within 20 minutes he was on the phone and had to meet the individual who brought a background in project recovery. The consultant agreed to meet, but his condition on meeting was that the meeting be a constructive dialogue, indicating that was the hallmark of his collaborative style.

The consultant went to meet Frank at his office, and Frank immediately left him with artifacts to "review for 20 minutes followed by a quiz". The three artifacts left were as follows:

- *The PowerPoint Deck used at project kickoff, briefly defining the output of the work. The high-level scope was documented, overall objectives, and the project team members from the sponsoring organization, as well as vague identification. The remainder of the deck spoke broadly about deliverables, but was unclear on specific actions. While a long deck, it spoke mostly about issues rather than the overall focus and benefits.*

- *A partial Project Schedule that showed a middle delivery section of the project, but was missing completions, clear accountabilities by name, and was both linear and iterative in nature. Simply, it appeared to assume that everything would be completed on time, so there was no contingency and its dates were optimistic. Many of them had already passed without indicated completion.*

- *A Change Request for one aspect of the project, outlining a simple change that allowed actions to be taken on multiple items. Since the consultant already knew the capabilities of the package, he recognized that the Change Request might not have been made had those capabilities been understood and thoroughly explored, since the request depicted a function that was native to the package without modification. The Change Request document was a standard template used by other organizations with no modification, although some information was overkill and redundant. The vendor identified an impact of 45 days linearly to the plan, shifting a deliverable from the middle of one month until the end of the following for development. There was no indication of the disposition of the change, and the project schedule included no updates to reflect the impact.*

The consultant spent the next 20 minutes marking the document up for comments with an eye toward an open discussion of the issues he'd noted. When he had asked if there was a "Project Plan", he was told both that there was a Project Schedule, and that the Kickoff Deck should be viewed as the Project Plan. After making observations in the limited time-period, Frank led him into a room where he asked "I'll bet you've never expected a quiz, did you?" The consultant responded that it seemed a better opportunity for dialogue on the root causes and Frank's overall goals and challenges as they had been explained to him.

The consultant began with a question: "In your view, why do you believe that we're here, and why did you invite me specifically?" Frank's answer was that he had a consulting role open and that the consultant was there to interview. The consultant clarified his question further and explained what he knew about the situation to help confirm his understanding of Frank's issues (as outlined above). Frank confirmed the consultant's understanding by saying, "That's about right" and offering nothing else. The consultant also made the observation that the acting Project Manager had not been invited to the discussions. Frank responded defensively with the following comments:

- *All projects have issues.*

- *If we didn't have issues, we wouldn't be speaking with consultants.*

The consultant pointed out some of the gaps in the information he'd reviewed, and suggested that it painted a very incomplete picture of the situation, but what he could derive suggested some fundamental issues that could be productively reviewed in the time they had scheduled. Frank declined any change in his approach, instead opting for his own interview style which was a strict Q&A, and in which Frank would be asking the questions of his choosing. The consultant listened, and decided to indulge Frank as he asked the first question, which was a reading comprehension question about the Kickoff Deck.

As the consultant began to answer, he was cut off from continuing within the first 10 words and was childishly admonished by Frank that "this was not the question he'd asked," restating the question as if the consultant were an elementary school child. The consultant thanked Frank for the opportunity to meet, but felt further use of their time would be unproductive. Frank did not deal with the rejection of his approach, and slandered the consultant with subjective comments, including saying that the consultant "had a hell of an attitude for someone seeking a consultant role", while the consultant observed in return that he fully understood the root-cause of the situation. Frank couldn't have been faster ushering the consultant out the door. The consultant left the artifacts on the conference room table and exited, Frank was very happy to hold the door as he mumbled expletives under his breath.

What's wrong with this picture? Review the following questions and develop your own answers to these:

Q1: Define some of the issues with this effort.

Q2: Define Frank's management style, and suggest how this might affect the outcomes.

Q3: Define why the interaction between the consultant and Frank did not work, and why the consultant concluded the discussion.

Q4: Identify the culture of Frank's organization using the case above to support your stance.

Q5: Define the likelihood of a successful outcome to this project – meaning on time, on budget, within scope and to customer satisfaction.

Q6: As an outsider, what do you feel would need to change to produce different outcomes?

Q7: The consultant indicated that he fully understood the root-cause of the situation. What do you think he meant by the statement, and what do you believe the root-cause or causes to be?

Q8: Identify Frank's own issues. Be as broad in your answers as you'd like.

Q9: Did the consultant act fairly? Ethically?

This is perhaps one of the longer case studies I've provided because I wanted to cite examples of how stylistic differences and methods of communication and collaboration differ within various organizations. There are a few items that I gave specifically as clues to this case study about the organizational culture, Frank's personal style, the issues in vendor interaction, and views toward accountability to name a few. I've intentionally provided a great deal of information to digest here so we can walk through each of the questions I've outlined. I promise that my questions will be more instructional than Frank's.

Q1: Define some of the issues with this effort.

This question is so rich with examples that one needn't look very far to see that Murphy's Law was running amok with this initiative. So let's think about some of the observations, as I've listed my own thoughts to this:

- We've defined that there was a lack of formal project management knowledge and discipline. The first clue was that the project manager was pressed into service from another role, and her background did not include project management. The same observation held true with the program manager; had he been experienced, he would have noted the problems with the effort and provided guidance or direct assistance. So we have inexperienced resources without experienced support. Little wonder that within 2 months of kickoff, they're already seeking help – projects that are behind schedule at the 15% completion mark will usually not recover.

- Another comment mentioned is the "Project Plan" artifact, which the consultant was first told was the project schedule, then told to consider the Kickoff Deck as the plan. Neither would have been correct because it's not good practice, and a Project Plan tends to be a living document. It's also not a good way to formalize communication guidelines, meetings, value propositions, executive sponsorship, and so forth.

- A schedule is simply that and it's useless if it's created once and never updated, or held so rigidly as to not permit flexibility in the deliverable. I mentioned above that the schedule only showed one section of the project, and there was no completion or accountable party information.

- The Kickoff Deck is designed to socialize the value of the project, introduce the team and create the working relationships, and outline the objectives at a broad level. It's normally created once, and then remains an artifact.

- The artifacts shown didn't include the business specifications for the individual business units; simply a general statement within the Kickoff Deck. Operation, workflows, current-state compared to desired-state were unknowns, so the operating environment for a business analyst was unclear.

- There were multiple unclear accountabilities. Among those were the tasks and how they were split between 2 different vendors. To see what each vendor was to perform, you had to review the schedule, which wasn't updated. It's easy to understand why there is trouble in managing vendors when there is no clear plan for them to address.

- The organization did not understand the product, resulting in a proposed change request that had an impact on the critical path of the schedule by 6 weeks at a high cost (and delivering functionality native to the product). Without clear understanding, a vendor can use that to their advantage.

- No transparency. Did you notice that Frank's answers were both evasive and defensive? Both suggest that Frank wasn't seeking help or a corrective stance to the project, but someone who could conform to Frank's style.

- Frank and the third party in this story viewed a Project Manager as a "do'er", not a strategic resource delivering initiatives. That type of person is normally given a title of an "executor" or "expediter" since they have no authority and operate only under direction. As we explore Frank further, you'll understand how we reach this conclusion.

- Communication is poor. Simply, there is no dialogue. Notice in Frank's approach to discussion, he wants to reveal no detail, nor did he invite the current Project Manager to meet with the consultant. Frank's approach toward discussion was one of "he asks, you answer" and when the consultant didn't immediately say the exact words he wanted, he was quick to be cutoff.

- Lack of root-cause analysis. To know how to correct the problem, the consultant needs to understand how it started. Since Frank seems only to want to talk, and expects his directs and consultants to listen and react, it makes open-dialogue exploring root-causes difficult. In this case, it wasn't even possible.

- Unclear expectations. Notice that the prior consultants were removed from consideration due to their "reactive" style when faced by Frank. However, when Frank was faced with a "proactive" and "problem-solving" approach, he disliked that as well. So what were Frank's actual expectations? We'll never quite know.

Q2: Define Frank's management style, and suggest how this might affect the outcomes.

We're given some important insight and clues into Frank's style and approach, so the following are some observations:

- Autocratic. There are clues given to an autocratic style. The strict Q&A nature of the interview is one, and the response to questions is another. The undertone suggests an individual who isn't comfortable with equal dialogue, or with being questioned about progress and approach. Therefore, others may be forced to "react" to his style versus being able to engage him since he may view them as only superior-subordinate, and a subordinate should simply follow orders.

- Rigid. Again, see Frank's interview style. When the consultant tries to engage Frank in a dialogue, Frank responds negatively and reacts by insisting that his own process be used. Even when his own process is used, Frank still responds negatively to the stimulus of hearing another response other than what he expects. As a result, it's possible that the current Project Manager could be providing useful information that Frank simply dislikes or that doesn't conform to his style.

- Evasion. I've captured key points in the conversation that explain that Frank provides evasive responses to questions, or responds negatively to any question or comment he believes is critical of him.

- Self-Centric. Returning to his comfort-zone of questioning ("I ask, you answer") versus productive dialog, Frank tells us that he is the focus of the discussion, not the jeopardized project.

- Poor Self-awareness. When the consultant at the end of the conversation depicts Frank's flaws, Frank chooses to be defensive (we'll get there next), and he remains unaware of how others respond to his behavior. This is noted by the consultant's response to spend no further time meeting results in him accusing the consultant of having an attitude. In reality, the consultant is responding to the negative stimulus given by Frank by stating that further conversation won't be productive.

- Defensiveness. I gave this one away already in the Case Text. Frank's response to being faced with the issues on the project results in a concise answer and reluctance to consider that discussing the problem might be a more productive approach.

- Emotionally Immature. Frank demonstrates his inability to respond to rejection through his response to the consultant terminating the conversation, and mumbling expletives as he shows the consultant out. It demonstrates a poor level of professionalism. Name-calling is never a professional response. His grumbling depicts someone who doesn't accept criticism or rejection.

Q3: Define why the interaction between the consultant and Frank did not work, and why the consultant concluded the discussion.

I've given away much of this in the previous answers, but let's recap this in a simple answer.

Frank's style was a rigid approach, and all interaction needed to conform to that approach. Anything else breached Frank's comfort-level. Frank was neither adaptive nor receptive to candid dialogue.

The consultant's style was constructive dialogue and collaboration. The consultant knew that he was there to solve a problem, and made that clear in agreeing to the meeting. This underscores Frank's lack of comfort in an adaptive style.

When the consultant could understand that Frank was not receptive to an adaptive style, and demonstrated a lack of openness to listening or open-dialogue, he thanked Frank but recognized that the relationship could not work unless Frank changed his style. As Frank had the issue with the jeopardized project and had specifically asked to speak to the consultant, lack of openness to answer clarifying questions indicated that this would not be a productive engagement.

Q4: Identify the culture of Frank's organization using the case above to support your stance.

There could be many answers to this question, because we don't know about the entire organization; only the people reporting to Frank and the vendors engaged into the effort. So I'll suggest potential answers:

- Autocratic. Demonstrated by Frank's rigidity and authority-tinged approach with the consultant, it might be fair to assume that any decision he made must be obeyed.

- Closed-Communication/Dysfunctional. Notice the mention that the current project manager was not invited to participate. It is unclear that the current Project Manager would have even known that a selection process was being carried out to replace her. What is clear is that this was not transparent, and the opportunity to ask questions of the current Project Manager on her perception of issues didn't exist.

- Isolated. There's no clear information to suggest that an open-communication model exists; however, Frank's reluctance to consider the consultant's approach to the dialogue suggests that Frank's view of the project may not consider all the facts, or that those on the project are not comfortable in providing status.

There are other possibilities, so I've listed only a few that are clear from the information provided.

Q5: Define the likelihood of a successful outcome to this project – meaning on time, on budget, within scope.

We're provided with some valuable clues that help us with this question. Let's think about the following:

- A lack of clarity on requirements. Since the project was kicked off, but the status of requirements were not clear, it's reasonable to assume that a cry for help during this stage of the project indicates a challenge or risk to on-time delivery. Business analysis was stated as behind schedule, for instance.

- A lack of clarity on project risks. They're not in evidence, nor in the Kickoff Deck, so perhaps some have been realized.

- Stated problems with vendor management. This could suggest that the vendor has not completed its deliverables on time, or they do not meet quality standards. Both could be part of the underlying issues.

- Criticism of the project manager in driving the process. Recall that we're dealing with an inexperienced Project Manager on a strategic initiative.

- Unknown/potentially inadequate support from the acting Program Manager. The program manager has no formal background, so this could be the blind-leading-the-blind.

- Inadequate/unclear documentation. As a result, the vendors may not have clear expectations. Without seeing Statements of Work, this remains unknown; being told there are vendor management issues (as above) suggests concerns and potential trouble.

- Communication Issues. A lack of open communication to address issues could contribute to delays in decisions, and subsequent delays on the effort.

- Change Control. Already in the process, the vendor is taking advantage of a lack of knowledge by Frank's organization of the product, and suggesting a change that would result in a 45-day delay if adopted.

Given those factors, it can be inferred that successful delivery (time, cost, scope) without extensive re-planning is unrealistic. The anecdotal information suggests that an inexperienced team is facing issues, and lacks experienced guidance to bring delivery back in line.

Q6: As an outsider, what do you feel would need to change to produce a different set of outcomes?

This case is so rich with examples that we could literally spend much of this book sifting through the factors that could change to produce different outcomes. I will provide a few ideas, keeping in mind that this is not a comprehensive list of the things that should change for this organization.

- Expectations. In the Kickoff Deck, an end-of-year date was given for project completion, but a definition of success was never provided. Without having completed business analysis, it's difficult to presume this is possible. If the project is now behind schedule, the damage has been done, and a new definition of success is required along with realistic expectations.

- Communication & Accountabilities. Without a clear communication plan, either in document form or a RACI Chart, accountabilities can be unclear.

- Leadership. Frank demonstrated a non-adaptive style (we mentioned "rigid" several times in describing him), so chairing and sponsoring an effort aimed at a major change for the firm's financial advisors seems to be a mismatch to his personality and professional style.

- Culture. Considering Frank's style, it could be inferred that open-communication is not a part of the organization's culture.

- Formal project management processes. The observation was made that their Change Management document was borrowed from a template, but their project schedule was uninformative, and there was no Project Plan document governing the effort. Some level of rigor would be beneficial, especially if external vendors are involved.

- Understanding product capabilities. We noted that the vendor was charging a fee for functionality that already existed in the product, forcing an end-date change. A savvy customer would have validated the functionality before making such a buy-decision. This demonstrates a lack of competence in executing informed purchasing and evaluation decisions.

- Collaboration. Frank's own communication and management style did not demonstrate collaborative ability. It can be inferred that his organization would operate in much the same manner. The Case Study provides some indication of this.

This is obviously a partial listing. As this is subjective for each evaluator, it is difficult to provide a comprehensive list; also we only know what is stated in the Case Study, so much can either be inferred or assumed from examples. Use this to think of areas in which you might grade the capability of the organization, and changes that might be most productive.

Q7: The consultant indicated that he fully understood the root-cause of the situation. What do you think he meant by the statement, and what do you believe the root-cause or causes to be?

It's very possible that a few things crossed the consultant's mind, many of which we've discussed in other questions. This is a question for the reader to evaluate for himself or herself. We'll return to the consultant's own answer momentarily. Place yourself in the consultant's position undertaking the same steps, and use a separate sheet to outline some notes about your thoughts:

Q8: Identify Frank's own issues. Be as broad in your answers as you'd like.

Again, this is an opportunity to put yourself in the consultant's shoes for a moment, and consider the information given about Frank's actions, words, and temperament. We'll come back to the consultant's own responses to this question on the following pages, but on a separate sheet, outline your thoughts on Frank. Consider also whether Frank's temperament is suitable for a leadership role focused on client delivery and customer satisfaction.

Q7 From the Consultant's view:

The consultant believed a few things had been the case.

- Frank lacked flexibility and was not adaptive. His style was far too rigid to be productive. The consultant described Frank's style as being a hammer, and constantly requiring everyone to be a nail.

- Frank lacked the emotional maturity and professional demeanor to productively collaborate with others.

- Frank lacked experience with such efforts, but could not be persuaded that someone else might have experience and other approaches.

- Frank believed that a Project Manager was a directed executor rather than a consultative resource with experience in these types of initiatives. Therefore, the expectations were skewed.

- Frank would not listen to answers. Considering the walk down the aisle, the consultant felt the marriage would be rocky.

- Frank's questioning style was pedantic. It was better suited to interviewing a small child about reading comprehension, not a professional tasked with a strategic effort.

- Despite the agreement that the conversation be a dialogue, Frank continued to be evasive. Collaboration would not be feasible.

- Frank was having trouble truly accepting that his approach, not the individual, might be a root cause to the challenges facing the effort.

- Lack of Project Management understanding (i.e. a Project Plan is not a Kickoff Deck), and refusal to discuss gaps.

- Inability to understand that consultants could be more than "hired help" and be a useful strategic presence in an organization.

- Frank's outburst near the end proved he wasn't management material, and was operating beyond his capabilities.

Q8 From the Consultant's view:

The consultant had this to say about Frank during the interview process:

- Frank's arrogance was unbecoming. Comments such as "I'll bet you've never expected a quiz, did you?" set a poor tone for a discussion of how the consultant might help them succeed.

- There was never an effort to interact collaboratively, nor treat people as anything but inferior to him. The attitude was that the person from whom he sought expertise was beneath him.

- Frank seemed unwilling or unable to fully accept there was a problem. Being faced with this put him on a defensive posture. The conversation would have been more productive had it centered on the problems being encountered and transparent dialogue.

- Frank seemed to have only his own agenda from which he refused to deviate, judged by his interview approach and evasive answers.

- Frank could not view himself as being a part of the problem.

In addition, the consultant offered the following observations:

- Someone at Frank's level should have had a higher public profile or been seen in his field as more of a subject matter expert in a particular discipline. The consultant found none of that in his research on Frank.

- Frank came across as socially awkward, afraid to interact and ill-at-ease with a conversation not in his direct control.

- Frank appeared to be the type of person who "was never wrong" or too thin-skinned for criticism. That sort of flaw could hold him and his entire organization back from both recognition and further achievement – if he could see this on a first meeting, others likely knew this behavior also. Frank may be the sort of person who opens his own wounds and makes them even worse.

Q9: Did the consultant act fairly? Ethically?

The last lines of the study give us some indication to the consultant's actions. Since the premise of the dialogue was clearly stated, and although Frank did not want to interact in that manner, the consultant was honest in his statement. *"The consultant thanked Frank for the opportunity to meet, but felt further use of their time would be unproductive."* Rather than spending further effort, the consultant thanked the potential customer for his time and diplomatically excused himself. Regardless of Frank's reaction, the stated intent was dialogue, which by definition is not one-sided.

As to ethically, the clue is provided in this sentence. *"The consultant left the artifacts on the conference room table and exited..."* meaning that the consultant did not breach information that could have been Intellectual Property of the organization, or remove anything that he didn't already bring with him. I would suggest that his actions demonstrated appropriate and ethical behavior for the situation.

It is hoped that the above Case Study was insightful in its length and detail. I've provided this out of an actual case with some minor modifications to protect confidentiality (obviously, Frank is not the manager's real name, for instance). The point behind this case study was to address narrowband thought – a trait Frank exhibited that we'll discuss – and to talk about the idea of a 12-Step Program for organizations that come across this at various levels.

Before doing that, the purpose of this chapter was not to ridicule Frank, but to use him as a teachable example of organizations that fail to realize that they suffer from a "Barrier to Success".

Barriers to Success

All organizations have people that fall into a middle ground between competency in one discipline and lack-of-competency in their current role, despite insistence that they are suited for the role or the impression made on superiors. I used Frank as a long introduction to 2 topics, this being the first. We often refer to the Peter Principle[12] in referencing individuals who have surpassed their level of competency through progressive promotion, or the assumption that because someone has demonstrated adequate capability in one role, they can perform equally competently in a next progressive level of responsibility or complexity. When they can no longer deliver results resembling their previous accomplishments, they've progressed as far as possible in that organization.

In the case above, we can infer that several people achieved that level. The project manager who was pressed into the role because, presumably, she had performed well enough in other roles to merit consideration; the program manager who lacked experience in program management, but presumably performed well enough to warrant consideration within a new accountability; and Frank, the IT Manager who lacked the necessary social and professional skills for his level, as evidenced by his awkward social interaction.

All three represent barriers to success:

- People who prevent success either actively or inadvertently by their capabilities
- People mismatched in their role based on their capabilities and competency
- People who are misaligned with the organization's strategic goals, or whose actions prevent their realization

Right Talent, Right Role

Removing the barriers requires recognition of their existence, and a plan to ensure the right match of talent to role. Organizations routinely experiment with different tactics in the name of "opportunity" or "career growth" when these may not be the right actions for their strategic interests.

I recently learned about a position advertised for a Program Manager on a very strategic product rationalization effort – combining duplicate products into a single customer offering. After much external interviewing, the company had rejected the external candidates in favor of an internal candidate who later turned-down the position. This forced the company to go to the expense of resuming the recruiting exercise with new candidates and be well into the process of selecting a second round of finalists to review when the original internal candidate had a change of heart and wanted the role. The organization re-extended an offer that was accepted.

> *Q: Why was this foolish?*

> *A: It sends everyone the wrong message, and rewards the wrong behaviors. Human Resources paid for expensive time and effort to recruit twice for the same role, and the candidate demonstrated indecision, which could indicate that he is not committed to the role and prone to jump to something else later. It also shows indecision, which may translate into poor performance for the organization. Meanwhile, solid candidates are sent conflicting messages about the organization's ability to act decisively, so the organization looks foolish.*

I had a similar experience in hiring for a role on my team in the past, and extended an offer to an internal candidate, who complained about conditions in the offer. Since the candidate was dissatisfied with the offer, I asked HR to retract it and remove that candidate from further consideration. He demon-

---

[12] Refers to the work published by Dr. Laurence J. Peter and Raymond Hull, 1968.

strated behavior that I'm happy to have seen earlier versus later when it would have had an impact on an important initiative. That organization's Human Resource group also didn't view him positively in the future.

In summary, success means finding the right talent and deploying it where it can be best used. It requires planning, resource management skills, and the ability to make critical decisions – promotions, change in deployment and corrective action – when the needs arise. Organizations cannot afford to think the best candidate is always within their walls, despite the message it sends about growth and opportunity, and employees need to be educated that their skills should be compared with others on the market. Managers should feel under no obligation to select an inferior candidate for a role simply because it promotes the culture of career growth within an organization.

Frequently, the lack of ability to find the best talent, or the ability to broaden internal talent out of a comfort-zone, results in poor choices for the hiring manager and inadequate results in initiative delivery.

A 12-Step Program for Initiative Success

Alcoholics Anonymous has been famous for creating and coining the concept of a 12-Step Program[13]. Before we begin to apply this to Initiative Management, however, we need to change the tenor of a few steps to begin to see how this has application in understanding and improving overall competency.

First, let's look at the original 12-steps as originally outlined by Alcoholics Anonymous

1. We admitted we were powerless over alcohol—that our lives had become unmanageable.
2. Came to believe that a Power greater than ourselves could restore us to sanity.
3. Made a decision to turn our will and our lives over to the care of God as we understood Him.
4. Made a searching and fearless moral inventory of ourselves.
5. Admitted to God, to ourselves, and to another human being the exact nature of our wrongs.
6. Were entirely ready to have God remove all these defects of character.
7. Humbly asked Him to remove our shortcomings.
8. Made a list of all persons we had harmed, and became willing to make amends to them all.
9. Made direct amends to such people wherever possible, except when to do so would injure them or others.
10. Continued to take personal inventory and when we were wrong promptly admitted it.
11. Sought through prayer and meditation to improve our conscious contact with God as we understood Him, praying only for knowledge of His Will for us and the power to carry that out.
12. Having had a spiritual awakening as the result of these steps, we tried to carry this message to alcoholics, and to practice these principles in all our affairs.

The notion of a 12-Step Program is certainly not new, and this example from its genesis demonstrates that it can be applied to a variety of situations.

So why shouldn't there be a 12-Step Program for Strategic Initiative Management? If admitting we have a problem is the first step toward recognizing how we must address it in a structured and con-

---

[13] Alcoholics Anonymous (June 2001). Alcoholics Anonymous (4th ed.). Alcoholics Anonymous World Services. ISBN 1893007162. OCLC 32014950

tinued approach, those steps could certainly be applied to create a process that could be targeted and followed by managers for continually improving their own awareness of staff, personal and team-competency, collaboration, and self-awareness. The notion would certainly have applicability in the Case Study outlined at the beginning of this chapter, which we'll discuss shortly after we outline the changes in the steps as I've shown in a draft proposal of a 12-Step plan.

A few things have been edited for this to not be considered sacrilege. For instance, my intent is not to deify initiative managers, much less malign team members who may lack specific competencies, but to help bring these together with the goal of improving interaction between all parties.

With some modifications, I present a 12-Step Plan for Managers to assess their progress toward an overall goal of collaboration, initiative success and strategic alignment.

Introducing, 12-Steps for Strategy Alignment and Initiative Success:

1. We admitted we were not achieving success using our current approach, and that the process, objectives and goals had become unmanageable, without assigning blame or fault to ourselves.
2. We came to believe that others with a greater competency within a discipline could restore sanity and help align strategy.
3. We made a decision to let go of the notion that we must control the entire process, but placed our trust in collaborative and competent teams to manage the process against our strategy.
4. We made an inventory of the current business and strategic issues and our ability to address them.
5. We admitted our competencies and limitations, and sought a support structure capable of acting on our strengths and addressing our weaknesses.
6. We were entirely ready for others to collaborate with us in achieving those strategic goals.
7. We demonstrated both our leadership qualities as well as our own humility.
8. We made an inventory of all our strategic business partners, suppliers, and stakeholders, and reached out collaboratively to ensure our alignment and cooperation.
9. We directed our efforts to understand our business requirements and strategy, and ensured the best interests of the business were always fundamental goals.
10. Our organization continued to address challenges and issues within our initiatives by continual monitoring, support of team deficiencies and weaknesses, and prompt decisive actions to support strategic goals.
11. We sought to improve our 360-degree communication skills with our management, stakeholders, team members and customers, remembering to align our efforts in a manner that effectively executes our organization's strategy.
12. Our organization recognizes the individual high-performers within our teams toward broadening skills and challenging them further, along with practicing these principles in all our affairs.

Let's examine Frank, now that we've nearly worn him out like an old record. From our Case Study, we can see Frank was barely committed to Step One. While he recognized there was a problem, his controlling nature prevented him from fully realizing Steps Two and Three. Using this example, had he progressed at least to Step Three, the steps beyond that would be shorter hurdles, but each would focus on a collaborative approach.

Strategic Initiative Manager's Postulate #1

There is one careful presupposition that we can draw from all the above:

"Poor management hinders good employees."

How many organizations have dealt with the other side of employee recruiting: Valued and competent talent leaving due to ineffective management? Citing the Peter Principle, we know that an employee can be promoted into management because of demonstrated competency in non-management tasks, yet never demonstrate effective leadership nor prior experience in a leadership role. It's not uncommon for that to be the <u>only</u> career progression for individual performers who become poor collaborative influences in an organization.

Having worked in a wide variety of organizations through my own career, I watched as people were given more senior titles based on their technical skill, not based on their ability to collaborate or communicate; the results were usually a disaster for both the manager and his direct staff.

In one case, the organization had the foresight to provide for both a management and technical career path that allowed very senior technologists to continue beyond a certain pay-grade and level based on technical competency, recognizing that management wasn't a realistic career-path for everyone. The result was successful for many of the former managers who returned to individual contributor roles – most recognized their own lack of interest and deficiencies in management, and accepted those roles as a smart way to stay within the organization with the opportunity for advancement.

While this is one way to counter the flight of capable staff, many organizations are not progressive enough to better address this as an issue. As a result, a very capable employee works beneath a far less capable manager, and his or her career progress is hindered as a result. To close this chapter on a more positive note, I'd like to offer some observations and advice as a successful manager who has managed happy and positive employees:

Employee Satisfaction Comes In Many Forms...

And here are a few ideas and suggestions:

- "Do Unto Others...": Treat your staff in the same way you want to be treated.

- Maintain an open-dialogue with everyone equally. Make sure that you spend time with them one-on-one routinely at set intervals, and maintain routine dialogue day-to-day with them.

- Include them whenever possible. If you have a meeting with a business customer, include them so they can get firsthand information. Compare notes as well to ensure common understanding.

- Recognize. Make sure they know your sincere recognition of their effort, especially if they've gone above and beyond. And don't be afraid to ensure that your management understands the effort from your team.

- Coaching. Make sure every employee has both a set of objectives that are clear and achievable, as well as a personal development plan. Challenge them to broaden their skills or knowledge in some way that prepares them for opportunities, and helps create a diverse team that benefits the organization.

- Feedback, both types, and both ways. Annual reviews are the wrong place for surprises, so any employee should already know where they stand, and what steps they should take (see Open Dialogue above). And let your employees know that you want to hear the good, bad and ugly about yourself – only the thinnest skinned managers don't accept feedback as an opportunity to improve (see Case Study #14 for an example).

- "Kick 'em out of the nest." Encourage your employees to broaden their horizons, and let them know that their career aspiration should not be "to work for you forever". When you see an opportunity for them to grow or do something that will benefit them, let them know and encourage them to network for other opportunities.

- "We're in this together." If your employees know that you'll support them when they're making the right decisions and meeting with resistance, they'll appreciate that more than being left out in the cold when it mattered most.

- "Pull no punches." I've always found that sugarcoating is best left on cereal and not in a conference room. If there's bad news to be had, tell your team honestly and explain how it affects them. They may initially be angry about it, but they'll respect you more for your honesty.

- "Information exchange." Meet regularly as a group so that everyone interacts and has an opportunity to exchange ideas. I've managed groups that were distributed around the globe, and it's very beneficial to have a teleconference so that people feel comfortable with one another, despite the difference in geographies. Use that opportunity to ask for ideas.

- "There will always be greater and lesser persons than yourself." This line from the Desiderata[14] denotes a stance toward humility. Humility is admitting you're wrong, you're not always the expert, you're not perfect, and you make mistakes like everyone else. When people see that you can be humble and still be a strong manager, they'll share a different respect for you, and they'll have a much different level of loyalty toward you.

- "Share the credit." When you recognize and promote your team, you're already promoting yourself. The secure manager isn't afraid of making sure his staff gets their deserved recognition because he knows he'll automatically benefit.

- Know when it's time to be a boss, and time to be a friend. Business relationships can happen outside the office, and they can work when everyone is emotionally mature enough to recognize the differences between work and social environments.

- Make sure your team knows "you". And get to know "them". If you treat them as hired help, they'll act that way; if you treat them fairly and professionally, they'll generally return the favor.

---

[14] Attribution to Max Ehrmann, 1933

Chapter 10:
The Quality Conundrum

"Which Comes First: Chicken or Egg?"

Managing quality within an initiative often results in a decision point as to where quality is checked in the process, and when or how often that check is made. It's a conundrum that countless Initiative Managers have faced when developing a plan and considering when to perform testing before release.

Very often, it's the last step before turnover to a User-Trial or Customer Acceptance.

When you put that in perspective, you've written a failure plan into the initiative for a number of reasons. Let's consider a split case study where we can begin to discuss the circumstances, conditions, and outcomes in perspective:

> ### Case Study #15, Part One: Quality, the afterthought.
>
> *A large organization had contracted the business requirements, development, and deployment of a custom-built back-office workflow system to a third-party consultancy. The goals of the engagement were as follows:*
>
> 1. *Replace an existing legacy technology base that would no longer be supported by a third-party software vendor.*
>
> 2. *Extend functionality from one component of the back-office to all business groups.*
>
> 3. *Extend the robustness of the platform by developing around the defined business rules, provided by the various business units.*
>
> 4. *Deliver projected headcount savings (20%), increased capacity (5 years live data online for recall), and reduce processing time by two-thirds from its current levels.*
>
> *Within 18 months of beginning the engagement, the project was behind schedule and well in excess of the budget for its deliverable. More alarming still, over 5,000 enhancement and break-fix requests were made, and the number grew by the day. Without a firm regiment of change control in place, change requests were submitted without regard for business impact, many of which counteracted other requests. Morale on the development team, which was composed of both third-party consultants and in-house developers, was sinking quickly, as was customer confidence.*

Overall effectiveness of change and quality slipped to a 40% defect rate. Out of every 10 changes implemented, 4 would be rejected or simply not work. Quality Assurance was, at best, a haphazard affair done late on the day of a deliverable deadline without rigors. The sponsoring customer, while having good personal relationships with the consulting team due to a "please the customer" orientation, was not satisfied with progress; the approach of demanding continued scope changes wasn't effective.

A new Project Manager was hired by the organization: His first 2 orders of business were (1) to disengage the Third-Party consultancy, and (2) to get control over the chaos.

As with many of the other Case Studies outlined, this follows a pattern that shows the mistakes being made with some cause and effect. It would be easy if the new Project Manager walked in on Day One and been provided this level of background to begin organizing and executing on his charter. In the case of the new Project Manager, it wasn't a simple task to reach the conclusions that we'll see in the second part of the study.

From the first part of this study, we recognize that quality was considered as an afterthought in the process, and when a release was in a time-crunch for delivery, quality assurance was the first item to suffer. It also appeared to lack an organized process, given the description of it being a haphazard task.

The other useful detail is the number of requests, many of which were "break-fix" situations. A 40% defect ratio provided some indications.

The project management profession speaks about the 3 pillars of project constraint referred to as either "the triple-constraint" or the "Iron Triangle". In the case above, it's depicted that the project was running well beyond budget (cost), behind schedule (time) and that the defect ratio (quality) left significant room for improvement.

There are other challenges depicted by this short study. We'll focus on these:

1. Quality as key to customer satisfaction.

2. Change control as key to ensuring overall quality.

3. Both Quality Control and Change Management as key to demonstrating value.

Let's continue with the study to see how the situation progressed under the new project manager.

Case Study #15, Part 2: Quality + Change Control = Success

The new project manager began to probe all the aspects of the problem, starting with controlling and prioritizing the changes in the environment so that future changes were carefully considered. Working with the business liaisons and project sponsor, they prioritized the requirements for upcoming releases according to both their criticality and their business value. Some defects would remain in the system as long as a process was in place to handle them.

He then focused beyond that to understand the Change Request process. After review of the changes, some issues became clear.

- *Many requests lacked clarity*

- *Several were duplicated requests, just phrased differently.*

- *Several requests contradicted others*

- *Many contained no description about the current problem, or information on its resolution. They were requests that simply requested, "Fix this".*

- *There was never clear documentation of the business rules accompanying the request (were the developers supposed to guess?)*

As the Project Manager and business units honed their fixes, the Project Manager also set about addressing quality from several different perspectives:

1. *Understanding of the business rules and requirements. If information was insufficient, it was "returned to requestor" to clarify. Many never made it back because the requestor had forgotten why they made that request originally, or had learned enough about the software to understand their request was not relevant.*

2. *Creating a more comprehensive request process: Specific business liaisons could authorize a request; all were reviewed to clarify understanding; any that had a business value were accepted; documentation of the current and desired states, business logic, business requirements, and use conditions were mandated with all requests. This "gatekeeper" process resulted in a higher quality of information provided, and a resulting improvement in understanding.*

3. *Establishing a permanent Quality Assurance function with personnel who were trained on the software as it evolved. Each tester used the Business Requirements Document to develop their testing logic.*

4. *Creating a parallel Development/Test Scripting process that worked based on business requirements to develop test conditions that validated the change under a variety of conditions, some not always expected.*

The changes in the Business Requirements process were iterative, but adopted quickly by the development team and resulted in improvements that drove product quality gradually higher. As the developers began to understand the testing process and how thoroughly testing would now be done, their process for unit testing their changes also became more thorough. Once changes were compiled for a final test, it resulted in exhaustively testing the application and driving product quality toward a zero-defect goal.

Within 15 months of his original start, the 36-month effort that had been envisioned for building and deploying the agreed scope of the application had been completed. Three months ahead of schedule to a more confident and satisfied customer.[15]

The last statement in the study is somewhat tricky, since a few things happened to reach that agreed completion (see footnotes). We'll revisit this in a moment.

In the meantime, let's return to the three challenges and how each was met:

1. Quality as key to customer satisfaction. The efforts undertaken to understand the customer requirements, focus on the efforts needed to achieve them, and deliver what the customer requested (often beyond what they'd considered as user scenarios) resulted in quality improvement across the board. The customer received precisely what they requested.

2. Change Control as key to overall quality. By creating a more comprehensive change process as well as specific gatekeepers, specific people could understand the changes actually re-

---

[15] Note that recovery of such backlogged efforts when delayed after the 15% completion mark generally have a minimal chance of complete recovery. The situation above considers the changes that were agreed to scope the effort with Change Controls, process controls, and gatekeepers.

quired, and could clearly document what these entailed. The world of over 5,000 requests quickly disappeared; a new world emerged where the requests could be counted only into the low hundreds, and could be effectively managed. This did not mean less change; it represented more effective change.

3. Both Quality Control and Change Management as key to demonstrating value. By managing both ends of the process – the detail behind the requested work, and the management of quality throughout the process – the level of overall quality improved since more attention was given to what was delivered to the customer, rather than meeting an arbitrary timeline.

In fact, you'll note my point on the delivery of fewer defects within a timeline that was 3 months ahead of the original schedule for completion. As customer frustration increases, the tendency is not to stop and examine root-causes for the problem. Rather, in the rush to want changes by the numbers, the customer kept shoving more changes inadvertently through the project pipeline with little regard for what each change represented. By only viewing the numbers, 5,000 changes was destined to grow to 6,000 and beyond. By examining the root-causes, more information could be gained in understanding how the change request process had broken, and the necessary steps to return it to sanity.

Once the project was revised, the overall scope could be assessed and the necessary changes to complete the effort made with higher quality.

Requirements Drive Product Development...and Quality

The above example creates a compelling case for creating a branched execution at the completion of business requirements into separate tracks: One being the product development path; the second is the development of the quality track, which should begin with the development of Test Planning, Test Scripting and Scenarios, and other quality initiatives derived from the point of view of the business requirements.

If requirements drive the development, staying in lockstep through a test plan that maps to both positive and negative testing jump-starts the overall process.

In many cases, this won't be performed in complete isolation by either a business analyst, a customer subject-matter expert, or the QA tester, but should be some combination of all three parties to ensure that the requirement is understood, and its intended use and conditions have a high degree of clarity. It provides an ideal time to ask questions that address the intended use and workflow of a product.

For instance, if someone were to spend a day in the life of an assembly line worker observing their interactions and motions, they could understand how modifications to a product will positively or adversely affect them. My contention, and I've managed similar initiatives successfully using this process, is that a branching of the process will provide valuable information as an upfront investment of time. While many will argue that this delays initiative progress, I'll offer up the following observations:

1. In time-constrained circumstances (hard deliveries, time-boxing of teams), quality assurance, testing and validation are the disciplines that suffer most. As noted in this Chapter's case study, delays upstream squeeze testing time when deadlines loom. Often, those delays can be traced to a lack of understanding of business requirements that result in insufficient work product deliverables in an initiative. Were the time invested at the beginning, it would promote understanding, quality and development throughput as it did for the organization in the study.

2. Quality in most organizations is an end-check rather than comprehensive thought process. Have you ever wondered why the interest in Six Sigma has increased over time? The focus is to reduce defects by applying a process and understanding the root-cause of those defects. In

the Case Study, the Project Manager did a similar exercise without using a Six Sigma formula to meet the same goal. Six Sigma processes can be very beneficial when used properly; they're not a panacea but help drive attention to understanding root-causes. By giving all quality processes a parallel path, the tests are ready to execute the moment the product is ready, and delays can be mitigated.

3. It's an investment in understanding the customer. When you better understand that customer's processes and issues, you can target richer solutions to address those needs and anticipate future needs (consulting organizations, are you listening?).

It's Not the Symptom; It's the Root-Cause.

After reading the above, do you still believe this is an "either/or" proposition? The reality is that it's neither but must be both for the process to truly be successful.

As we learn about managing the customer expectation, just as the project manager did in the prior Case Study, we also learn about the true focus of their pain. The role of a good Initiative Manager is sensing that pain, and understanding the root causes to solve the underlying problem versus just treating the symptom.

In treating one symptom, we must understand the other affects our action may have. One of the best parallels that most of us can relate to are pharmaceutical commercials in which the US Food & Drug Administration (FDA) requires that warnings and side effects be clearly advertised when the drug is promoted or advertised on television, radio, or in print. For anyone who has heard these, and comedians such as Jeff Foxworthy have poked fun at the practice through comedy skits, the majority of a 60-second commercial is filled with a listing of warnings and potential side-effects that, when considered as a whole, often seem worse than the original condition that the drug was originally designed to treat. In a few cases, pharmaceutical companies have even aired follow-up commercials required by the FDA to clarify even more side effects and symptoms.

It's a point well taken in that we need to consider that every action can be followed by an equal or opposite reaction[16]. The focus should not be the prescription we take away from our physician to relieve the pain we're feeling, but to focus on the factors causing that pain in the hopes that they can be treated or cured.

Earlier in the year that I wrote this book, I spent a good bit of time with a shoulder condition that resulted in pronounced pain at my shoulder and bicep, combined with a loss of feeling in much of my left hand. Think of it as similar to the tingling feeling children describe as their "hand being asleep" (the sensation when nerves or muscles are deprived of blood flow or you've lain on your hand too long), just 24 hours a day. My family physician could prescribe me a dermal patch to relieve the pain, but we still didn't know or understand the root-cause that created the issue, nor did it eliminate the numbness. So thoughts ran through my head of surgery or other treatments, but it wasn't until I'd taken the extra step of checking the real root causes through X-rays and MRI's we could understand the underlying problem: compression in my cervical spine and a torn bicep. I was relieved when I found out they could be easily treated with physical therapy, and I'm feeling much better and stronger today as a result.

My case was perhaps somewhat different in that I could not pinpoint the exact event that triggered it, but could narrow it to 2 possibilities: Both involved over exertion, and both involved a man in his 40's that could use more muscle toning. Since we could narrow down the symptoms – the pronounced pain, the tingling sensations, the loss of feeling and range of motion – this provided some clues on how

---

[16] Reference to Sir Isaac Newton's Laws of Motion, 1687

we could resolve the underlying issue. In fact, most root-cause analysis is done by tracking back from those symptoms to reveal the underlying cause.

Symptoms Leading to the Underlying Cause

Earlier in my career, I managed a development group that was responsible for supporting a Report Generation System, based on transactional data and a variety of underlying queries. We'd experienced issues with system performance at a variety of times, which slowed system performance against the live system (much of our reporting information needed accuracy with within the previous few minutes, rather than waiting for replication against a separate server that could handle more robust queries). Behind all of this was a large database that handled transactional data.

When we discovered this early in the lifecycle of the product, a system that had great excess processing capacity was brought to a grinding halt, and the game of finger pointing had begun. Each side wanted to point at another for the problem – application developers wanted to blame the database architects and administrators; database administrators wanted to blame the application development teams; business customers wanted one throat to choke from their frustration.

I held a meeting with the database administrators to get their side of the story, but I also wanted to understand what they saw, and why they felt as they did. So we gave them as much information as known and began finding recognizable queries against the system, which were being generated by our up-to-second transactional query tool. I then spoke with the business customers to understand their user experience – this involved both asking them the types of queries they had generated, as well as the outcomes of those. I was suddenly deluged with complaints that revealed that the customer had requested data from the tool but none ever returned, and a message appeared indicating that the transaction had timed out. We took this a step further and compared the database queries with the user experience.

The query tool within our application limited the result-set to 50 items, and the user training taught the users to refine their queries as much as possible to return relevant results. Instead, they were requesting a result set that included nearly all transactions within a certain category for a very long period, something never envisioned. The application had set a time limit of 60 seconds to respond so that the user would not be unable to continue if an error was encountered.

Behind the scenes, that query continued to run, although the user never saw a result. When we duplicated the query outside of normal hours, the result time was well over 3 minutes and included over 20,000 records. As a result, we made 3 significant changes:

1. Changed the application to provide a "next" function, which would return the next results when more than 50 were received.

2. Revised the database code to improve query delivery efficiency.

3. Retrained all of our customers on the tool, its proper use and capabilities, and types of information to request.

Incidentally, no one's throat was choked as a result. Rather, it demonstrated an example of a collaborative effort to find the true root cause of an issue versus treating only the symptoms. Treating the symptom would never have revealed the underlying problem, and could have created several new ones. Focusing on the root-case analysis to develop the right answers resulted in an improved understanding of the application by the users, and an immediate change in performance; focusing on cleaning and fine tuning the underlying queries sent to the database resulted in somewhat more concise and efficient code, confirming that capacity was never an issue; and slight modifications to the application resulted in bringing slightly more data to the user and improving the perception of responsiveness.

This leads me to Buck's Postulate #2:

"Someone will find a way to use a product, service, or system that was never intended."

The pharmaceutical industry has known this for years, and has termed the use as "off-label indication": a drug developed for a specific purpose could be found to have another life with a different useful purpose. For instance, how many men knew that the hair loss drug "Propecia" is actually a smaller dosage of the drug "Finasteride" which is used to treat male prostate issues?

Defining and improving Product Quality

In Case Study #15, we emphasized a business problem partially driven by quality. By changing several processes, we changed the landscape and directly improved quality.

The process was a two-pronged approach that resulted in a clear outcome. This section will probe further into quality delivery approach by first defining the level and grade of quality desired. The goal of any organization is to strive for a defect-free environment. The reality is quite different, and the drive toward further quality gains also meets with the "Law of Diminishing Returns"[17]; the addition of more input may not realize the originating level of gains and will recognize a higher cost. For many organizations, a reasonable middle ground between high-cost/high-quality and low-cost/lower-quality will emerge. As an organization drives closer to a zero-defect goal, the underlying cost of finding and fixing remaining defects becomes larger since the defects are usually less apparent.

Therefore, it is necessary to define the quality standard desired, and the definition of success should include what some organizations have defined as "Key Product Quality Parameters"[18], referenced as KPQP's, or the level of quality that is acceptable for the sponsoring party to agree that goals have been achieved. Discussion is needed to determine the standards against which the initiative is being benchmarked as part of the quality planning exercise, along with the standards needed to complete User Acceptance. There are some common methods:

Blocker versus Non-Blocker
1. Agreement that defects ranked as "Medium" or higher, and any defect that blocks usage of the product, be addressed before product launch.

2. Any defect that does not affect overall usage or the user experience, or is ranked as "Low", be addressed subsequent to product launch.

3. Rankings cannot be subjective, and should be independently reviewed with a sponsoring party.

User-Acceptance Passage:
1. The product is found to be defect-free by a User Acceptance process or a qualified Quality Assurance process that adequately exercises the product functionality.

2. New defects resulting from the changes in functionality which act as "blockers" must be addressed before launch.

---

[17] Adapted from the work of Anne Robert, Jacques Turgot and implied by Thomas Malthus in his *Essay on the Principle of Population* (1798); first accepted as an agricultural law but later expanded to include economics and other disciplines.
[18] Defined via public literature on the KPQP Method in conjunction with Public Domain data; also referenced as KPI's, representing Key Performance Indicators as an expression of product performance and accepted variances or tolerances.

3. Defects that are the direct result of inadequate documentation of requirements, or errors/omissions, be excluded from becoming new requirements within the same quality review cycle.

This is not a complete list of considerations, and intended as a guideline for applying a quality litmus test against defined circumstances. Depending on the industry and application, quality sign-off parameters could include the following additional requirements (which must be defined in the KPQP above):

*   Specific tolerances to conditions (e.g. temperature ranges, pressure ranges, amounts of force applied, weight certifications, safety specifications)

*   Specific throughput requirements (e.g. withstands pressure of 2000 psi, withstands flow of 100 gal/min, handles 10,000 transactions/second)

*   Specific mean or maximum response times (e.g. must respond =< 1 second, must be capable of operational time of 99.97% or < 30 seconds of downtime per day)

As mentioned, this is an example list. When planning an initiative, these might inspire some guidelines to consider and can be expanded based on the initiative.

Incidentally, if your business is based upon both the quality and availability of data (e.g. a market data vendor, a brokerage), formulation of a strategy to ensure data integrity should be a primary consideration before all others. Having worked for such organizations, the decisions upon which customers invest millions of dollars rely on the quality of that data. Losing the game here results in losing marketshare and fighting to regain it. Your initiative expectations should consider the expectations of your customers in the same way you would expect if you were your own customer.

Summary Points

The closing paragraphs will focus on the importance of quality as a consideration, using Case Study #15 as a focal point.

Our study organization began with an end goal of performance, reducing transaction time, improving efficiency by reducing manual processes, and creating a leaner organization. The symptoms of the situation provided only part of the overall story. We recognized that the symptoms experienced by that organization depicted other underlying causes, which we could discover, correct, control, and use to focus on improving quality.

The resulting process used several steps to address and improve quality outcomes:

*   Detailed specifications

*   Gate keeping, including prioritization

*   Elaboration of the Business Requirement, including:

    o   Current scenario

    o   Envisioned (to-be) scenario

    o   Design requirement details

*   Interaction between technical and business customers

*   Interaction on requirements for detailed understanding, which lead to:

    o   Detailed Test Cases

    o   Detailed Testing Conditions

        o   Positive/Negative/Regressive Scenarios

- Focus on addressing requirements

- Continued improvement on revealing and documenting potential issues for future discussion

- Iterative phasing and grouping of requirements to deliver business specific value, with a goal of measurable improvement within the group

There's one more important item in this process: **Pre-and-Post Metrics**.

We need to create a baseline starting point for the changes to be measurable. Defects were measured at 40% at the beginning of the Case Study. This forms a measurable baseline for improvements to be measured and compared, and will demonstrate effectiveness of our quality process. Some additional measurement criteria to consider may include:

- Number of iterative fixes or changes per requirement

- Number of defects found in quality testing

- Time required to conduct quality testing

From a customer perspective, consider measuring the following parameters to ensure the desired outcomes are achieved:

- Efficiency, both pre and post

- Cost, both pre and post

- Throughput, both pre and post

- Headcount, both pre and post

- Failures or defects, both pre and post

…Among other parameters that will vary based on the initiative and requirements.

Also, the organization's approach to quality must be carefully thought and consider the objectives to be achieved. Using the above Case Study, clearly moving from a 40% defect rate to the desired end state will be a process of continued improvement and investment (which often can be self-funded). It will also depend on the organization's current and desired maturity level with constructing and maintaining a quality regiment that best suits its goals.

Rather than close this topic with a single summarizing thought, I'll cite several:

- Quality is not an afterthought. It's planned as part of the initiative.

- Quality is not a check before turnover. It is a mindset that we fundamentally change to achieve measured improvement.

- Quality is not omniscient. It requires defining the goal to be achieved and the steps required to achieve it.

- Quality is not a fix, but a very well planned and executed avoidance system.

- Quality assurance should confirm our understanding of the requirements, not be a gatekeeper to rejecting change.

- Quality is a parallel process to all other activities, and must work in conjunction with product development and customer interaction to be truly effective.

Understanding these tenets changes the game without either dropping the ball or creating overhead.

Chapter 11:
An End-to-End View

Where Do Our Roles Begin and End?

I previously mentioned a key point about metrics across the entire product lifecycle. As part of an overall examination of Initiative Management, this is where I diverge somewhat from self-contained methodologies and frameworks, and migrate toward a more end-to-end focused agenda. So I'll qualify my comment to recommend that Initiative Managers must take a strategic view of the enterprise, not merely transition their effort once the "Completion" phase of a traditional project has been signed-of by the customer.

Where most approaches fail is in the compartmentalization of responsibilities, while the overall end-to-end view of initiatives is absent. Consider the following:

- *Most of the IT spending in organizations is based on year-to-year maintenance of the existing infrastructure, not the implementation of new capability. This includes the networking, application and user support, data centers, hardware maintenance, bandwidth costs, individual or group software licensing costs, and the required care and feeding of the applications entering and existing in the enterprise data center. Of course, many of those applications and older infrastructures need to be retired and replaced with updated technology and capabilities. The challenge of the Chief Information Officer is to run a lean an operational enterprise, since organizations cannot to fund increasing operational costs without also undertaking innovation and abandoning older markets.*

Readers of this book may understand or realize that many technology departments report to a Chief Financial Officer rather than directly to a Chief Executive Officer. We can speculate on why, but it helps the organization keep close accountability on what might otherwise be runaway technology spending. That's one commonly held view, besides limiting the number of direct reports to a CEO.

The challenge is to serve the new requirements of customers effectively while maintaining operational standards. Compounding that challenge is a dwindling share of the overall financial pool for resources.

Many years ago, I ran a PMO for an organization whose parent company's Technology Operations Division handled operational budgeting. While there, the Operations Group asked for an 8% increase in funds over the prior year, despite our having migrated to less-costly infrastructures, retiring some applications and using less of a footprint in the data center. They were surprised when I asked for a breakdown of our utilization costs for the division, and challenged them on the details – the rationale was that we've reduced our requirements, so why did our costs increase? It was the beginning of a larger discussion for the organization as they were unable to show financial transparency or justify their request.

While the matter was eventually dropped for that year, it didn't go away as the organization realized their cost-containment wasn't effective and did what most do to shave costs: Reduce headcount.

The beleaguered Heads of Infrastructure in many organizations don't have an easy job because most don't get to see a roadmap of initiatives that will require support after implementation. This holistic view doesn't exist in many organizations, and hinders the ability to effectively understand and control investment.

Where Do the Answers Lie?

The UK's Office of Government and Commerce developed the Information Technology Infrastructure Library (ITIL)^{TM} Standard[19] as a set of practices and policies for managing IT services and technology operations. More information concerning ITIL^{TM} can be found on its website: http://www.itil.co.uk/. ITIL^{TM} has become a de-facto standard in the management of processes and procedures, and provides a system of templates that can be adapted to the individual enterprise. The focus of ITIL^{TM} is more operational, and in some cases the costs of ensuring ITIL^{TM} compliance among all constituencies can outweigh the end benefit if the scheme is not tailored to the maturity and culture of the organization.

Incidentally, this is especially true in the event of mergers between organizations that are ITIL^{TM} practitioners and those that are not. One of the goals of ITIL^{TM}, however, is to provide a level of transparency for how IT budget is spent, and to quantify the results of that investment while simultaneously improving service management across the enterprise.

While not specifically endorsing ITIL^{TM} as the authoritative infrastructure statement in this publication, I'll refer to some of its broad concepts in helping shape the holistic view of end-to-end initiative management. Where possible, I'll adapt these concepts to the wider audience of products, including those that are not necessarily technology derived.

Total Cost of Ownership (TCO)

Behind all of this lies a discussion of the overall costs of an initiative, and why all should be considered in the product life cycle being managed, not simply the beginning and end of the project, or transition to a future product.

To relate a short story, as the Manager of a PMO earlier in my career, one of the Chartering Reasons for that PMO was to provide financial transparency into both the costs of the project and the subsequent running costs. In the example above, I mentioned the 8% increase in operating expense and the lack of granularity behind that increase, which drove us toward probing our expenses more granularly.

Every capability has a life cycle. Cellular phone owners know this well, since they've likely had more than one phone during the past few years. The computer you're using today is not the same computer (or even Operating System in most cases) that you were using 10 years ago. Every capability runs its course, and earlier in the book I mentioned a long series of products that have become obsolete or replaced within our lifetimes. So it also goes with business capabilities.

Once we release a product, the process does not stop there, nor should our view of initiative management. Thus, when we have an idea to introduce a capability or product, we should consider the frequency of revision required to stay current with or ahead of the marketplace, or the point at which that

---

19 ITIL and IT Infrastructure Library are registered trademarks of the UK's Office of Government Commerce.

capability is no longer relevant and will require replacement. That decision juncture is missed in many organizations, and why I've structured this section separately in the lifecycle: It's the concept everyone misses.

If you guessed there was an example of this, you're right!

Case Study #16: Sourcing Costs as TCO

The Assistant Vice President of a performing organization determined that he no longer wanted to be in the business of document capture and indexing of correspondence and paperwork – something that was the critical entryway into the organization's electronic workflow system for customer requests, business requests, and other transactional forms relevant to the business. He undertook an effort to source the function to an outside vendor familiar with the types of documents the business used, and could handle the task. He interviewed 2 vendors and selected one.

During the next phase of this effort, he engaged the development team to rewrite their existing code to accept a data feed in XML format, which would cross-reference the indexed document images once the vendor was done capturing them. The effort involved about 320 development hours of an in-house developer's time in coordination with the vendor.

The vendor had some difficulty in finding qualified people to perform the work satisfactorily, so they arranged with the customer organization to transition all but 2 of that company's current employees to office space they rented: across the street from the company's facility.

The Assistant Vice President pronounced the initiative as a success despite the higher cost of doing business with the vendor versus the current cost for the organization to have kept the function intact. That number included the 2 people who were not retained. A one-year contract was signed at a set rate for the business. The equipment originally used for document capture was crated and shipped offsite to a warehouse; other groups never occupied the floor space that was made available (therefore, no savings in rental costs for the floor-space).

Before the one-year anniversary and renewal of the contract, the vendor returned to the performing organization with a firm proposal for a 3-year extension for that business, at a significant markup. The vendor had accepted the business unprofitably during the first year and recognized an erosion of profit margin. If they could not agree, they would need to use their 60-day notice to the customer to discontinue their operations and not renew their office space lease. Moreover, their costs had risen because they had to pay the organization's former employees the same rate they were receiving before their transition. The customer did not renew.

The customer was fortunately able to reinstall their existing equipment, fallback to their previous arrangement, and restart the function, but not without some further costs that included:

- *Paying the severance to the former workers who had been displaced to the third-party vendor and later brought back.*

- *Bridging their years of service toward their pension plan, including the year they had spent with the third-party vendor as incentive for returning.*

- *Providing cost of living increases.*

- *Time spent by development staff, facilities staff, and operational staff breaking down and reassembling the office environment within the same year, as well as implemen-*

tation and back-out of application and workflow changes, totaling nearly 500 hours of development time.

The Winners: *The employees who were paid an average of 34 weeks of salary for their severance, and were restored to their original positions with their pension plans unaffected. Several pocketed the money; some bought brand new cars.*

The Losers: *The third-party vendor for underestimating and under pricing business for that year, and counting on renewal increases to recoup their losses; the AVP who undertook a misguided and unprofitable effort, and who was promptly severed from the organization once the former employees were back in place.*

The example here demonstrates a lack of understanding of the Total Cost of the Initiative. The reason this happened is simple. The total cost equation was never factored, and had it been calculated, it would have revealed that the costs to outsource the function were higher than to retain it. While organizations may view outsourcing as a windfall, this is an example where it presents little value and significant risk to the organization.

Something else failed in this example: Proper governance. If the costs were greater to outsource than retain, this should have been more diligently questioned. A lack of a check-and-balance system in making such an agreement, misallocating the company's financial and personnel resources, and the net wasted effort could have been avoided had this simple equation been understood.

Why TCO and not ROI or Net Present Value?

When you calculate the return on investment, you are only including the invested money – that is the capital and financial disbursements of the project or initiative, and not the ongoing costs. Even a Net Present Value calculation usually considers only the value of the project at its core, and recouping the investment from the project apart from ongoing and recurring costs (power, heating & cooling, floor space, support costs, annual licensing, etc.)

The understanding of TCO might seem daunting for some, and for others it might spell doom to the initiative they hoped to champion or sponsor. The news isn't that at all. The revelation is that organizations have been shouldering those costs all along, but never considering them as a single initiative. Consequently, the best options may be declined in favor of a personal preference; the financials may not validate those options if better scrutinized.

This brings us back to the beleaguered Heads of Operations and Chief Information Officers hoping to serve their customers under tighter constraints, and the CFO seeking granularity in technology costs. The bigger picture that includes the total cost of ownership reveals those answers for both the project sponsor and others charged with supporting the capability once implemented.

I've used the common information technology scenario or business scenario for these examples. Natural gas and oil exploration can view through the same lens and recognize their TCOs through the costs of building the infrastructure for drilling and exploration, and the expected return value provided commodity prices (which can fluctuate wildly) maintain a certain price level. Simply, and perhaps oversimplifying a bit, it's both the inherent costs of exploration and construction, plus the cost of day-to-day operation for as long as the well is producing.

Why Metrics Are Important to this Style of Governance

I explained earlier our goal to capture the projected returns on an initiative. We need a baseline or a starting point of comparison for any relevant metric. Using the 40% defect ratio from the Case Study in the last chapter, if our goal was to be within 1% overall defects, and 0% critical or blocking defects released to the customer, we would want to know our starting point (40%) to address the root-causes and create a process that reveals and corrects defects before they're found by the customer.

Supposing that our development team had a major customer release every 3 months, the trend should show a steady or marked improvement toward that goal over a period of defined time until it is achieved. That premise also held true in Case Study 15, although we did not discuss the expected time frame in which that achievement was expected. Anyone using a goal setting process probably understands the acronym **SMART**, which is also applicable here. For those who might not understand it's application correctly, it's an acronym for the following attributes:

- **Specific**
- **Measurable**
- **Attainable**
- **Realistic**
- **Timely**

I'll demonstrate examples to align the expectation between SMART goals versus those missing the mark.

Example #1: *A project is being established to ship camels to the moon and back at a total cost of around 100 million Euros.*

- Specific – Questionable – the project goal is specific enough to understand as an objective, although vague on the number of camels to be shipped. Camels as plural simply means "more than one", so the goal could be considered achieved if two camels are shipped. Cost is defined.

- Measurable – Passes – this barely passes if we agree on the safe round trip of more than one camel. We can also measure this by being over or under the 100 million Euro budget.

- Attainable – Questionable – It's not very likely the goal can be met.

- Realistic – Questionable – given today's technology, it may be possible, though it's not very likely.

- Timely – Fails – there is absolutely no time parameter around the mission, so if this happened in 50 years, we might not be around to see it, but it might be achieved.

Example #2: *A process redesign project is to be undertaken for an insurance underwriting group that allocates $200,000 to improve an existing workflow to achieve a 20% gain in productivity within the next 9 months.*

- Specific – Passes – the nature, focus, customer, and outcome of the project are all very clear.

- Measurable – Passes – the mission statement tells us that within 9 months, the efficiency of the group should have improved by 20%, and that our cost target for the effort is a $200,000 investment.

- Attainable – Passes – the mission statement is clear about the goal, and provides a reasonable time frame for measurement and tracking of the improvements.

- Realistic – Passes – a realistic expectation has been set to determine what needs to be performed, for whom, the time frame during which it should occur, and is probably within the project team's control.

- Timely – Passes – the time parameter for performing and completing the task is clearly defined.

In a TCO-based situation, we need to understand what we're measuring, our basis for comparison, and our trending toward the goal. We can also understand before undertaking the initiative whether the expectations surrounding it are also realistic and achievable within the time expectations provided.

Estimating Ongoing Variable Costs

Don't be surprised if you ask, "how do I estimate the ongoing support and maintenance costs of a product's proposed life" and be greeted by a confused stare. Although it's a relevant question for our needs, there aren't many organizations yet prepared to provide granularity of analysis, as I pointed out in a previous situation.

In Case Study #16, we could see the objectives of the two parties were different. The contracting party's was to ensure this was done at somewhat reasonable cost, albeit above current costs. The third-party firm believed it could withstand the loss in the first year if they could recoup that loss subsequently. Neither was transparent about their goals. Fortunately, that is more the exception than the rule, and most service providers can estimate the costs for an effort based on an understanding of requirements, prior experience, and their ability to meet targeted deliverables. For many organizations, this provides a compelling reason to consider third parties for contracting work since the overall costs can be locked into a contract and properly estimated upfront. It provides comfort and reassurance that the contractor is assuming the risks to their margin by providing a fixed price to their service.

Does it mean that organizations should contract all work outside because it's cheaper? As proven by both Case Study #1 and #16, not always and not necessarily.

Businesses are finally reaching a better level of financial granularity where TCO equations are more possible than several years ago as organizations learn more about estimating and gauging the year-over-year costs and maintaining better cost control.

I once liaised on an effort between an application development manager seeking a managed testing environment for their application and an Operations Manager who struggled with estimating the costs to host such a facility. A third-party that presented a year-by-year cost for a similarly managed service prompted the question. After some encouragement and discussion, the data center manager could break down his costs with some buffer factor for the unknown, and present a compelling reason for managing that environment themselves – it was 30% cheaper than going outside. I mention this because this characteristic has some variability, and is emerging as something that more adept managers are beginning to do in justifying their budgets. It's worth both asking and challenging people to think about annual costs – both fixed and variable – to confidently produce a projected Total Cost of Ownership.

Summary:

We challenged the compartmentalized view of the Project Manager and proposed a process roadmap that migrates the Initiative Manager into the **Idea** and **Definition/Validation** Phases of the Life Cycle. We suggested that the insight of project management should be used across all facets of the Initiative, including the implementation and monitoring of the capability once implemented. We reviewed the idea of Total Cost of Ownership as contrasted with Net Present Value (NPV) and Return on Investment (ROI) models that return an incomplete picture of the capability cost over its expected lifespan. We discussed the value of metrics as key to the calculation of value. As we move closer to a clear picture of an end-to-end framework, we'll detail these points further.

Additional Exercise:

The following exercise provides some scenarios for consideration. At a high level, evaluate the current options, and elaborate the rough costs given the constraints and information provided:

Scenario: Replacing aging system with newer technology.

A major company wants to replace a Mainframe System that is outdated technology, but does not wish to make the investment in either a Client/Server or Web-based solution as the current process and system are understood and serve their purpose without incurring major data conversion, development and training costs. They are under the following constraints.

1. *Their annual support costs for their Mainframe are $170,000. The rate increases by 10% per year and carries risk as parts become scarcer with age.*

2. *Their operational support costs are $185,000, which includes 24x6 support for the system, placement in a data center, power and cooling, and connectivity to their offices. Traditionally, the utility costs have increased by 7% annually, and personnel and benefits costs have also increased by 7%.*

3. *Current development support costs are fixed regardless of the solution, and those are $125,000 year, with an expected 5% increase each year.*

Given this data, evaluate the following scenarios:

1. *A do-nothing solution across a 5-year lifespan.*

2. *A solution that replaces the aging Mainframe with a newer more powerful machine at a fixed cost of $250,000 with an annual support cost of $45,000 and a 6% increase each year; the reduction in power and cooling and data center foot print with the same headcount costs bring total operational costs to $150,000 with the same expected 7% annual increase; a one time installation and configuration charge of $130,000 for a third-party to perform work. Development support costs do not change.*

Considering the data given, calculate a 5-year investment in this technology on both the "Do Nothing Solution" and the "Replacement Solution", presuming that Year 1 includes the project costs. Answer the following questions based on your analysis:

(a) *If the costs of the project are compared with the "do-nothing" scenario, what is the first year delta, and why?*

(b) *What is the percentage difference in cost between the solutions in years 2 through 5?*

(c) *At the end of 5 years, what is the delta in cost between the 2 solutions?*

(d) *If the goal of the project were to save an averaged 20% across a 5-year lifespan, would this project meet the stated objective?*

Answers will appear at the end of the next chapter (Reminder: If you cheat by looking up the answer now, you're only cheating yourself.)

Chapter 12:
Change or be marginalized.

Changing How We Engage in an Increasingly Agile and Changing World

It's been clear to be for a while that there are a few models of Project and Program Management Organizations. The most familiar or the one that typically comes to mind when a Project Management Organization is mentioned is known as a "Coaching" or "Reporting" PMO. I'm reminded of an old adage:

"Those who can, do; those who can't, teach; those who can't teach, teach teaching."

Since I haven't given a Q&A from my perspective in a while, I'll start this Chapter with the following question:

Question: Does your company have a PMO? Why or Why Not?

Answer: I've seen several examples where companies have both had PMOs, have started PMOs (I've been responsible for establishing a few), retooled their PMO strategy, and disbanded their PMO. I can point to a common thread among all the successful examples.

Those PMOs that have been most successful were chartered with specific goals in mind: Develop PM competency, support common practices in the organization, improve business project delivery, improve success rates of all project components, delivering with shorter time-to-market, or ensuring financial oversight and direct cost savings.

The stigma attached in many organizations that have tried/failed at PMOs has been that they view the practice as a single model organization, usually a coaching or reporting organization better suited to executive level dashboards and extracts but demonstrating little or no value to improving project success or delivering value -- i.e. if a project is "red", they'll report why but offer little suggestions for mitigating. The result is that most organizations view project management as little more than administrative support to those doing the real work rather than a central strategic focus to delivering successful initiatives.

Where PMOs have been disbanded, it's been for that reason, and the remaining project and program managers were cast into business unit supporting roles where they deliver far more impact.

Any successful PMO must start with a metric baseline and consensus from key strategic stakeholders to define the success criteria they wish to see, and continue following that delivery beyond the completion of initiatives to ensure that value aligns with customer expectations. On 2 personal notes, avoid the temptation to get paralyzed by process and find a pragmatic and iterative approach suitable for that organization.

As I began this book, I considered my originally targeted audience. When I discovered Case Study #14 (we all remember "Frank", don't we), I realized that I'd stumbled into an entirely different audience for the book – the executive that longs to see change and becomes frustrated with its lack of progress.

You might notice that I began this book with the intent of transforming the project into the "initiative", and that's the language I've increasingly used as we've progressed from Chapter to Chapter. As I approach defining and describing the methods and practices behind effectiveness, some additional steps will help us understand where initiatives succeed and where they fail, and the commonality among the successes.

The initiatives and efforts that succeed are overwhelmingly those where executive sponsorship and interest has been most visible, and where the organization has been shown how success translates tangibly for the organization. In those cases, the top of the organization and the bottom are closely aligned in their overall goals. The following short example makes this clear.

In May of 1961, mere months after his inauguration, President John F. Kennedy set down a challenge that our country watched and followed closely. His exact mission statement was simple:

"I believe that this nation should commit itself to achieving the goal, before this decade is out, of landing a man on the moon and returning him safely to the earth. No single space project in this period will be more impressive to mankind, or more important for the long-range exploration of space; and none will be so difficult or expensive to accomplish."[20]

It was both a gauntlet and a challenge for the country. On July 20, 1969, that challenge was met by the first lunar landing, and the subsequent return of three astronauts safely to Earth. It was a challenge and a mission coming from the highest levels, and resonating to everyone in the nation. That memorable statement eclipsed the remainder of that address, but it set the direction for communications satellite implementation, the creation of new jobs, and the current system of weather satellites that helps predict weather patterns across the planet. If your car has a GPS system, you can thank that effort as well.

While our efforts need not be as massive and costly, clearly the foundation for that mission was set from the highest levels, communicated clearly, and adopted by everyone as a "cannot miss" target.

With that as a premise, I'll segue into the next topic.

Alignment/Engagement

Any organization that has embarked on employee engagement surveys and truly evaluated the results in quantitative terms will recognize the value of the information contained in such an effort. In large organizations, they provide valuable information on understanding core values, objectives, the organization's mission and target markets, competencies, and areas for improvement or adjustment.

Employees often view this is an opportunity to give unfettered feedback on their management, the styles of communication used, and the collaboration or isolation found around the enterprise. The ma-

---

[20] Special Message to Congress on Urgent National Needs, delivered May 25, 1961. Text excerpted courtesy of the JFK Memorial Library.

jority of these surveys have some sort of ranking and rating, whether on a 1-5 or 1-10 scale, of how the organization is addressing those goals, and where it should focus the most. But the information collected is useful in another way that is seldom explored, and I'll refer to this as "Bow-Tie Syndrome" [TM] [21]. Please see the figure captured in Figure 12-1 for details.

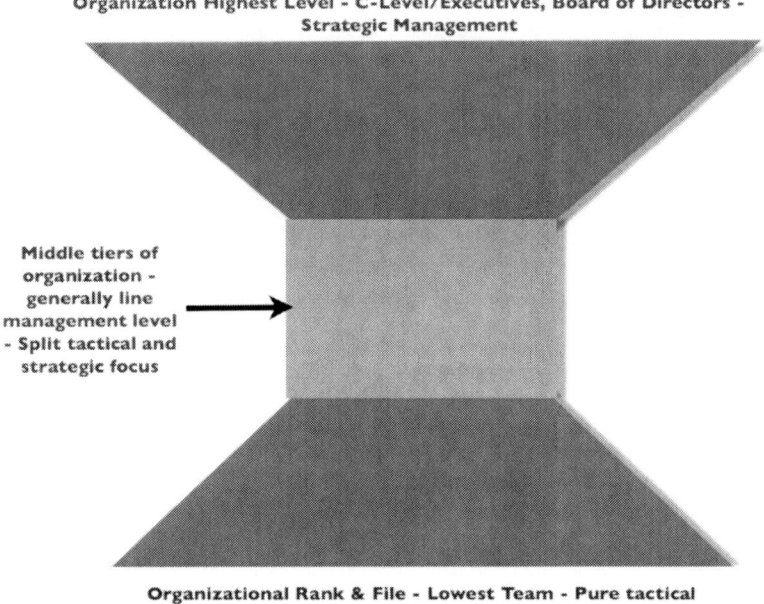

Figure 12-1: Depiction of Bowtie Syndrome for Engagement/Alignment

Many organizations may find that the core mission statements, rankings of satisfaction, understanding of objectives, their relationship with management, and other questions are exceptionally well aligned at the top and bottom of the organization. A CEO might examine the data and see very little variance from his level to his direct reports, and slightly more variance as he drills to the next level down. He'll probably also look at the data across the organization, and find the average of alignment seems to be clear across the whole of the organization (or at least close enough for satisfaction).

If you follow the trending by doing a forward and backward pass within the organization, you'll find that trending should reveal the middle point where the data has much higher statistical variance than the averages. Seldom is the data evaluated thoroughly enough to understand the spread through all the various levels and the separation within those levels to identify where alignment breaks or begins to squeeze.

I refer to this as the "Bow-Tie Syndrome" [TM] for that reason, because when represented visually using both a forward and backward pass, it demonstrates a central blocking point where the interests do not properly align and the highest variance levels will be found. It's also viewed as the "bottleneck"

---

[21] Trademark pending, General National, LLC

within the organization. Either way, it's likely where you'll find the root-cause of the problems, and where engagement and satisfaction can be the lowest.

This is often attributed to an attitude of "everyone hates his or her boss", though that's a sweeping generalization of the problem, and a good data analysis tool employed with such an engagement survey will likely demonstrate that as inaccurate.

Changing this sort of organization requires careful probing, since these surveys are usually completed in an anonymous fashion[22].

Items to Consider in Alignment/Engagement

I won't organize explicit detail but rather offer some considerations for improving alignment and employee engagement.

- **Culture** – is the culture of the organization collaborative or authoritative; how involved are employees in the decision-making with their management; how comfortable do they feel in working with other groups; how cooperative or responsive do view their group and others; does the culture recognize their efforts.

- **Performance/Rewarding** – does the culture properly recognize or reward top performers; are there opportunities for work variance; are projects and assignments providing the right challenges; is compensation fair compared to peers in their group or other organizations.

- **Opportunity** – is there opportunity for advancement or lateral movement in the organization; is there opportunity to build knowledge and skills that can benefit the organization; does their management encourage or discourage their growth.

- **Management** – does their direct management understand their motivations; do they feel they have an open-dialogue with their direct manager; does management recognize their effort; do they feel supported in their job role.

- **Mission/Objectives** – do they understand the organization's mission statement and core values; are those upheld; do they feel their work contributes to those values; do they believe their management supports those values; does their work align with those values; do they understand how their roles affect the organization's objectives.

I'll examine culture for a moment, since it's a core element of ensuring alignment and engagement.

Culture

The first item to consider is how well each person knows and understands the organization. It's a difficult stretch if your organization is a Fortune 25 company with tens of thousands of employees, not as much if you're a smaller organization where employees should have closer relationships and tighter interaction with one another. This is an opportunity to find the dysfunctional pieces of the organization and begin prioritizing them based on their misalignment with goals.

Honesty is important during the process of change, and the results that you'll receive from an anonymous engagement survey will provide an opportunity for honest feedback if approached correctly. I've used the following Chart to define traits that can have a positive/desired or negative/undesired impact on organizational culture. While not a complete list, it helps set tone and direction.

---

[22] I qualify the anonymity of such a survey since most will also ask about your role, location, number of employees managed, and other differentials that can reveal the respondent. Having worked in an organization where I acted as one of two US-based presences for a globally located manager, simple elimination would have indicated to within a 50% chance that gave a response.

Chart 12-2

Cultural Adjectives	
Desired / Positive	**Undesired / Negative**
Collaborative	Political
Adaptive (to change)	Chaotic
Democratic / Participative	Toxic
Responsive	Passive / Aggressive
Creative	Autocratic
Communicative	Defensive / Rigid
Respectful / Professional	Critical
Accountable	Isolated
Rewarding	Indifferent

The differences in the terminology are intentionally obvious to help underscore the point that the positive traits result in a more productive culture, and an opportunity to achieve better results and alignment with core values and objectives.

WII FM – "All me, all the time"

We've discussed this acronym previously, but it bears repetition here: Employees in general, if you look through the lens identified by Douglas McGregor in his "Theory X/Theory Y" research[23], are identified as either less motivated (Theory X – lazy, avoids work, requires strict supervision) or more ambitious (Theory Y – looking to succeed, works through problems, finds creative solutions).

Think of managers who subscribe to Theory X as more negative (the glass is half empty) and Theory Y subscribing managers as more positive (wow, I have a half-full glass, I can do something with this). The goal in most organizations is to move closer toward the Theory Y school of thought, where job satisfaction is a strong motivator, and employees view the organization as responsive to their needs. The Theory Y worker is much less likely (not unlikely, but less likely) to ask the WIIFM question.

Everyone in some way wants to understand their impact and how they affect the organization. I once knew a manager who addressed a gathering of technology folks within his company and introduced himself very simply: "I manage the company payroll system – how many of you like getting paid?" The audience both chuckled and clapped, realizing that he'd just given others the incentive to help his group when they needed it. That's one example, but a good one that drives home the motivations that employees like seeing: He appealed to both sides of the spectrum.

The goal in dealing with WIIFM is translating it into terms that are meaningful to the employee but aligned with the organization's mission. It's a continuation of the employee engagement process where the employee understands how they contribute to the end goal, and where the thought process changes from self-centric to goal-centric. By the way, it doesn't happen overnight and requires adoption at all levels. The challenge of overcoming the Bow-Tie Syndrome ™ is performing a thorough drill-down to find the variances and then presenting the case for cultural changes. Depending on your starting point, it can prove challenging.

- **For the Initiative Manager**, it requires the visibility, tangible backing and presence of the sponsor whenever and wherever possible, as well as sponsor interest in the outcomes. Where

---

[23] Douglas McGregor: Theory X and Theory Y. Workforce; Jan 2002, Vol. 81 Issue 1

the sponsorship and value-proposition is clear, the objectives and mission are more likely to gain compliance.

- **For the Senior Manager or Executive**, the WIIFM proposition for you is that your effort gets more direct attention than one in which your presence is absent or behind closed doors. When the news isn't good, share in the disappointment and motivate; when the news is good, make sure the initiative team sees your satisfaction. If the sponsor takes an active interest, rest assured that the team takes notice and will follow that example.

Engagement/Alignment Barriers

We've all seen organizations that have been resistant to change. As of the writing of this book, one great example is General Motors. When fuel prices spiked in the mid-decade of the 2000s, GM was still mass-producing large SUV's because they could make more profit off the sale of one SUV than they could a smaller and more fuel-efficient car. Never mind that people had stopped buying large vehicles around the world and were craving less thirsty cars, few of which GM Dealers offered in the United States despite offering them outside the US for decades. As of this writing, the company announced the closure of their Saturn division – ironic when you consider the goal of that division was to compete with Japanese auto manufacturers.

We've also mentioned the barriers that come in the form of individuals and managers, or individuals who take a short-shrift view of collaboration.

Employees' work is often rewarded based on their personal objectives. These may not be aligned with the organization's goals, creating a conundrum: Do I follow the objectives my manager has set, or do I follow those that the organization views as strategic?

We likely know what the answer should be, which is often different from what that answer is. The resulting outcome is simple: Unclear priorities. Clarifying them requires both the top down and bottom-up approach we outlined in the Bow-Tie Syndrome [TM] to find the resulting root cause and clarify the changes in priorities.

Proving the Concept

I've depicted some of the behaviors, root-causes, and background on why organizations behave as they do. Each organization develops its own culture, or evolves over time based on their leadership, their marketplace, and their personnel assets. Not all organizations will adapt to change in the same way, nor is it correct to suggest that cultural (or any other) change happens quickly. The investment takes time, and often takes the form of an example effort or "pilot", otherwise known as a "Proof-of-Concept". This generally involves taking one effort that can be controlled and monitored to determine the aspects that will and will not work within the performing organization. This is a good barometer for a number of reasons:

1. It provides useful data around the expectations, timing, and challenges your performing initiative teams have in the Phases of Team Development: Forming, Storming, Norming and Performing[24], with potentially Transforming as a follow-on phase[25].

2. It validates efficiencies in working and performance differences, provided that you have similar products and a baseline for comparison.

---

[24] Model of Group Development and formation first proposed by Bruce Tuckman in 1965, "Developmental Sequence in Small Groups"
[25] Tuckman's work was later amended to suggest a subsequent phase in which synergies continue to develop and the team produces greater performance as it continues its work.

3.   The team's feedback proves useful, and the results of the experience will explain the changes in behavior observed or perceived by each team member, and their satisfaction with the experience.

Change or be marginalized: The Relevance of the Classic PMO

In Chapter Five, and to a lesser degree in Chapter Two, I spoke at some length about the fact and fiction of starting a PMO, insisting that more than one potential model exists for the Chartering of a PMO.

As of 2007, 54% of organizations surveyed had implemented an Enterprise-Wide PMO[26], an increase from 35% in 2006. Still, the project success statistics provided in the June, 2008 Standish Report show a 32% success rate for projects. Many are simply overwhelmed, others are struggling with the adoption of tools to manage project flow and capacity, and still others are not capturing a repository of statistics on which to base metrics, determine best-practices, or demonstrate factors resulting in success or failure.

My purpose in reciting these statistics is not to deride the existence of a PMO, but to dispel the notion that simply instituting a PMO automatically ensures or improves project success. Given the statistics above, the compelling evidence suggests otherwise. It also suggests that the classic approach to the PMO role in many organizations has not matured from being a manager of project information (the Coaching/Reporting model) into a partnership on strategy execution.

A survey of 968 business technology professionals conducted in 2008 by InformationWeek[27] provided the following factoids for consideration:

- 75% described the Information Technology workload as "heavy" or "crushing"

- 40% indicated that Information Technology has little to no control over project flow.

- 35% use a "best guess" method to determine the capacity to handle more projects.

Can we conjecture on what these suggest? Yes.

They suggest that the Project/Program Groups within most organizations have little or no active partnership in the strategic prioritization process, and potentially lack the tools for managing the roadmap and pipeline of work, or the control of resources needed to perform effectively.

In the current market, I've previously written comments on some of the reasons why this problem isn't being taken as seriously as it should:

- The perceived role of Project Managers. In many organizations, they're viewed as organizers and note-takers, scribes and facilitators, status checkers and e-mailers. They are viewed more secretarially than managerially, less as leaders and more as a dumping ground for administrative work.

- Remuneration packages are insufficient to attract best-of-breed strategists. During the 2008-2009 recessionary period, many organizations took the opportunity to drop the rates for project management consultants to mercenary levels, resulting in lower overall competency at a lower price.

  Experience being viewed secondarily to number of credentials and resume/CV buzzwords. With the arrival of recruiting Vendor Management Systems (VMS), many organizations sim-

---

[26] 2007–2008, Center for Business Practices, PM Solutions, Havertown, Pa. Results based on a web-based survey conducted in June 2007 of 435 global program managers.
[27] "Tech overload". *Information Week,* April 14, 2008.

ply scan a resume for a specific keyword, relevant or not, and present only the candidate who is optimized for breaking past the VMS filter. Beyond that, it can be difficult or impossible in many cases to validate credentials if the candidate is being less then ethical.[28]

- Appointment or promotion of "accidental" Project Managers, or people serving in the role without sufficient experience, training, or guidance/mentoring to help assure successful outcomes (please see Case Study #14 for an example).

These are just a few factors that challenge the chances for success before an initiative has even gotten underway. Consider the following about appropriate experience, skills (soft and more tangible), and compensation: If you expect to find talent that can fit a strategic mindset and mold, it either must be cultivated and groomed internally (the "investment approach"), or gathered at a price commensurate with that experience (the "acquisition approach"). If this concept is difficult to grasp, please review the section on Constraints in Chapter 4 as it also applies here.

I liken this to a customer group I once supported whose eyes were larger than their stomachs. On one occasion, I sat down with them to discuss their needs and desires. They provided a smorgasbord of items that were critical to for their next release, including a replication of the infrastructure in multiple locations, increased capacity, new features and functions, and the ability to add new business units into the system. They requested a price for all of this. I prepared estimations and quotations on work, and presented options for phasing and implementation. The conversation went something like the following exchange:

> *PM: Well, as you've requested, I've priced out all the options you've listed, and gathered it into what can be done separately or together. This Excel sheet will allow you to manipulate that data into several different scenarios.*
>
> *Customer: OK. How much would it take for us to do everything we wanted?*
>
> *PM: $9.5 million.*
>
> *Customer: Ok, let's say for example we only had....hmmm...what was it...$1.67. What could we do with that?*
>
> *PM: Buy the large coffee at the Mini-Mart. Then maybe dream.*

I mention this to segue to my next topic, but will close this topic with a final thought. **Buy the right tool for the job**. If the job requires a jackhammer, a hammer and a dull chisel won't suit your requirements well. As evidenced in the above statistics, you'll likely be disappointed in the results.

Prioritization

The example exchange I mentioned above – OK, it wasn't quite that bad, but it was close – provides some realism and insight into typical business-aligned thought. In an ideal world, we'd be able to fund everything we wanted. While that's what we'd like, we often need guidance on what is and isn't feasible. Within the Initiative Management space, this holds true on a variety of levels that we'll explore more fully now.

Initiative Prioritization (Strategic)

I've managed in a variety of organizations where customers would love to have every item on the menu, and during the budgeting process, the organization's finance group might deliver the harsh reality that they'll not only need to pare back what they wanted, they'll likely need to spend less than they

---

[28] Some Project Management organizations maintain an active registry of credential holders. Six Sigma as a credential cannot be as easily verified since there is no central certifying body. Foreign held credentials, including degrees, certifications, and coursework, are more difficult to validate and often go unverified.

did the previous year. This generally results in a prioritization exercise in two forms. The first is deciding the critical items that must be addressed; the second involves rationing money among the strategic items that should be completed to enter emerging markets or be competitive in existing markets.

Rather than the 20 projects envisioned on a list for this year, perhaps the financial resources exist only to perform 4 or 5. In reality, considering the statistics I listed earlier, there may only be enough resources to truly do those 4 or 5 well, not the 20 originally envisioned. This is a necessary step to squeeze out the unnecessary spending that will tend to occur in any organization

Each organization will find some way to rate and rank those projects based upon their business value to that organization in terms of market-share, revenue growth or other factors, and hopefully a healthy dose of Total Cost of Ownership will also be considered. This represents a high level step toward identifying the truly strategic projects to the organization. It's not the only step to decide the initiatives that can or should be undertaken.

This pass is the high-level strategic view.

Initiative Options (Tactical)

When we come across issues that require escalation to an Initiative Sponsor, we normally bring along recommendations and suggested solutions. However, when we consider how to approach a business initiative, why do we usually bring one idea to the table and base our thinking around that as the sole option?

If we truly needed to price out the costs of approaching an initiative – provided we understand the situation and how to address it – we may not consider the most cost-effective options, much less the results of the "Do-nothing" option, which should be considered by default in any analysis.

In the prior Chapter, I provided an analysis of 2 variants of a project to replace an aging system. That case provided both the costs of doing nothing versus the costs of taking action. It also provided a case for the subsequent years of the ownership and ongoing costs of that system. Having that information and the comparison of options available provides new insight into the discussion to make a more informed choice.

When considering how to do something, the tendency is to base our planning around a single option, not the alternatives. As a result, we may strand money that could have funded another strategic venture, or returned at year-end because initiatives didn't spend quickly enough. Anyone who has ever worked in a Purchasing Department role recognizes that they can't take time off at the end of the year since departments will scramble to spend the last of the funds they've stranded!

Therefore, the goal of planning and prioritizing is twofold:

1. Find the right mix of strategic initiatives that can and should be funded.

2. Bring options for executing each of those alternatives that provide options to the sponsor.

Structuring Options

One school of thought suggests that at least 3 options be presented[29] for each initiative. While 3 may be the only possibility, I will suggest another option be added to the selection, so that a recommendation resembles the following:

---

[29] By the way, I violated this in the Chapter 12 example purposely to emphasize the difference between the options and create the exercise

- Do nothing – the option of taking no action, which may or may not have an associated cost.

- Low-cost option – provide the initiative capability with a minimal or bare bones configuration, and explain the ramifications.

- Moderate-Cost option – provide a somewhat more robust initiative capability, though some desired features may not be available, and the impact clearly identified.

- Full-Cost Option – providing the capability as originally envisioned, feature complete, impact also identified.

If you'll contend that this stacks the deck toward one solution or another, I'll counter that I've provided a wider range of scenarios than simply suggesting "all-or-nothing", and provided the sponsor with the ammunition to make a decision intelligently or argue the case that more budgetary dollars are required to complete the strategic vision.

This is why I've suggested four as an option for comparison. If we only used three, and one by default is a "no-action" solution, this leaves only room for either a low-cost or high-cost option, and no middle ground. By presenting a moderate solution, the sponsor has another option to compare that may meet many of the core strategic requirements, and permits a more granular prioritization.

Relating This Back to the Classic PMO Model

Project Managers were once considered to be the arbiters of change. Their job was to manage the implementation of a project or capability that focused on value to an organization. In Study 2 and Study 2a, I focused on the concept that there is no single concrete model to what a PMO must be – the charter of the PMO depends on the organization it serves and value perceived. When I've spoken with organizations about their expectations in a PMO, I've asked, "why they want one" and "how would they measure its success", the two questions posed in Study 2a. Both are logical questions, and address the notion that there is no "PMO-in-a-Box" kit for managers to open and suddenly expect success. Nor would I trust one if it were marketed.

If we stop viewing Project Managers as change agents, and only view them as administrators, we'll be disappointed when all we receive is administrative assistance on a challenged effort.

To that end, the difference in approach of this book targets a more holistic view of change and management of Initiatives at the Enterprise Level. I contend that most CEO's don't want to sort through fingers pointing at each other when an effort is challenged, but will look toward one leadership resource to guide the effort back on track.

I'm not suggesting that many Project Management Organizations don't do an admirable job of aligning strategically with their partner organizations or don't deliver initiatives well; nor is my intent to malign my colleagues in the PMO community or project management in general. The changes caused by leaner and more agile business methods, regulatory and auditing challenges, and cost restraints require all of us to think differently and consider different approaches to an ever-evolving profession. It requires us to abandon the notion of "thinking outside the box" by seriously questioning the relevance or necessity of the box.

If the success rate does not meet the new requirements, despite all the knowledge gained as a practice or profession, perhaps the processes aren't as valid in the current business environment as we presume them to be, or the profession has isolated itself into complacency and irrelevance. While I hope that does not happen, what I've suggested thus far leads me to a conclusion that a better approach is needed for success, and that projects can no longer be seen as finite "beginning/end" efforts from which a traditional project manager emerges and wipes hands clean at a formal project sign-off meeting.

Isolating projects does not provide the foundation for enterprise-wide collaboration.

Enter a broader picture entitled "Initiative Management", and the accompanying role of "Initiative Manager" charged with much of the end-to-end life of an initiative.

From over 22 years of having lived through the entire lifecycle, I've personally understood the issues that emerge from incomplete planning and not considering the ramifications of a post-deployment product. I hope that it becomes clear that as times change, our thought process must broaden to consider the entire spectrum of how our solutions strategically advance an organization along with maintaining and improving cost, productivity, and service standards.

Chapter Twelve TCO Exercise (Answers)

You'll recall the questions posed in the previous Chapter on the Total Cost of Ownership Exercise and our comparison of 2 possible options. One was to take no action (the "Do Nothing" Scenario) and the other was to opt for a replacement with newer equipment (the "New System" Scenario).

Answers:

(a) *If the costs of the project are compared with the "do-nothing" scenario, what is the first year delta, and why?*

The answer was $220,000. This considered the Operations Costs, the Cost of all one-time fixed investments in the project, and the Maintenance Costs for both Development Staff and Mainframe annual costs. Please note that this answer does not consider depreciation costs just to keep the equation simple. Had we considered the costs over a 3 or 5 year depreciation cycle, the delta would have been much lower since the cost would have been spread across multiple years.

(b) *What is the percentage difference in cost between the solutions in years 2 through 5?*

Year 2: 34.24%; Year 3: 35.15%; Year 4: 36.07%; Year 5: 36.99%

This was derived by dividing the costs of the new solution by that of the old solution, to reveal a TCO savings on one solution over the other. Again, depreciation was not considered as in the prior question.

(c) *At the end of 5 years, what is the delta in cost between the 2 solutions?*

$605,473.78, approximately. Translated to a percentage difference of 21.68%.

(d) *If the goal of the project were to save an average 20% across a 5-year lifespan, would this project meet the stated objective?*

It would have exceeded this expectation by 1.68%

Chapter 13:
Formulating the End-to-End Model

Project Management: 1969 –????

Over significant research, I've failed to find a single approach that addresses the entire life cycle of a product from idea to retirement. While this is a generally broad-brush stroke across a number of organizations, I'll attempt to qualify that remark somewhat to provide some perspective around the notion.

To extend the concept more graphically, see table 13-1 for more detail on how I've broken down the Matrix of Initiatives.

Table 13-1

Organization Size	Maturity Level	Number of initiatives	Project-suited	Strategically suited
Small to Medium	Low (CMMI Level 2 or lower)	Limited	Yes. The organization likely can control their investment and closely monitor their condition	Not a candidate
Medium	Low-to-Medium (CMMI Level 1-3)	Several, some cross business units	Potentially. Depends on the sponsor's involvement, overall breadth of initiatives, cost and resource constraints.	Potential. If organization is struggling with success of individual projects, a more strategic focus could be productive.
Large	Medium (CMMI Level 1 to 4)	Many, always involve multiple business units	No. Projects become contentious and lose a strategic focus, since the mandate for each may be tactical.	Yes. Opportunity to align strategy against enterprise budgets, resourcing, and TCO for results.
Massive	Any (may depend on division)	Many for each business unit, multiple BU's.	No. Project focus is too small to map resourcing, strategic spending; individual initiatives nearly impossible to map to strategy.	Yes. Stronger alignment to strategic focus, greater visibility to budget and resourcing, proper selection criteria.

For a smaller organization that undertakes very few initiatives each year, a project-centric focus can provide the right level of value. For individual business units within an organization that can control the resources dedicated to a project, as well as the funding and governance around selection, the notion of "project-by-project" management can still be relevant.

The majority of issues will arise as the number of initiatives grows, and centralized outlook and control of those initiatives loses its alignment toward achieving strategic goals. Among the tenets I set forth earlier was that if something yields no value, it shouldn't be undertaken. This can be a difficult concept for individual business unit managers (i.e. forego their objectives), so some sensitivity must be given to the overall communication around a switch to strategic management (especially if the business unit itself is no longer a strategic component for that organization in the future).

The point of the matrix above is to demonstrate that the larger an organization grows, the further it may have a tendency to move from corporate goals and strategic objectives as it desires to keep more of the funding pie for efforts that only directly impact that business unit. Having said that, the fundamental components are the next step.

Strategic Planning (High Level)

Organizations generally need to consider the governance around planning initiatives, including ranking and prioritization against the available budget. This will likely involve multiple passes of those factors to reveal the available budget that can be devoted to initiatives.

1.   Each Business Unit (BU) Manager prepares his estimations, including available options for each as alternative approaches, and presents these in ranking order for budgetary review.

      a.   A short business case – no more than 2 paragraphs or 5 bullets – should accompany.

2.   A pass of the item cost compared to the available budget is done, and suggestions are returned to each hiring manager to either re-prioritize or realign their efforts with the organization strategy to fit that budgetary number.

      a.   Exceptional cases must follow with the business logic, business risk of inaction, and the clear case of options for the items.

      b.   Any "must-do" exceptions should be guided by the net impact to income or revenue should the current capability fail without an appropriate funding level.

3.   The process should be done for no more than about 3 rounds until decisions can be made against the priorities, "Must-do" and further discretionary items.

4.   All units must do this, whether your baseline is Zero-Based Budgeting (ZBB) or using the prior year and revenue trending as the goal.

Organization/BU Level

Before the budget process, the organization should have some general idea of the strategically aligned vision, and the initiatives in the portfolio that address that direction. To organize and condense that data into digestible form, I'd recommend the following steps:

1.   Identify, rate, and rank each of the initiatives under consideration, and develop the business case for each. Condense the business case into a short mission and values statement for each that refines it into 2 Paragraphs/5 Bullets or a combination thereof that can fit into a presentation slide (PowerPoint, Keynote, or other).

2.   Prepare a compelling business case for each, especially those that are multiyear efforts.

      a.   Itemize the appropriate deliverables and associated value for each year.

      b.   Identify how the investment will be monitored to ensure that an 18-month effort doesn't extend longer (e.g. how will you deliver specific iterations of value, if possible; when can the return on investment begin to be realized; can value against stranded costs be delivered, can stranded costs be deferred for longer, etc.)

3.   Prepare for multiple iterations as the strategic fit is refined, aligned, or addressed within the fiscal year (FY) budget. Ensure that a clear business case for truly strategic and "must-do" items is clear, along with any revenue risk for each.

4.   Ensure that he initiative can be undertaken and investment spent within the FY. This also means that performing resources are available, or that the initiative can be undertaken once budgets are approved.

Caveats - "Must-Do's" or "Revenue Protection"

I spoke about the "must-do" items, or those that put revenue at risk if not undertaken. Examples can include bolstering capacity, updating older technology, or refinements to products to meet market/regulatory requirements. There may not be a clear "return" on the investments made on these items, and often a case must be argued on the revenue opportunity placed at risk if the effort is not undertaken.

Your business may require that a capability is available to the customer continually; when this doesn't happen, outages can be clearly remembered and their impact felt by your customers, who may decide that a competitive offering is a wiser investment. We refer to this as "revenue protection" – ensuring that the revenue gained from one enterprise is protected from degradation, somewhat different to the impact that an insurance policy provides (indemnity protection).

It's essential to note if you are considering a "strategic" approach to Must-Do's or Revenue Protection situations, this is purely a short-term tactical maneuver and requires a longer-term strategy for mitigating the risk of loss:

> **Example:** *An organization in the data provision business operates much of its data warehouse on a platform that was built in the prior decade and maintained through an acquisition. During that time, the system has suffered from frequent outages and required additional hands-on support. Their approach to replacing this capability was twofold.*
>
> *1.   A multiyear initiative to re-architect this capability with future capacity and growth in mind, as well as "future-proofing" from obsolescence where possible within the design.*
>
> *2.   Maintain the current capability until the new capability was operational. This acknowledged the cost of potential failures using prior years as a basis for trending, plus the cost of other maintenance (software licenses, etc.)*

In this example, the first item was strategic in nature, and was already underway. If funding was not continued to complete the initiative, the current investment would have been stranded, and the existing capability left to maintain the service. The second item was the tactical measure to maintain the existing service until the new capability was on-line. This demonstrates a "must-do" (item #1; technically, it could have been deferred but not without degradation of service) and revenue protection (both #1, for ensuring future revenues, and #2 for ensuring continuous service through the transition).

Caveats - Capability & Culture

Another consideration is whether the initiative is within your organization's current capabilities, or matches the culture that you have or are seeking to achieve. Is the organization capable of aligning with the expectations, and does the organization's culture help or hinder that progress?

In earlier examples, I referenced the difference between CMMI^{TM} Levels - Level 1 representing pure heroism and Level 5 very tightly defined processes. An organization does not go from one to the other suddenly, but passes through measurable stages as the culture changes in gradual and visible terms.

All of us have probably watched television and seen remarkable examples of people who have won battles with weight loss, along with how they achieved their goals. All of them share the same common themes to their story:

- It didn't happen overnight. It took quite a bit of time to go from their first day state to their end-day state, and it will continue to be a process to stay there or progress even further.

- It required discipline. You don't simply will something and then wait for it to happen; you take decisive actions to make it happen.

- It required changes in their life and their habits to achieve that progress.

For an example of this type of dedication to cause, you need look no further than Jared Fogle, the commercial face for Subway. Jared did each of the 3 criteria I mentioned to lose 245 pounds from his frame. It demonstrates that change can happen, but also an example that your culture must be ready to accept the change, and will need the capabilities to learn and be supported in the process.

It's an important consideration.

Additionally, when I reference "capability", this also depicts the organization's ability to successfully undertake more complex efforts, and how those efforts are staged. Many organizational cultures can be overwhelmed by exceptional undertakings, underscored by comments such as:

- "We'll never complete that in our lifetime"
- "I don't think I'll be around to see this go-live"

It's negative thinking, and needs to change. Gradually. And the organization needs an assessment to determine its readiness for change. Let's continue this point in another perspective.

Gradation of Change (a.k.a. Iterative Methodologies)

Iterative Methodologies, have grown in popularity, especially if we're in a manufacturing or technology setting, and deserve a significant mention. Some examples of iterative approaches (though not an exhaustive list) include:

- Rational Unified Process (RUP)
- Lean
- Agile/Agile with SCRUM
- Feature Driven Development (FDD)
- Test Driven Development (TDD)
- Extreme Programming/Project Management (XP/XPM)

So we don't become lost in buzzwords and terminology, each approach uses iterations and delivers something of value in short periods of time, using a variety of steps or sprints suited toward the methodology precepts and the culture of the adopting/performing organization.

There are other methodologies not on this list, and all have approaches that are not contradictory or in conflict with either solid project management methods or the teachings learned from any reasonable project management resource. The benefit of an iterative methodology is the breakdown of work from a very large effort (perhaps multiyear) into pieces that can be seen, understood, and presented within shorter periods of definition; thus, their reference as "iterative methods" as each uses multiple iterations to deliver specific deliverables or objectives.

Using Feature Driven Development as an example, each iteration focuses on a specific feature or set of features that reveal a capability to the end customer. The sum of those iterations, when complete, reveals a fully developed product.

All of these methods can be used strategically as organizations adapt to change and effectively use resources in an efficient and value-driven manner. I'll liken this to the manufacturing of a car being only somewhat like the definition of a product or piece of technology. Each begins with a base and is improved or enhanced significantly as releases (model years) follow. That turnaround is quicker than a design that develops an entirely new product from scratch. The reuse and repurposing of existing capabilities presents a more compelling proposition than constant reinvention of a product (evolution of features versus "build-from-scratch")

This is the current paradigm of rapid change. Adjustment requires persuading your organization to align with that level of change, and alter the negative thinking we witnessed in the common quotes above into positive responses.

A side note: One method that I specifically did not mention as desirable (if it can be termed as such) is "Cowboy Coding" – a set of methods that leaves the product developers and technicians on their own to do what they want in the manner they want with total autonomy and no interference. While it may work in many environments and can encourage experimentation, without strategic guidance, it's more likely that Cowboy Coding will drive an effort off the rails.

"When Does It Make Sense to Retire a Product?"

Many organizations struggle with a "soft-underbelly" – a tendency to maintain aging platforms that cost more to maintain than the revenue produced. This is common with aging products when replacement products are introduced. Think about the last cassette tape that you bought. At some point, any capability will be replaced by another, and perhaps books-printed-on-paper will be completed replaced by media at cheaper cost for the publisher and the environment.

The point of replacement should be satisfied when the following formula is met:

$$R <= C + M + L + S + I$$

Where R = Revenue; C = Cost; M = Marketing; L = Licensing (Annual Fee/Subscription costs to outside parties); S = Support; I = Incidental Costs.

When the revenue trend is sloping toward a decrease, plans should already be on the drawing board to refine or replace the capability with a more strategic and market-relevant product. The Bottom-line: If the capability is costing more to maintain than the revenue supporting it, it's time to change markets or migrated customers to new newer capabilities by demonstrating their benefits.

Why Isolation Hasn't Succeeded

Up to now, I've spoken about Project Management traditionally happening as an isolated component of strategy, not overseeing the lifecycle of the strategy. In the Classic Inwardly Focused PMO Model, the Project is the deliverable. The Program, if we've reached that state of maturity, outlines how those projects help to form a strategy or align efforts together to make more effective use of resources (financial, physical, or human). For most organizations, the effort begins and ends with the delivery of the initiative. The Project Manager or Program Manager is happy to conduct a turnover and walk away. The battle may have been won, but what about the rest of the war?

This is where disconnects begin between traditional "inwardly focused" Project/Program Management (focused primarily on "People, Process, and Tools") and where the next frontier of managing overall initiatives must lead us. Businesses are demanding that project management be more tightly aligned to product, business purpose, and organizational strategy. Demonstrating results rather than simply implementing processes, training and tools will be key as businesses become more competitive and time-to-market pressures increase.

I ended the previous Chapter discussing the lack of an overall approach that views the entire product lifecycle rather than the individual components among themselves, and save but for organizations who have delegated that responsibility to people termed "Product Managers", it's not an approach that contains a definitive roadmap and set of methods and processes that comprehensively examine business challenges.

Isolating each individual unit in the process has led to dysfunction of all processes. While potentially this isn't as bad as designing all pieces and components in isolation, it often leads to solutions that may seem fine in product development but unsatisfactory for the supporting organization. As to ramifications, you can imagine a customer complaining about the product they've been sold that cannot be properly supported. The lack of cohesive interaction between organizations results in some of the following outcomes:

- Customer dissatisfaction
- Loss of market-share
- Wasted resources
- Ineffective investment
- Decreased internal morale

And that's just a partial list of symptoms or outcomes.

So what would a model of Shared Accountability look like? Let's consider the steps in the approach and begin to shape the underlying landscape.

Capability Lifecycle Framework ™: A STRATEGIC ROADMAP FOR END-TO-END CHANGE

Idea/Inception:
Most organizations begin a strategic initiative with an idea. It could range from an untapped market, to a market with potential growth, to innovations within an existing market, and a wide range of factors between. The idea may be vetted through a concept, focus groups, prototyping, or a combination of those and other methods. For instance, Boeing's 707 aircraft involved a repurposing of the jet engine component found in the military B-52 aircraft; as a result, Boeing became among the first companies to develop a civilian-use jet aircraft.

Definition/Validation:
The idea is further refined toward future objectives, and undergoes scrutiny and validation to determine worthiness as an initiative and the priority it should receive.

Initiation:
This is the stage-gate for the initiative as an Initiative Manager is defined, the initiative is socialized among key stakeholders, and a high-level budgeting estimate is determined. While some planning elements are involved, this is not yet a planning stage as several key deliverables need to be outlined:

- An Overall Initiative plan must be developed outlining the objectives, participants, sponsors, key resources, and success criteria for the initiative.

- A Risk Management Plan developed, which will become a living document to the Initiative and subject to continued modification as risks are closed or realized. Each risk requires an action to be taken, as well as a projected impact if realized.

- A Communication Plan that outlines the communication formats for the initiative, identifies the key meetings, key milestones, gating stages for sponsor approval, and may include a Responsibility Assignment Matrix (RACI, Matrix Document) to further clarify the who/what/when/why of the individual accountabilities.

- A Change Management Plan that addresses how changes will be considered, evaluated, and approved/amended or deferred. The accountabilities of those involved in Change Approval and their impacts, along with a change assessment process, will also be outlined.

- A preliminary schedule developed for major deliverables, subject to review, along with proposed phasing.

- The beginning of the Business Requirements cycle

- Initial identification of KPQP's and the required Quality Standards.

- Documentation of current state metrics for baselining.

- The beginning of Test Case and Test Script Development cycles parallel to Business Requirements.

- A Kickoff meeting to socialize the initiative.

  o This provides the sponsor opportunity to elaborate on the strategic alignment and how this impacts the organization.

  o It creates an opportunity for a "we" value proposition, or collaborative and contribution-focused behaviors – why this is important to the team, answering the "What's In It For Me" question.

Planning

This process will have kicked off during the initiation phase. High-level estimations will be refined based on elaborated knowledge of the initiative and any changes to definition. Elements and outcomes include:

- Refinements to the initiative schedule.

- Refinements to resource planning.

  o Augmentation planning.

  o Alignment of tasks to ensure completion within schedule.

  o Review of resourcing -- changes required on over and under committed resources.

- Determining the critical path, mitigating risks that will interfere with completion.

- Revisions to the Responsibility Assignment Matrix.

- Review of Documentation.

- Identification of any issues to be elevated to the Initiative Sponsor.

- Socialization of the Quality Plan with all members of the team, including expectations.

- Review/modification of risks.

- The cycle of Business Requirements continues, and should be moving toward completion before the end of the cycle.

- Schedule modifications, including phased or iterative implementation of deliverables.

- Internal and external stakeholder discussions, including project impacts with Operational groups, Infrastructure Groups, identification of deliverables needed for production life cycle transition.
    - o Service expectations – whether feasible or adjustments required.
    - o Incident expectations – whether feasible of adjustments required.
    - o Problem Management expectations – whether feasible or adjustments needed.
    - o Capacity requirements – whether current project will be sufficient or the expected point at which this becomes a greater issue.
    - o Monitoring/Alerting expectations – what to monitor, how to monitor, thresholds for alerting.
    - o Documentation requirements – confirm that the expectations of the Initiative match the documentation requirements; discuss any variances and reasons.

Execution

The normal working phase of the initiative and where most tasks are completed. This includes product revisions or iterations based on clarification and initiative elaboration. Items to consider that may have also occurred during Planning:

- Change Management.
- Continued review and modifications to the Initiative Plan, including escalation of risks to cost, deliverable modifications (content or date), and quality impacts.
- Continued Test Script/Test Plan development to completion, eventual execution of the Quality Cycle.
- Modifications based on:
    - o Change Management
    - o Quality issues
    - o Resources
    - o Risk monitoring
- Sign-off on gating deliverables, based on milestones.
- Configuration Management.
- Development of transition documentation in conjunction with Development and Business Analysis:
    - o Run books
    - o Supporting guides
    - o Training for Operational Support personnel
    - o Common or FAQ issues to be expected
    - o Troubleshooting
    - o Escalation
    - o Routes to internal/external support
    - o Disaster Recovery/Business Continuity Procedures
- Structured review of final issues with Quality outcomes/KPQP's
    - o Decision to gate to next phases
- Finalized documentation available to:

- o   Customer Community
- o   Initiative database (PPM System, Document Repository, etc.)
- o   Sponsor
- o   Stakeholders
- o   Operational personnel
- o   Infrastructure personnel
- Planning of Training Delivery

Pre-Launch/Transition

Validation of the Quality Experience completed during the product's unit testing and commencement the formal Quality Assurance cycle. Steps will include:

- Preparation of a controlled, non-production environment for User Acceptance Tests (UAT)
- Delivery of product training to personnel, including testing personnel:
  - o   Formal handover of QA results
  - o   Formalize the QA regiment, aligning it with business requirements.
  - o   Results of any product version regression that has occurred.
- Migration of product to (UAT)
  - o   Production Migration process test for Operational/Infrastructural Personnel.
  - o   Document revisions based on experience.
- Submit Operational Production Change Management requests before launch.
- User validation
  - o   Log and rank issues by priority
  - o   Decide on changes needed versus deferred
- Fixes based on validation (medium or higher priority, blockers).
- Confirmation on validation as gating:
  - o   Schedule post-implementation fixes, or iterative updates to include changes identified.
  - o   Change Management, Business Requirements, and Documentation.
- Sign-off for Launch:
  - o   Revise any Operational Change Management documentation (amend for changes in date/time/components)
- Complete staging and announcements for launch:
  - o   Final walkthrough with business people as preparation.
  - o   Final walkthrough with Operational/Infrastructure personnel.
  - o   Miscellaneous preparations – interactions that need to change to accommodate launch.
- Turnover of product to Operational Personnel for launch

Launch and Post-Launch

The supporting tasks that surround the launch, including the Initiative Manager's support for any onsite activities, escalations, or non-production related fixes and workarounds or alternate procedures:

- Post-launch comparison of Pre-Launch and Post-Launch environments for any variances.
- "Product Live" communication.
- User and Operational personnel trailing for 48-72 hours post-launch to support first issues or note behaviors.
    - Observation of product use
    - Documenting variances from intended use
    - Documenting issues from use or misuse of product, determine actions to be taken.
- Periodic review with Operational Personnel for issues, corrections, subsequent defects, planned workarounds, troubleshooting not previously noted.
- Revise End State documentation.
- Confirm that End State requirements have been met.
- Sign-off into Operational Use – Gating for Post-Implementation Steps.
- Continued Monitoring of the Initiative's "Capability"[30].
- Reporting of details on periodic basis to the Product Owner[31].

Post-Implementation Lifecycle

After implementation, the cycle for extensions to the capability will occur on an agreed-upon schedule by the Sponsor/Product Owner. Those steps will involve further but less intensive iterations of the cycle beginning at the Planning Stage, and likely become a working routine for the group.

Rather than repeating the steps in order, it's appropriate to suggest that the overall plan for the Initial iteration of the project will decide on the features and functionality to be included in Phase 1 or Release 1.0. Subsequent releases will follow a more lightweight path beginning with the following considerations:

- Review Documented Features desired and fully funded.
- Review Change Management items deferred from the previous release.
- Prioritize to be incorporated into future iterative build phases between technical and business personnel, and Product Owner.
- Detail any Operational Impacts and modification to existing documentation through an update bulletin or other tangible means with Operational and Infrastructure staff.
- High-level task review to determine the scope, resourcing, and requirements to develop quality plans, business documentation, and test plans/scripts for proposed additions.
- Execution on an order of magnitude best suited to the change.[32]

The release cycle should be detailed and planned on a pipeline or dashboard document that is socialized as a program-level document for the constituents of that release to digest and understand. This addresses ongoing product refinement.

---

[30] Introducing this term as synonymous with the output of the Initiative, the "product". The product has a specific capability that can be met or exceeded. Periodic reviews of capacity, monitoring, problems or incidents reported to the Initiative Manager and Sponsor (Product Owner) will reveal metrics, trending, and other statistics that were agreed to be measured at Initiation.

[31] Once the Initiative transitions from Pre-Launch to Post-Launch, the sponsor becomes the Product Owner, or will designate a Product Owner who will assume this task post-launch.

[32] An initial product release will require very fundamental planning, which should consider the steps and items of the lifecycle. The order of magnitude for subsequent releases becomes less proportionally to the content of the release. A release requiring 3-4 changes would be far more lightweight than a release containing 60-70 changes.

Within most frameworks, the ongoing portion that is not normally considered is the complete end-to-end perspective, which we'll now discuss in continuing the framework to its subsequent steps.

Production Continuity

This state provides a foundation for dialogue with the supporting functions of the organization that are responsible for ongoing upkeep, maintenance, and updates to the application, separate from structured initiatives that are identified in a release cycle.

Minimally, on a quarterly basis (or more frequently as issues present), a discussion of the state of the capability should occur. Topics for discussion should include:

- Overall metrics:
    o Outage times/service levels
    o Number of incidents/nature of incidents
    o Number of problems/nature of incidents
- Capacity trending and variances from planned or expected capacity lifecycle.
- Performance statistics – through monitoring capabilities, your infrastructure groups should provide insights into this.
- Any variances from expectations.

Along with Operational Metrics, the Production Continuity Phase should also include:

- Comparison of expected versus actual outcomes – simply, has the business value proposed been realized, or is there a trend that shows progress toward that goal?
- Analyses of any business utilization issues – is there compliance with using the capability, is it not used as intended or are customers "working around it"; determine reasons.

Communication and Control

These represent ongoing activities that exist regardless of the stage or phase of the initiative. I've listed them here for explanation and clarification:

1. Communication is a parallel thread to all activities within the Initiative, and the Initiative Manager should be mindful of that. At the beginning of the Initiative I mentioned the formation of a Communication Plan, upon which these activities are based. Communication is like air – it surrounds us, we live with it, we breathe it, and it's essential to both life and the success of the Initiative. Rather than devoting a section that prescribes its intersections within the Life Cycle, I've listed it here as a constant thread crossing all Initiative Phases, since all phases will require communication at their core.

2. Control. Although some may debate the precise origin of controlling components for the Initiative, I suggest that control begins at Initiation of the Initiative, where resources are involved and managed, expectations established, and the Communication Plan (which should outline team interaction) created and discussed. The Control is therefore exercised by the Initiative Manager throughout the process in line with the effective management of the Initiative toward its strategic objectives. We don't create set points for a controlling process; it happens as the Initiative progresses. When demonstrated a linear diagram, I'll represent this as a separate thread within the lifecycle.

Adoption of the End-to-End Model

To the casual observer, this will ultimately make some degree of sense. A compartmentalized view of projects doesn't translate well into collaborative organizations, nor does it recognize the intersections that will naturally occur when a product transitions from one stage of the pipeline to the next. It also focuses energy around a "product" rather than a "process", with an underlying objective of improving the customer experience (internal and external) as an outcome.

Naturally, not everyone will be excited about this view since it requires cross-pollination of duties between defined disciplines. I'll cite examples from my experience in the technology sector:

Example:

A traditionally structured organization has had a linear process with several constituencies for several years. They've located some gaps in that process that resemble the following:

1. *Lack of documentation for all phases, including lack of business documentation for development, lack of developer documentation for testing, lack of test result documentation for regulatory auditing, and an overall lack of support documentation for installation and ongoing maintenance.*

2. *Lack of planning for each phase of the lifecycle, including involvement of key support resources before production turnover, and a lack of training of users planned into the process.*

3. *Transition from phase to phase is sloppy in nature, if it occurs at all.*

4. *Timelines for each phase are not transparent.*

Does this sound like your organization? Does it sound like a good case for Program Management? The answer to both could be "yes" but keep in mind that Program Management as an offshoot of Project Management still takes us only to a certain point, at which time the Project/Program involvement trails off and the Project/Program moves on toward another initiative.

On the following pages, I've provided a high-level view of the "Capability Lifecycle Framework (CLiF)" ™, beginning with the Model that outlines the stages of a product from Idea through Retirement as a day-in-the-life view.

Our discussions will center on the Lifecycle Model proposed and how each intersecting phase is introduced, and examine the Communication and Control threads, along with other elements that are not outlined at high level as we begin to paint a more detailed picture.

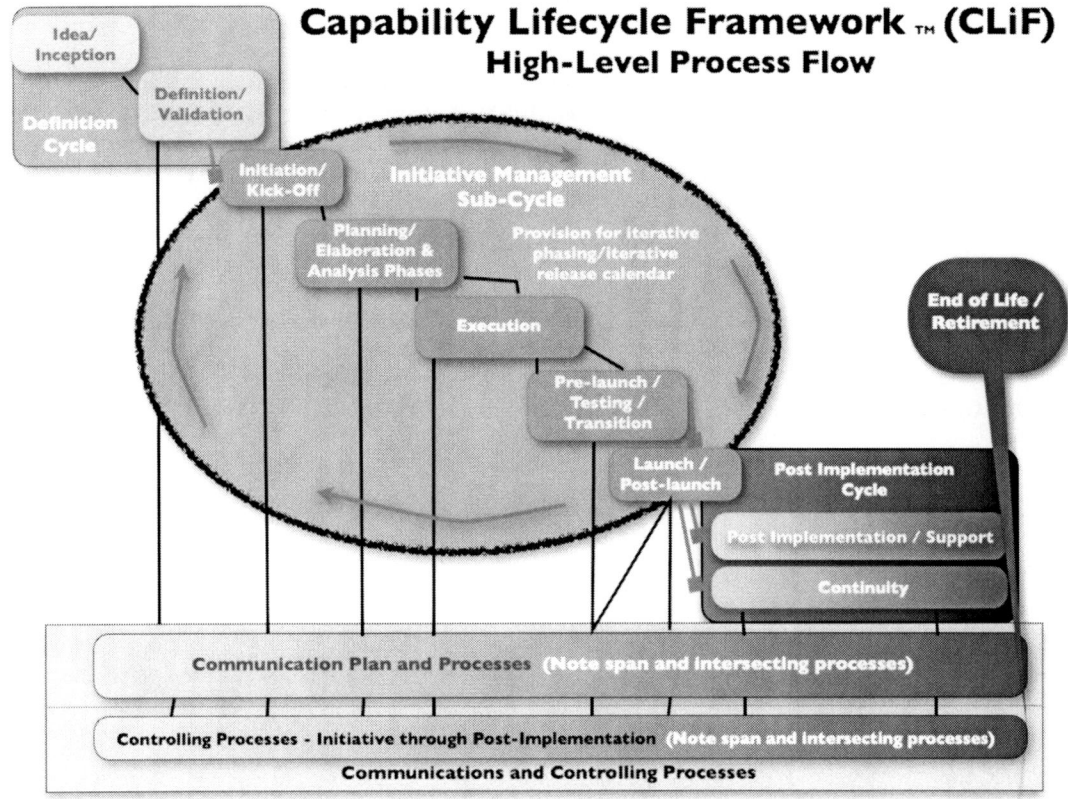

Figure 13-2: Capability Lifecycle Framework Model - High Level Process Flow

Idea/Inception

This is where we begin the process of formulating the product idea, beginning with the conceptual model to be proposed, the rationale behind the concept, and the initial strategy alignment of the concept.

For clarity, let's break this into appropriate subtasks:

• High-level concept - what are we doing

• Marketing Strategy - what is the market opportunity, and how this initiative leverages that

• Alignment to organization strategy - how does this represent the organization's direction and goals

• Clear statement of "what, why, when, where, and how much" at high-level view.

Definition/Validation

The initial concept from the Idea/Inception Phase is further vetted, and defined with greater clarity as the picture of the envisioned outcome is further elaborated into a proposal that can be prioritized, estimated at high-level, and vetted against competing proposals. This is where the business case behind the idea begins development and where research will take place. The results of market research, focus groups, corporate priorities, and organizational objectives can begin to confirm the alignment of the potential initiative with the strategic goals of the organization, and high-level estimations on cost, effort, resourcing, and budgetary planning can occur.

Should the Initiative concept pass this gating stage, it continues toward review, prioritization and funding, proper governance, and approval to progress as an Initiative.

In the earlier comments about this Phase, I did not mention the specific individuals that should be involved in the validation segment, as these can vary based on the scope and type of initiative under consideration. For instance, a new technical capability could be well within the current capacity of the organization's data center to handle, or may require upgrades or enhancements to existing equipment, if not additional equipment to address planned capacity issues.

It is therefore imperative for the success of the entire lifecycle that all relevant stakeholders be included during the validation phase once enough information is known, and ramifications can be assessed at a high level. This process cannot occur in isolation to be effective, as no single source will possess all the required information.

For clarity, the following are sample subtasks within this phase:

- Refinement of concept, potentially a Proof-of-concept (POC)
- Validation of costs, resourcing, and impact
- Confirmation of capabilities
- Communication among affected parties and major stakeholders
- Preparation for governance

Note also that Controlling processes and Communication begin at this point as relevant parties are engaged into the potential Initiative. This cycle will continue through the lifespan of the Initiative, once approved, funded, and scheduled.

Initiation

As noted in the prior section, this process follows the generally accepted standards for the Kickoff of an Initiative within the performing organization. All the individual activities defined in the earlier section on **Initiation** are performed, so will not be repeated herein, but explained in detail as we break down the diagram into smaller components.

Planning

As you'll note in the CLiF Process Flow, this will have begun within the Initiation Phase and continued refinement during Planning Exercises with individual groups, team members, and internal/external resources assigned to the Initiative. This will be further detailed in a separate diagram so that the interaction between the phases becomes clearer.

For both Initiation and Planning, the Communication and Controlling processes will continue to run in parallel as standing activities, also represented by the alignments in the process flow.

Execution

For many organizations, this becomes an issue of preference in their product development methodology. As we spoke earlier about Methodology Adoption, the framework I have defined -- as noted by the box surrounding the "project-specific" processes -- allows for either iterative or non-iterative development patterns to be followed. Should the performing organization opt for multiple iterations or multiple development cycles, they should consider the following:

1. A turnover sufficient for stable Production Support and Continuity should be performed in explicit detail before the first iterative production release. As a result, the process will likely be longer in its first iteration than in subsequent iterations once participants are familiar with the process and expected requirements.

2. There may be overlap into Production Support for every iteration. Depending on the nature of the iterative release, some release mechanism will involve Release Management resources to handle the "lifting" or migration, as well as facilitate the activities associated to the release. It is also possible that iterations may be staged as "silent releases" -- ones that are transparent to the end client, but result in either stability improvements or some enhancement to functionality that requires a less intrusive delivery. Your organization may elect to adopt a very lean process for such releases, but still should document their existence and prepare appropriate contingency plans.

Execution in an iterative environment may result in the segregation of testing into multiple stages to permit earlier feedback on progress and quicker detection and resolution of defects. As elements of the initiative are ready for testing, the process should permit potential cycles of feedback to account for greater defects initially. As the performing organization becomes more adept with the process, they will generally develop a much greater understanding of the test cycle's tight integration with the same functional and technical requirements used to construct the product. Errors or defects not routinely captured during unit and assembly testing are more likely to be trapped within the formal testing cycle. Please refer to the previous explanation for the expected steps.

Pre-Launch/Transition

This provides both the "first-look" at the proposed product, as well as an opportunity to engage the sponsor and stakeholders in the quality experience. Formal elements of this cycle include the following:

- Delivery of training
  - User training delivered
  - Supporting organization/Operational training delivered
  - Documentation turnover
- Migration of product into User Acceptance Mode (UAT).
- User Validation
  - Feedback on issues and defects
  - Correction of defects found based on priority and criticality
  - Decisions on whether less critical fixes can be deferred into a subsequent phase or release.
- Confirmation and Customer Sign-Off
- Staging/Communication of Launch
- Turnover to Operational Personnel for Product Launch

Fluid but controlled communication is critical to success during these stages, and many organizations have preferred to make use of methodology components that lend to this. For instance, in SCRUM, a daily standup meeting is used to review the previous day's work, outcomes, issues, and plan for the day ahead. It can also be successfully used as a communication vehicle between key customer contacts should issue clarifications be required. If SCRUM is used, a SCRUM Master will be designated to maintain control over the meeting -- in essence, someone who will facilitate according to the methodology's parameters.

Launch/Post-Launch

This is where the Pre-Launch and Post-Launch environments can be compared. When the product is launched, a short period of coverage support can be implemented to handle any major changes or the anxieties associated with adopting a new product or process.

Where the turnover to a Production-Stable state is later mentioned, involvement and direct engagement from the supporting staff would be recommended to understand issues that might arise during their day-to-day support of the product, as well as understand common issues to facilitate workarounds or corrections needed.

Post-Implementation Lifecycle

This is the running state of the product from Version 1 and beyond, and represents an accepted stable state that is mutually agreed by the supporting party and the developing party. This is a formal process by which the product passes into a production lifecycle, and future changes would be expected. It represents an opportunity for the Product Development and Production Support groups to review any gaps, changes to documentation, and issues that are the outcome of transition into this phase.

A further diagram will show the constructs of the interaction between Pre-Launch and Post-Implementation so that the communication between the elements is better clarified.

Continuity

This becomes the ongoing lifespan of the capability within the organization. During a stable running environment, it facilitates continued communication between sponsorship, product owners, and production support resources to identify ongoing issues, capacity projections, and any critical feedback needed on the capability for review and action.

It also provides an opportunity to capture the reporting metrics required to understand if the expectations of the capability are being realized -- in short, do the metrics reveal that the projections used to justify the initiative have been met, exceeded, or fallen short -- and provide insight to where issues may exist that should be proactively addressed to achieve those targets.

I'll elaborate the elements and interconnection between these processes in the following chapter by providing further detailed diagrams for interaction.

Chapter 14:
Understanding the Capability Lifecycle

Making Sense of the Interactions

The prior Chapter presents fundamental information known and understood in the Project Management profession for years as practitioners, regardless of whether those practitioners have executed on these actions in the best manner possible for results.

The approach I've outlined accomplishes a number of objectives, however:

1. It elaborates a truly end-to-end approach with clear connections between the stages. We'll talk more about how this is better achieved within this chapter.

2. It addresses the communications, control, and interaction between phases in a manner that accommodates both iterative and traditional methodologies. In fact, it can exist neutrally along side nearly any methodology since it is non-prescriptive to most project-based and development-based methods of working, and considers their process flows within the final CLiF Model.

3. It provides a cradle-to-grave view of a capability, which has become more relevant in the face of scrutiny and adoption of dissimilar standards between product development, product support, and enterprise standards constituencies by aligning all at an early stage in the process.

The more known that is initially about an eventual product within an enterprise, the greater the chances for successful adoption and improved overall support, including product knowledge.

The following image breaks down the first phases of the Capability Lifecycle Framework (CLiF) Model graphically into lower-level views. As you review the diagramming included, please keep in mind the organizational flow of the phases, as well as the choice of colors used through the diagram.

The diagrams in this book will not be in color, largely as a result of cost constraints and the publishing process, as well as display better-printed clarity in book format. Color versions of the Framework can be obtained on my Website at http://www.GeneralNational.com. As a disclaimer, I've trademarked the naming and the diagrams, and am available to establish this regiment for organizations or through partnership. Information about these is also available on the Website. The Website Deck is in PDF format, and will reference the correct coloring that is noted in the individual diagrams in the book, as well as provide the specific details about the Framework. The diagrams here will represent a light grey to black paradigm in place of the green-amber-red colors used on the Website PDF.

I've broken down colors generally into a "Red/Amber/Green" effect as the process begins and continues through the lifecycle in the following manner:

- Green - Generally represents the beginning-through-implementation of the lifecycle and the first post-implementation period before anticipated obsolescence, or breach of capacity. Notice that the Idea/Inception is automatically Green until the Idea is either approved or disproven, at which time the process would end.
- Amber (Yellow) - Generally represents the approach of a new phase or decision point, or the approach of a closure. It may represent a stage where a Go/No-Go decision cannot yet be determined or is under review, or it gradually represents the movement toward capability decommissioning.
- Red - Generally represents a stopping point, an end-of-life/product retirement stage, or a critical stop in the process that prevents any further action.

For some of the cases, were the processes to be broken down more granularly, each stage could conceivably have Red, Amber, or Green potentials. Using the normal CLiF flow for an Initiative, the first diagram will be demonstrated outlining the first 3 phases, and their accompanying control tracks (Communication, Control).

You will also notice that many of the same process blocks will display a gradient color, since each will represent a stage of the lifecycle where a process can begin and end.

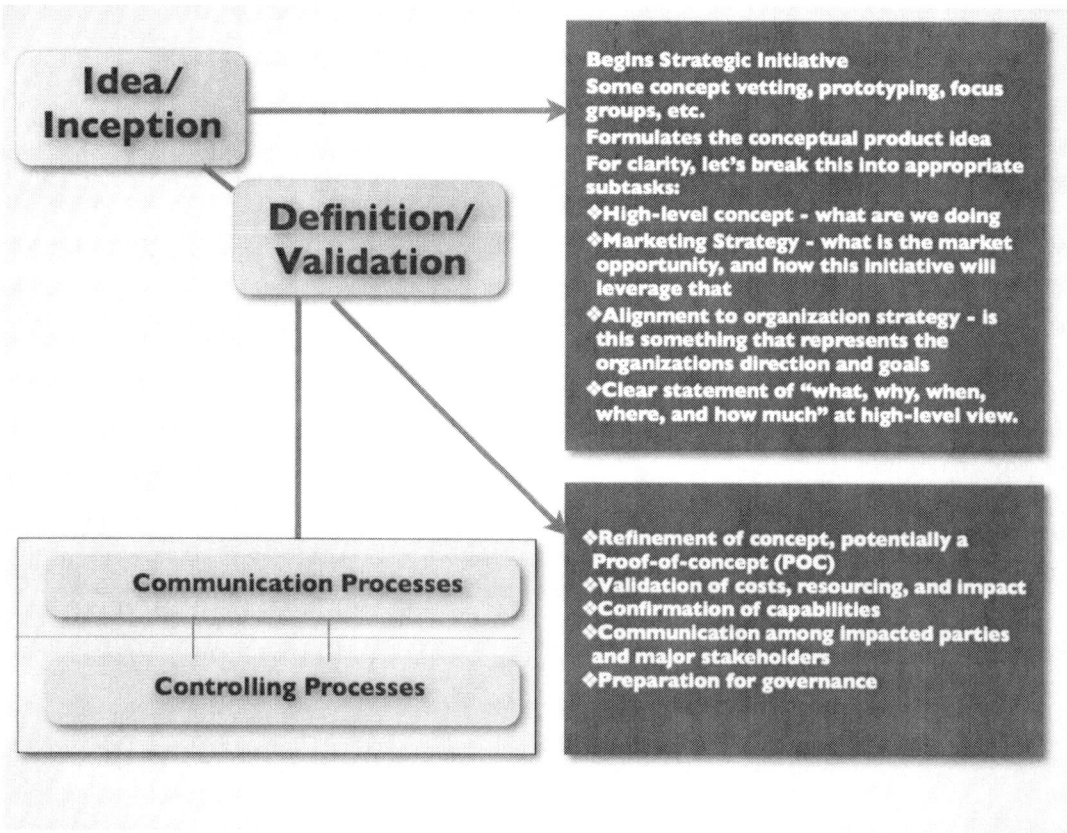

Figure 14-1 - Idea/Inception through Definition/Validation

Note that The Definition/Validation Phase appears partially within the Amber-to-Green Box, which represents Initiative-specific efforts. Similar to a typical project methodology or presentation, this will contain all the product development phases, and can permit for iteratively phased releases.

Also note that the parallel tracks of Controlling Processes and Communications at these stages remain green since these processes have just started, and as part of the overall lifecycle should not be triggering alerts or alarms until the product continues into subsequent phases. As the horizon for the product approaches (noted in Figure 13-2), these bars will approach red and go through amber, indicating that actions and decisions are required to maintain product continuity. This will be more evident later.

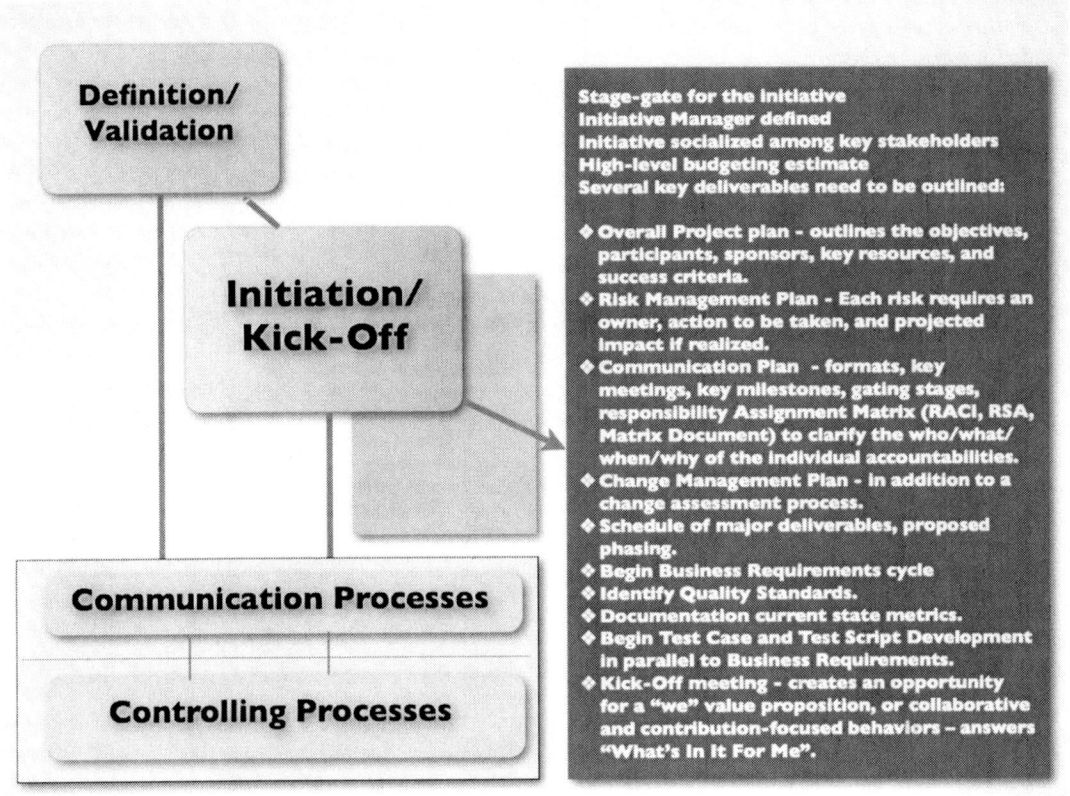

Figure 14-2: Definition transition to Initiation/Kick-Off

On the color diagrams available for download, a color variant is introduced to the Initiative Management Sub-Cycle from Figure 13-2 to differentiate project-level initiative work that may undergo several iterations and multiple releases within the product lifecycle. The variance between shades of Purple and Blue is used to denote Project/Program-specific work only, which is also noted within the green-blocked zone that I've used in Figure 13-2 to denote the expected area for such work. In Figure 14-3 following, I have visually represented the targeted processes more granularly. The Communication and Controlling processes will still remain static in shade (Green), as does the zone for Project Work, since we are still only starting the Product Lifecycle.

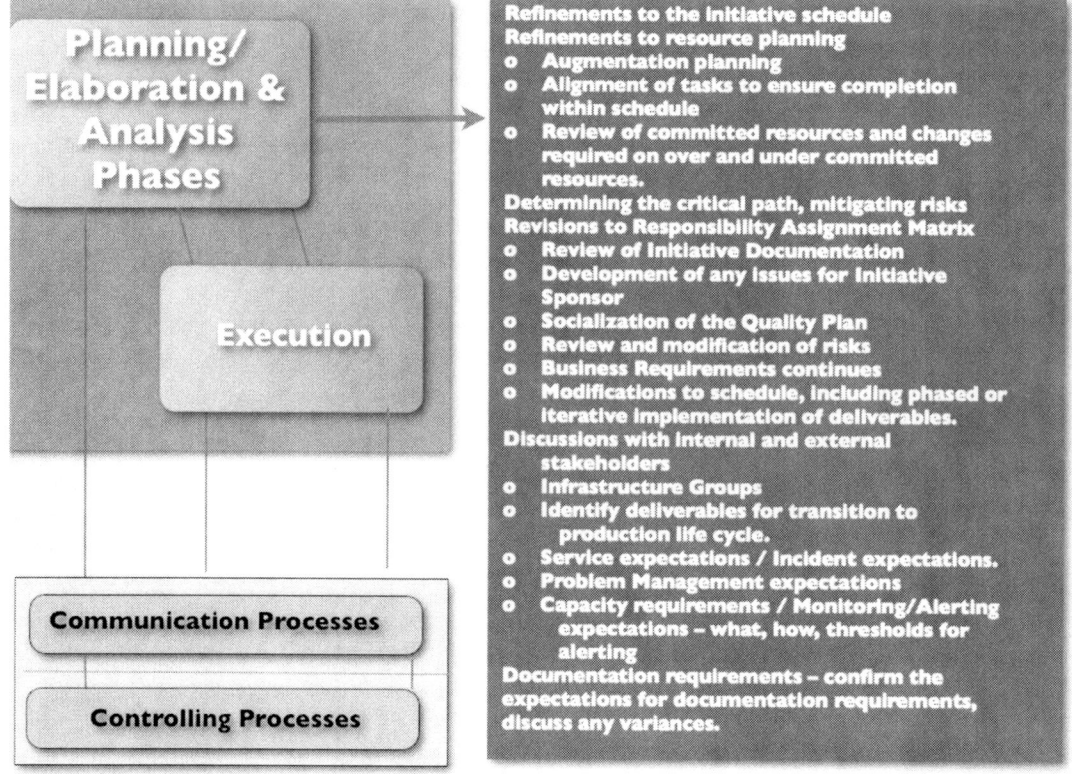

Figure 14-3 - Planning Stage

We'll return to Execution in the next Chart as well, since the Execution Stage may be affected by findings in the Validation Stage, or may be altered through Change Management functions normally germane to initiative undertakings. This is represented in Figure 13-2 by a circular reference when required, since the process may not be entirely linear in nature.

The placement of the blocks with some parallel location is intentional. In most development environments, especially when certain work can start while functional and technical specifications continue to be defined, the process can be somewhat staged in nature with development finally able to complete only after there has been a lock-down in the requirements. As with most frameworks, continued progress will depend on staging the requirements to provide a meaningful release, and at times that release will undergo several iterative builds as one release is locked for final development, and all changes beyond that deadline will follow into a prioritization queue for subsequent releases. Please refer to Part One of this book for a refresher on detail around Change Management controls and their relevance to this component of the process.

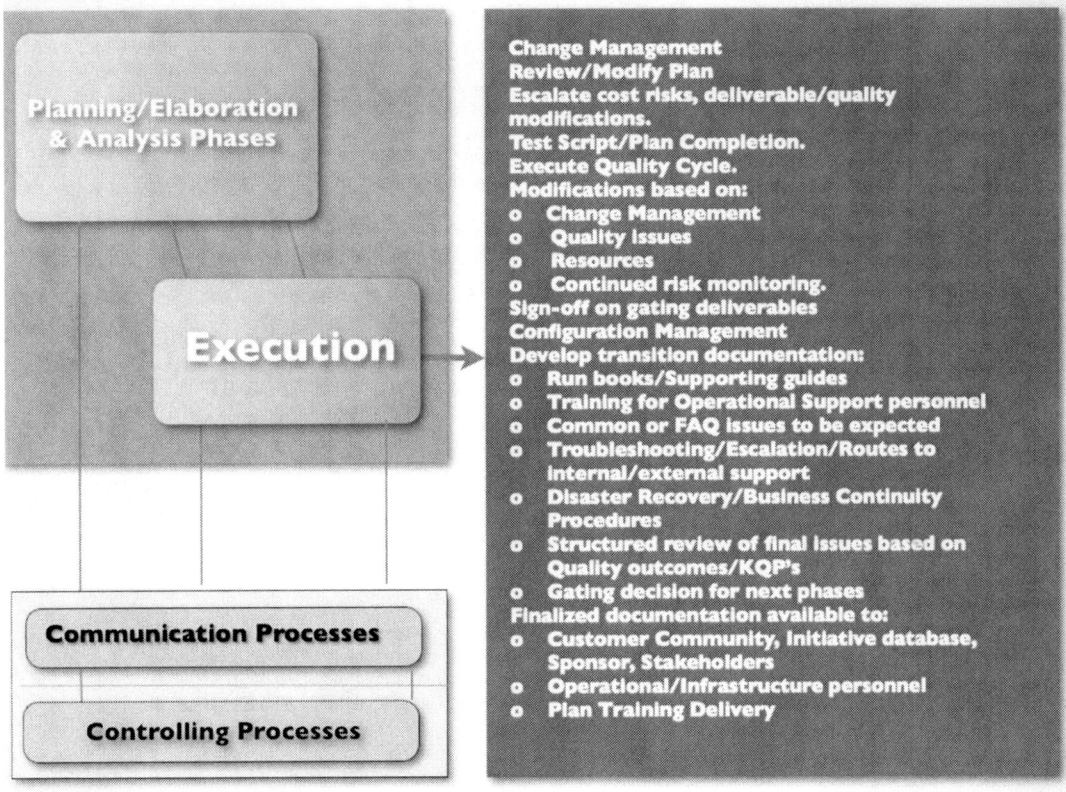

Figure 14-4: Transition to Execution Stage

In Figures 14-4 and 14-5, the process contains a loop between Execution and Testing that returns defects to the Execution phase where issues can be addressed based on criticality and priority. While the goal ideally should be to work to correct all issues, instances can arise that cause conflict between resolution and product release. As such, the written process provides for prioritization and suggestions on rating and ranking depending on the organizational priorities. Other reference titles on Change Management do a more than adequate job of speaking to this issue[33], and we've also discussed this point previously.

The objective is not for the loop to be infinite, but to provide a point of re-contact with the design/product-development process that ensures quality benchmarks are being maintained. CLiF recommends that a Change Control mechanism be implemented to address this need, but is non-prescriptive on the specifics of its organization use, policies, or other factors.

---

33 **ISBN-13:** 978-0070271043 - "Project Change Management" by H. J. Harrington is a very valid and useful reference in this regard.

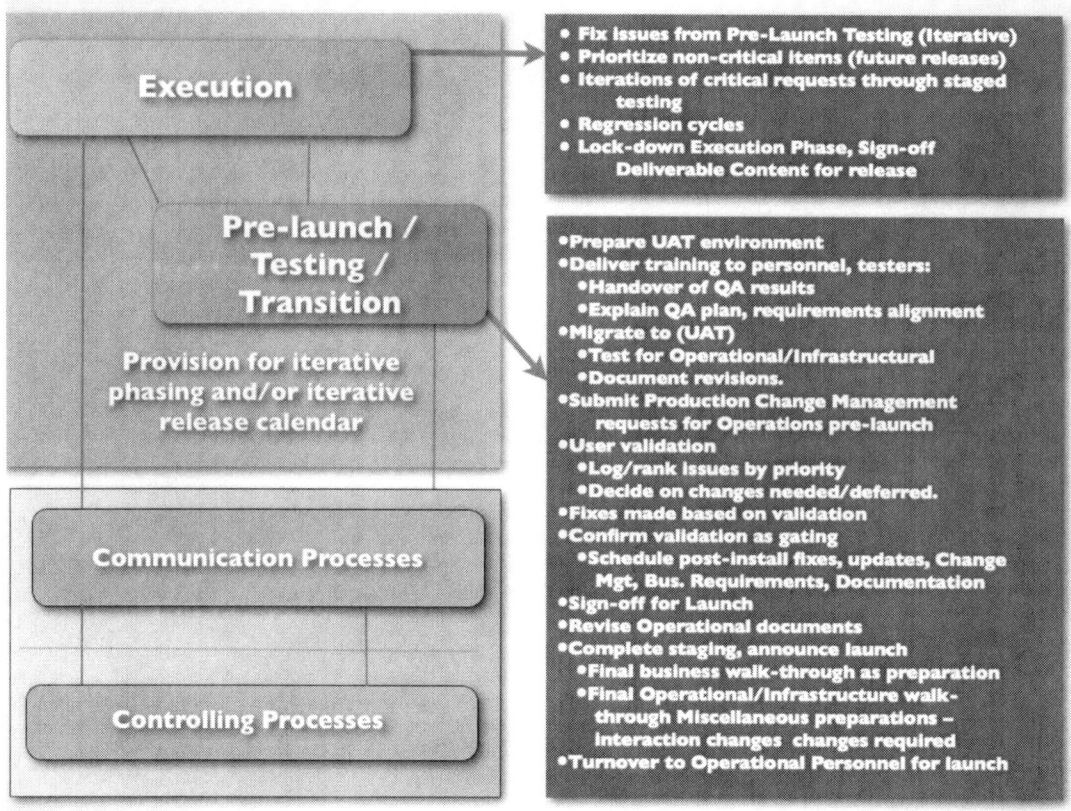

Figure 14-5 - Continued Execution through Pre-Launch Activities

From this point, we begin to approach a Launch of Product within the Lifecycle. Before we do that, a few additional points should be reviewed.

1. Engagement of Operational Personnel. Presuming that your Product Management environment is technology-based, the largest contributor to ongoing friction with the any product lifecycle -- one that this framework is designed to address -- is the alignment of product desires to operational capability. A good example of this is engaging on the implementation of an Open Source Software solution, using all Open Source products with which none of the Operational resources are trained or remotely familiar. Support may not be available externally for the product. As a result, when an incident or problem occurs, the Operational Support resources don't want to be left holding a hot potato. As an initiative is undertaken, it is critical for success that either (a) Operational Standards and Guidelines be followed, or (b) resources be devoted to introduce and train on the newly introduced products sufficiently for the supporting resources to be comfortable and capable of effective support, troubleshooting, and engagement.

2. Use of Product Roadmaps. I strongly encourage this where possible, especially if the roadmap for a specific product -- or, better still, all the products within a business unit -- provides a planned guideline for the ongoing requirements. Some items to consider that have been mentioned previously, but worth noting:

   a. Power/Space -- what are the requirements for ongoing power? Are redundant power-supplies/suppliers or generators required to cover outages? Can space be recouped once a prior capability has been decommissioned?

b. Capacity -- what are the initial capacity requirements, and what is the projected growth year-over-year? Will this displace other capabilities?

c. Resilience -- if there is a failure in one location, what are the business continuity requirements? Does a Service Level Agreement (SLA) need to be crafted, agreed, and funded? Can the system be brought down for maintenance?

d. Owned/Hosted/Software-as-a-Service -- can any of these arrangements work to release current staffing pressures or remove the workload to existing staff? Are the costs more or less than an owned capability?

The Roadmap will give key stakeholders the necessary insight to what is planned and allow for preparation and potential leveling of workload during the periods planned for Initiative Execution, Launch, and Post-Launch activities. It also avoids the element of surprise when services or attention is demanded too late for the required actions to be taken.

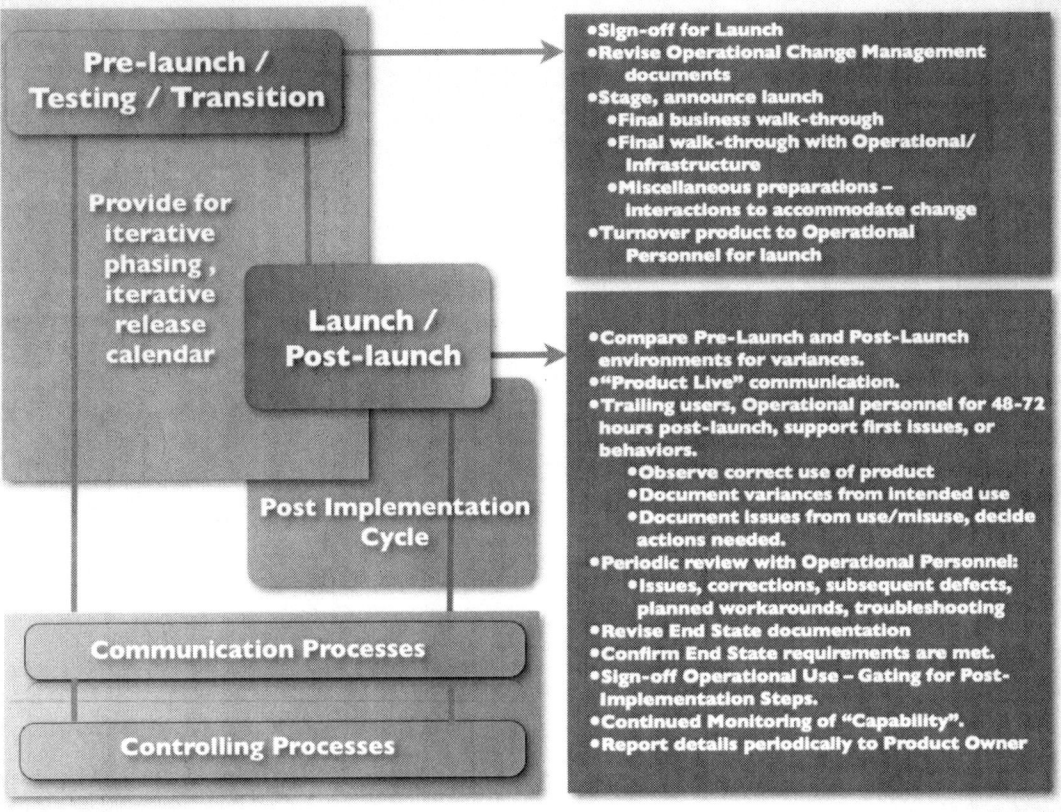

Figure 14-6 - Pre-Launch through Post-Launch Lifecycle

A review of the Product Roadmap should be a regularly scheduled activity for key stakeholders, and permit them to provide input or help set/reset priorities based on changes in business strategy. It also ensures that the capability can be accommodated when its launch is envisioned by providing the opportunity to align the desires for the capability with the resources needed to ensure each phase of execution. If those resources are otherwise engaged, it also provides for transparency at an overall strategic level to prioritize initiatives.

At the Launch/Post-Launch stage, we begin to see a marked difference in the process flow of the model. The capability is released from the Initiative Management phases and begins its transition to the Post Implementation phase. In future diagrams, we'll see how this process should flow as an ongoing cycle. Let's note the changes as shown above.

First, the "Launch/Post-launch" function begins to leave the Project/Program-specific work zone and becomes covered in the Post Implementation work zone. As specified in the steps of the process, there is a turnover of documentation (run books, diagrams, procedures, common troubleshooting, defect lists, workarounds, et al. to a production support group that will monitor and support the capability through the remainder of its lifespan.

During this transition, there are checks to ensure that the correct procedures and requirements have been achieved, scheduling of periodic reviews with Operational personnel to review any updates to the capability, and a gating "Sign-Off" which removes the Product Development resources from this section of the loop. This represents the formal handover, and permits the Product Development Team to continue work on either this initiative, or other tracks of work that map strategically to the organization's objectives. It also permits that group to focus on correction of known defects or iterations to the capability.

The "Communication" and "Controlling" threads begin grading toward a darker share (turning from Green toward Amber on the downloadable copy from the Website) as the product begins its lifecycle stage. This is represented in Figure 14-5, and indicates that the capability is beginning the production cycle where control will shift toward day-to-day continuity (see next diagram) and a focus on ensuring the required customer experience.

Whereas during the Capability/Initiative Development Cycle this area was static in shade ("Green only"), the focus during continuity is to a much larger contingent of customers. Thus, the communication cycle has broader impact and a potentially larger audience. If problems, issues, or incidents occur, the communication needs to be robust enough to cover those constituencies, as well as provide acceptable feedback estimating when the capability will return to the defined "Service Levels".

Rather than addressing a very focused group of customers during the initiative, shorter communications promoting broader impact are needed as the audience becomes much larger. Therefore, communication continues its importance for confidence in the capability to be maintained.

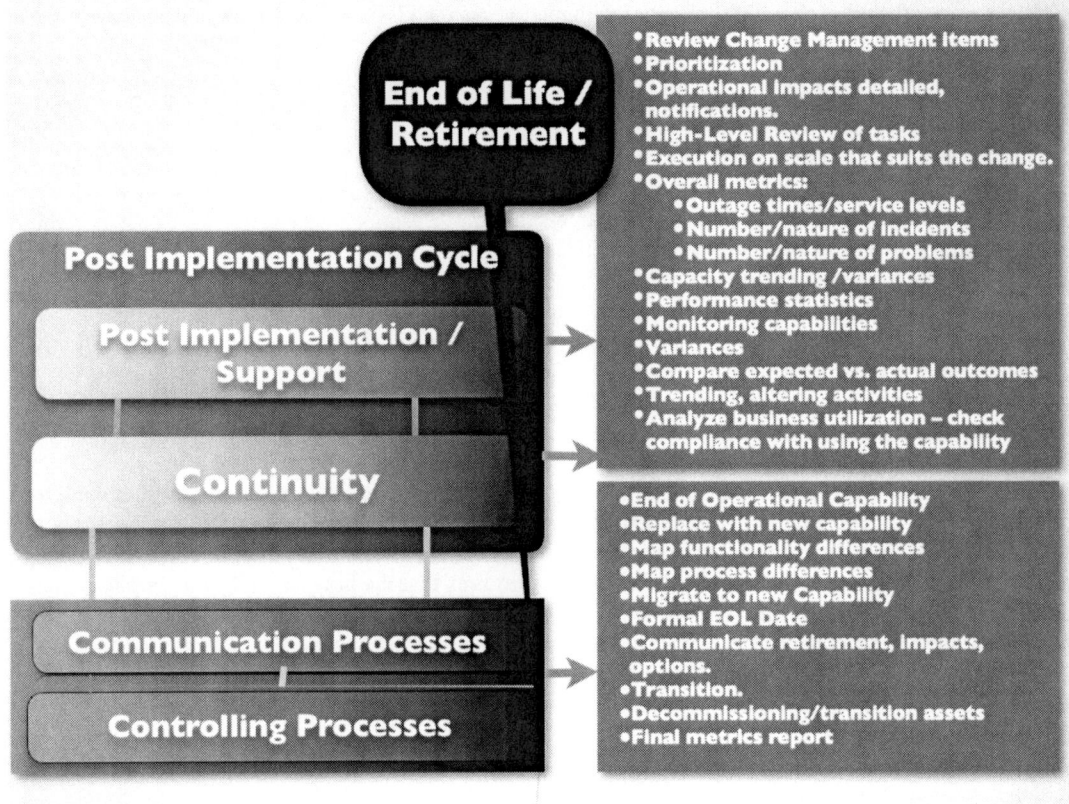

Figure 14-7: Post-Implementation Cycle through End-of-Life/Retirement

Controlling processes fall within the same category as the Communications Track. As we examine the Control Track and Continuity Phases in more detail, we'll note that the day-to-day support around the capability requires that a series of standards be met, including capacity monitoring, alerting, capability bulletins, maintenance or upgrade windows, and more. In addition, the systems to capture overall metrics should be in place and reviewed periodically.

There are a number of goals outlined through the Post-implementation lifecycle. Despite the short span in the diagrams for the Lifecycle Framework, this will undoubtedly be the longest portion of the Capability Lifecycle, and will require significant attention to detail.

In Figure 14-7, you'll note that the Cycle Box containing the Post-Implementation/Support and Continuity processes cycles slowly into a darker shade that eventually turns black (on the Website copy, turning from a Green state slowly toward Amber and finally to Red). Red/Black in this case represents decommissioning or "retirement" of the capability, which also signals the end of the Controlling and Communication Processes that also cycle to Red/Black. The diagram contains a hard ending line that represents a full-shut-down of the capability.

Retirement

Eventually every capability will reach a point of retirement, or a point of diminishing return where the benefits gained from the capability are outweighed by the detriments (costs, effort, etc.) in continuing the lifecycle of that capability.

At that point, a checklist should be completed that addresses the issues with closing the legacy (old) capability once the replacement (new) capability is launched.

End of Operational Capability

- Replacement of existing Capability by new Capability
- Mapping of Prior functionality to replacement functionality
- Mapping of prior processes to new processes
- Migration of customers to replacement Capability
- Formal End-of-Life (EOL) Date for shutdown
- Formal communication of retirement, impacts, options
- Formal transition
- Decommissioning/transition of assets
- Final reporting of metrics against planned baseline - did the Capability provide the expected outcomes, ROI and TCO desired?

As with any capability, there are tasks that must be completed before retirement, and those completed post-retirement. Supposing that your capability is a Personnel Management System; it has completed its expected lifecycle, and is now being replaced by a newer capability that better addresses the growing needs of its constituents. Retiring the capability requires that the new capability be in place, validated, and live before the retirement of the legacy capability. Once the replacement capability is live, has compliance by its constituents, and critical issues are addressed, it becomes time for the "now" legacy capability to be dismantled. This could include the retention of legacy data that will not be contained on the replacement capability, dismantling of hardware, and transition of assets to another party for disposal.

It also must include the final metrics captured from the system that would serve to demonstrate whether that capability met its targets for investment:

- Did it meet its Return on Investment (ROI) target?
- Did it meet the Total Cost of Ownership metrics in place?
- Did it meet service targets? Stability? Year-to-year incidental costs?

These examples are broad-brush strokes, since the overall planning would need to consider other transitional factors (data quality, data migration, data retention, training, etc.). However, they outline the minimal and basic steps that should be considered with any capability being retired.

Author's Notes

Iteration. In crafting a lifecycle process, I've been very neutral and non-prescriptive in suggesting any Project/Program Management Methodology. The goal of this framework is for those to be transparent processes and occur with as few or many iterations necessary during the Capability Lifecycle. For example, if the specific capability is a passenger vehicle, the lifecycle would usually have iterations annually that are released to manufacturing -- for instance, if the suspension could be improved to dampen road feel due to uneven pavement, this might be an incremental improvement versus an entirely new capability, and would likely be released at the next model year.

Most organizations will likely come across the reality that iterations or "releases" are commonplace through the capability lifecycle and consideration should be given to setting expectations for those iterations and structuring them for best business benefit based on both investment and cost controls. Again, this has been standard practice in the software development world for many years, and other manufacturers have adopted similar policies.

Iterative Methodologies return value when they accomplish one clear goal: **Being truly iterative**. To be effective as iterative, there must be a clear window for changes to be introduced, as well as a firm (or reasonably firm) lockdown for changes to be made to that iteration. Surprisingly enough, there are organizations that have been sold on the use of "Agile" or "Iterative" methodologies that still insist on leaving specifications completely open or delaying iterations continually to receive more and more feedback and input. As a result, they release less iteration and turn their product release process into a large "plunge". This is not an effective use of an iterative process, which will be far more effective when universal understandings about business requirements and specifications are clearly targeted and the window or parameters that can be achieved within those parameters are accepted.

Nested Processes. Mentioned above, the product development cycle may be iterative or at least require enhancement or modification based on customer requirements. CLiF presumes that capabilities are not simply implemented then left alone to run without aid or support. Seldom will you find a turn-key solution that does not require at least some modification to meet organizational requirements.

The nesting within the process will occur within the Product Development Cycle, and will resemble either a "release cycle" or a "product iteration" that includes the amendments to the capability. If you refer to Figure 13-2, you'll note the "clockwise" flow of objects in the Initiative Management Space, indicating that this may be a repeating process over several iterations.

Retirement Decision. Earlier, I mentioned a rudimentary formula for retirement of a capability that should occur as you trend toward decreased revenue compared to all costs to maintain, operate, and support the capability. The Chart in Figure 14-7 shows an example of this.

In the example, the organization should be seeing the downward trending at Year 5, and be focused during Years 5 & 6 on a less costly replacement before Year 7 to avoid a negative return on the capability. At Year 7, the system is expected to generate less revenue than its costs of maintenance.

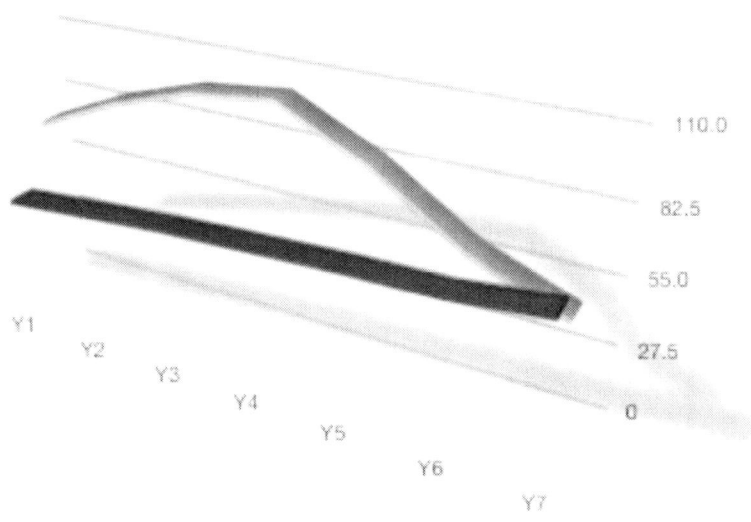

Figure 14-8: Example Retirement Decision Chart, based on TCO and revenue.

Clearly, none of this can be predicted at a Day One launch. In viewing the investment, the Initiative Sponsors should have a strategic idea about the realistic market opportunity and its expected duration.

This example underscores the concept of cost control using trend analysis to determine the point where capability operation will trend below anticipated revenues. This is a common occurrence and organizations will usually recognize this type of analysis. It should also be considered to adequately address the control of ongoing costs.

Related to Information Technology Spend. On average, nearly 80% of an organization's annual technology budget is spent on the maintenance of existing technology. The prior chart is relevant because of that factor. Once that cost can be predicted and controlled, the cost of the overall investment can be managed or placed in proper context. Among the goals behind the CLiF approach is to track spending patterns transparently and reveal appropriate savings, thereby making funding available for future strategic investment.

The challenge is how to squeeze more juice from the same 20%, or better still, how to reduce the current 80% to a more manageable level by avoiding unplanned costs or the results of poor execution.

Post-Implementation Considerations

The goals of the "Initiative Management Cycle" are fairly straightforward: Align investment with strategy through appropriate governance and execution excellence.

The goals of the "Post-Implementation" components of the Capability Lifecycle are (1) to confirm that the goals of the initiative continue to be met after launch by ensuring alignment organizationally, and (2) to streamline the acceptance process into a state of Operational Readiness. By focusing on early engagement in the process, the key interfaces will have proper visibility of the requirements and can provide useful feedback to improve implementation and continuity.

On the surface, this type of framework may appear daunting. By aligning quality appropriately to ensure that quality assurance did not present delays in the delivery of the capability, here too we are engaging critical stakeholders into the process to ensure they can support the capability and have the necessary tools to do so in the most cost-effective manner. This helps avoid unplanned costs and improves the understanding of the TCO behind the capability.

This also presents an opportunity for the participants in the CLiF Model to understand a complete end-to-end psychology by seeing the entire experience from all angles. Through continued practice and interaction, the product development teams gain an understanding of how to construct solutions that will help reduce support costs and design within parameters that can be effectively repeated based on experience. Correct use of the framework can reduce both costs and the required support infrastructure. It results in the development of standard processes and templates that are subject to reuse and form an easily followed guideline during migration from product development to support at the post-launch gate.

Several factors should be considered when developing the long-term planning for an ongoing Capability Lifecycle at the Post-Launch Stage:

1. Monitoring/Alerting. As part of developing the capability, thresholds should be developed and established that alert support personnel to several criteria that affect the customer experience. For instance, is the capability approaching a capacity threshold? A storage threshold? A user or licensing threshold? Security breaches or security alerts? The earlier steps in the prior chapter provide some insights as to the types of items that require monitoring or alerting to be applied.

2. Incident/Problem/Issue Tracking. Does the capability exhibit behaviors that degrade the customer experience? Is there a trend of similar events being reported with the capability? What is the support team spending the most time addressing, and could this be solved in some iterative enhancement to the system that alleviates the behavior? It's important to identify common terms and defini-

tions, but be able to provide a reporting on their impact -- for instance, one function reporting an error more frequently that results in troubleshooting or workarounds.

   a. Would an investment of $X resolve issues that => $X?

   b. Would that investment save money, or result in opportunity costs?

3. Service Excellence. When the Support Standards were defined, a Service Level Agreement (SLA) should also have been defined. Periodically, the SLA needs to be consulted and compared to the actual experience. The SLA will address the service standard applied, the escalation, and the average resolution of incidents/problems/issues for which the Support personnel have a defined procedure. The SLA will also define other standards that can be applied to the customer experience, as well as the level of engagement between the Product Owner and the Product Support Resources.

4. Change/Release Management. A procedure should be adopted that addresses how Changes and Releases are handled within the environment as part of the overall Capability Lifecycle. I'll address the compliance and regulatory concerns around this in a moment. Such a process should address the notification required to implement changes, change access control, packaging of changes for release, validation, and implementation into the product. This procedure should hold true in different formats for "Changes" (which should generally be either minor or an a critical/emergency basis) or "Releases" (which typically are scheduled and more encompassing, or require greater resource and effort).

Given the implementation of compliance systems in organizations, especially in the wake of Sarbanes-Oxley and other regulations, as well as disruptive events for a product or service, proper Change/Release Control methods are essential to the Continuity element of the CLiF. Those methods should have the following effective results:

   (a) Provide a clear procedure for implementing change, as well as removing a change in the event validation does not produce the desired result.

   (b) Provide a clear audit trail of components that have changed, the nature of those changes, and a transcript of how those changes were validated.

   (c) Provide a record of why the change was made, how it was requested, and the requestor.

   (d) Provide controls around access and security to ensure that the correct components have been changed at an appropriate time. In addition, this helps address unauthorized access so that unintended changes are not released.

All are valid reasons for proper Change and Release Governance.

5. Availability Requirements. I use this term primarily to reference either a data or information service, or a technology capability that may be required between certain core hours of operation. Provisions for ensuring the customer experience is managed accordingly may require resiliency or disaster recovery facilities, depending on the Service Level Agreement negotiated. This is especially a consideration for capabilities that are either hosted by a third-party or a Service (software-as-a-service). Since we cannot generally predict when a disaster may occur, or how that disaster could impact the customer experience, an SLA should depict the type of experience desired, and the provider should outline the costs of maintaining availability, whether used or not.

Consider also that the availability of a resilient or "backup" environment can facilitate transparent change management for any capability that has a short defined window for outage or Change/Release. Without affecting the customer experience, it may be useful in providing continual service in an uninterrupted fashion until normal service levels can be restored.

6. Request Management. The performing organization may wish to collaborate between the Supporting and Product Development organizations on maintaining a "Request Management Apparatus". This can take any form, but one party should be responsible for ownership with communication of

requests occurring on a periodic basis defined by the SLA. I've listed some examples below, using a technology capability:

(a) Requests for specific functional changes. For instance, a Business Requirements facility where the request for enhancements can be registered and reviewed for potential inclusion with the capability sponsor.

(b) Requests for singular changes (i.e. a report to be executed to retrieve data based on specific criteria).

(c) Requests for changes due to error. If error handling does not permit the customer to change a transaction in process, a Request System might capture the change request so that later audits would document and justify the change.

All of these present an opportunity for the Capability Sponsor/Product Owner and the Production Support/Continuity Teams to ensure continual dialogue on the continuity of the capability, and proactively address requests by response or direct action (enhancement, iterative change, etc.)

Summary

During this chapter, we deconstructed the diagrams related to the process breakdown for the Capability Lifecycle Framework, providing an end-to-end view from a visual perspective of the information outlined in the prior chapter. In addition, we walked through the retirement and ongoing support of a capability in a post-launch scenario and outlined potential considerations to include in a Service Level Agreement discussion.

In essence, we've provided the foundation for an end-to-end lifecycle framework that identifies the steps, considerations, and individual gating involved in that process. We've also identified that elements of the process will likely continue iteration up to and through a certain point in the lifecycle of the capability, and addressed the planning that should be considered in the retirement of the capability.

This is not intended to be a comprehensive listing of everything to be considered in a Capability Lifecycle decision, but a foundation for productive dialogue that should consider appropriate factors.

In the final chapter, I'll outline methods that should be considered when implementing an end-to-end framework such as CLiF, and how/whether it is capable of coexistence with other organizational processes.

Chapter 15:
Considerations & Closing

Implementing Strategic Initiative Management & the Capability Lifecycle Framework

In the prior chapters, we discussed the principles of an end-to-end model, the benefits derived from aligning strategic initiatives with organizational strategy and goals, aligning staff to the common strategic themes, and creating a framework that ties one process together through the implementation of a seamless set of intersections.

Inasmuch as I've attempted to present a fairly neutral face to the notion of an entire lifecycle process by providing the guidelines that can encompass nearly any methodology for project/program/initiative management, there are some questions that may be asked along the way when the discussions of intersections and potential concerns are raised. I'll attempt to address the thought process around these through potential questions:

ITIL

"My organization has subscribed to ITIL (Information Technology Infrastructure Library) for the management of its supporting technology infrastructure. How does this process reconcile against that?"

Reasonable question. The process considers ITIL and is not in conflict at all. In fact, the considerations of an ITIL-based environment for service and availability standards and procedures are completely compatible with this framework. ITIL provides production life-cycle support and continuity pieces in maintaining an environment focused on standardized processes and a standard collection of artifacts to be used for production turnover, Change Management, Service Management, Release Management, and provision of a continuity experience to the customer.

CLiF attempts to clarify the intersecting points between a process such as ITIL, or any other reasonable support process to which the performing organization subscribes (i.e. ITIL may be too ambitious a goal for some organizations), as well as the requirements needed by the supporting/continuity components of that organization, and the requirements that should be provided early in the lifecycle and socialized through fluid communication across both the initiative and support cycles.

If your performing organization has subscribed to ITIL, you're already following a framework for the supporting end. The ITIL framework, however, is largely silent within a Project/Program Management scope, and provides minimal guidance to when communication and socialization of initiatives should be done with Operational Groups who will be the end recipient. As a result, CLiF attempts to provide further clarification by providing gating points at which those groups should be considered key stakeholders and involved parties.

Methodologies

"Our organization subscribes to multiple Methodologies depending on the Product Development Group and based on the type or size of an initiative. How do we implement CLiF against the different processes?"

Very easily. CLiF provides the gates and gating principles against which an effort should be guided, and the requirements to gate into the subsequent phases using a set of practices to guide interaction and intersection. As mentioned earlier in this work, the process considers both iterative and non-iterative methodologies in product development. The single difference is that iterations will simply cause greater interaction with the intersecting pieces between organizational groups, and therefore require a higher degree of collaborative behavior.

For instance, Rational Unified Process (RUP) has 4 major phases: Initiation, Elaboration, Construction, and Transition. Using that method, as the initiative is elaborated, the requirements become clearer and more information can be provided between the Initiation and Elaboration phases to post-Transition operational groups for the care and continuity of that capability once implemented. This would continue for each iteration in RUP, and the information would be fluidly communicated to the Operational parties as there is an impact defined.

The key difference is the involvement of supporting parties earlier in the process for planning and impact assessment, and to ensure that product development efforts follow accepted standards that are supportable within that organization.

Universal Applicability

"Many of the examples used in this work cite technology implementation. Are the principles universally applicable, and can you cite a non-technology example?"

I've cited how this process might translate into a manufacturing process using the automotive manufacturing process, noting the iteration/refinement or enhancements normally done between model years for a vehicle. Using the vehicle analogy further, suppose that a recall is done on a particular model of vehicle over several model years due to a manufacturing defect. As part of that process, a retrofit can be created to ship to retailers for installation along with instructions and procedures for handling issues at a retailer level. This is another example of providing a turnover that ensures a seamless end-to-end experience for the customer of that product.

The same process could be used for any product or service offering being developed and subsequently supported through a different process. For instance, a soft offering that doesn't involve a technology product (say a manufacturing item) could be created, released, and the support for it could be turned over to a telephone support team for product experience troubleshooting. It is especially useful in a globalized workforce setting where instructions and procedures must be carefully and completely documented, leaving little margin for error and removing ambiguity and decision-making from the resource supporting the effort. Such a transition defines the correct intersections to ensure that potential issues, problems, and incidents can be handled using an appropriate mechanism.

Decentralized/Global Workforce

"My organization is global in span, and leverages matrixed resources that have established processes. What value can a Capability Lifecycle Framework bring to a decentralized enterprise?"

In short, the approach can bring a very high degree of value and may involve very little change other than the collaborative steps, the prescribed intersections that have been outlined, active sponsor involvement and influence (both seen and heard), and collaboration between the parties. Each group may already possess all the necessary elements, but the lack of collaboration might obscure them from view.

The framework requires a collaborative approach at its core, and two key individuals lead that approach: The Product Owner/Sponsor and the Initiative Manager acting as his supporting voice. The conversations introducing CLiF as a lifecycle process should focus on the timing, key collaboration elements, and the value proposition for having the right information and decisions early enough to make a difference. Most Data Center managers would rather have that information soon enough to be prepared. I'd venture that most others with a collaborative and strategic spirit would also welcome early and meaningful engagement.

Smaller Organization

"We run a small organization, with very small departments and efforts that are not large in scope. What can we gain from this process?"

Potentially, more of a focus on process maturity provided that your organization aspires to organized process and wants to depart from the normal heroism associated with a CMMI Level 1/2 organization. Otherwise, much of the detail on aligning initiatives for greater success and overall maturity will likely be more useful detail for small, leaner organizations until they've grown beyond the staffing level where simple heroics will be productive.

Having seen similar organizations be the target of acquisition, understanding and having such a process in place once acquired could provide greater incentive for the acquiring organization to adopt your process if you follow the more mature and seamless guideline this framework outlines; otherwise, once acquired, you might find yourself at the end of an unwieldy process that renders your acquired entity and customer base less competitive.

"Lean"

"My organization's management keeps driving home the message that we should adopt 'Lean' Processes. This process seems to suggest more steps and more documentation than a 'Lean Process'. How do I present a compelling counter-argument?"

Actually, that's one of the big fallacies about 'Lean' in all respects. People misinterpret 'Lean' to mean 'no documentation', in the same way that many Agile practitioners interpret Agile processes to infer 'no documentation'. Both are technically incorrect.

Both 'Lean' and 'Agile' as premises suggest that documentation be done, according to their value. Neither suggests constructing a surplus of unnecessary documentation serving no useful purpose. If you note the earlier Chapters, one of my Pragmatic Premises was to undertake only items that provided direct value. If there is no value in the additional work, do not undertake it. Lean/Agile and this work align on this principle, although often misinterpreted. Neither suggests a code-and-go-but-don't-document approach.

Documentation is a requirement. Transition is a requirement. Doing all the correct processes is still required. Lean and Agile only suggest that the documentation be succinct and have a specific value to someone. We don't contradict that at all. In fact, we strongly oppose any documentation that simply acts as a checklist for the sake of having a checklist. The Initiative Manager should strongly oppose any non-value-adding work to minimize distraction from core goals and strategic direction.

Methodology or Framework

"You've described the CLiF Model as neutral toward support model and project/program methodology. How would you define it if not a methodology based around specific characteristics?"

CLiF is a component framework that permits the user to plug in the requisite methodologies and practices for managing initiative work, as well leverage the components related to their support model. While we support adoption of industry standards such as ITIL and Agile or Lean, among others, we stop short of a specific endorsement of any one standard being prescriptive within the framework.

Consider that an organization may not value the overhead required by a fully-ITIL compliant process and has different ideas on how to manage and support their infrastructure. This framework exists to provide guidance on areas to consider as part of adoption. Homegrown Project/Program Management methodologies can also be used provided that there is compliance with the framework outlined in the framework's stages.

Gating Stages

To underscore the collaborative aspect of CLiF, I've noted that each major phase has a gating stage critical for passage to the next steps in the process.

Within each stage, I've listed the requisite activities and requirements to be considered to fulfill the gate requirements. Between the "Idea/Inception" and "Decision/Validation" Phases, you'll find a gating stage following "Validation" that requires the concept under consideration undergo due diligence to ensure alignment with strategic objectives. If it meets the requirements for investment, it would be gated into an "Initiation" Phase and treated as an "Initiative".

The participants within the gating stages represent all constituents of the CLiF, from product development to sponsorship to product support. This ensures that all stakeholders form consensus around the process, and that any objections are socialized along with options to address to the satisfaction of the stakeholder and sponsor, and within the constructs of the framework.

This symbol in the CLiF Model Flow Diagram in Figure 13-2 represents the gating decision process. For practical purposes, the gates defined in the diagram represent the minimum requirements -- gates could also be established at interim points between transition stages to gain agreement to progress to the next stage, transition, or turnover from Initiative to Lifecycle. You may refer to the diagrams for complete details.

Gating Agreements

The gating agreement process represents a contract by involved parties that the capability can be supported through subsequent phases, and continues to align with the organization's strategic direction. It also confirms agreement by all parties that the requirements to progress to subsequent stages have been satisfied. Sign-off/agreement should be captured as an artifact for reference purposes. Should deficiencies be noted that might prevent gating, the following actions can occur:

• Proceed, with agreement to correct deficiencies (time or dependency-bound) - deficiencies may be moderate and require correction, but not severe enough to halt other progress.

• Proceed, accept deficiencies without correction - deficiencies may be minor, or permit feasible workarounds.

• Not proceed until deficiencies are corrected - deficiencies are severe enough to warrant immediate correction, or would impact supportability, customer experience, or ongoing costs.

In all cases, the Gating Procedure should provide for a documented sign-off that indicates acceptance of the capability being progressed into the subsequent stage, and note the specific deficiencies with plans to correct these either in a subsequent action or timeframe. The signed agreement represents the contract between the collaborators in the process.

Concluding Comments and Thoughts

Lessons Learned

I've provided some key considerations in outlining practices, methods, frameworks, and case studies throughout this book. Their objective was to provide perspective on issues that are pragmatically important in managing to a much higher potential and raising the profile of Initiative Management -- a banner for Project/Program/Portfolio Management practices -- to a strategic level by aligning to core organizational objectives.

As a career-long Project/Program/Portfolio Manager, I hoped to share lessons that might provide constructive input to others in achieving greater levels of customer satisfaction and strategic alignment from their initiatives. I hope I've made all the right mistakes along the way so that you needn't. I'll spend the next several paragraphs outlining some additional thoughts.

Core Goals & Rules

Early on, we established the case for core guidelines to effectively manage both our teams and ourselves. Those qualities included pragmatism, 360-degree communication, collaboration, ethical actions, providing options, and promotion of value and alignment with strategic goals. It would be very easy for me to summarize the core requirement for those skills to be optimally effective:

- **Provide Leadership**

- **Demonstrate Humility**

Leadership. One would think "leadership" would be an assumed trait. By doing so, we overlook the possibility that some individuals lack those characteristics. When I reference leadership, I also mean a "balanced" leadership model.

A good initiative manager will provide both the qualities associated with a leader -- the ability to create and present a vision and encourage people to work in collaboration to achieve those goals -- and those of a manager -- the person responsible for handling the core details behind executing against that vision and ensuring administratively that the initiative meets its objectives.

People can be defined as "leaders" or "managers"; in very rare occasions does a person espouse both traits, or transition between them. Marlene Caroselli in her book "Leadership Skills for Managers"[34] does an excellent job of outlining the differences between each. Our objective should recognize when "leadership" is needed and when "management" is appropriate.

Humility. I've commonly used the phrase "Check your ego at the door". Understanding people also means understanding that each one has an important role within any initiative, and mutual respect for one-another demands that we understand that attribute, and accept that we aren't subject matter experts in everything.

I heartily recommend a line taken from the poem "Desiderata" by Max Ehrmann[35]:

"If you compare yourself with others, you may become vain or bitter; for always there will be greater and lesser persons than yourself."

It's an important phrase to understand, though one that most fail to recognize in their desire to prove themselves. Our job in managing or leading is often to pull together the cacophony of differing voices to achieve a result. Our ego isn't important. The achievement of the strategic goal is. The challenge is creating a team atmosphere that channels the innate egotistic behavior of others productively. For me, that takes the form of a few characteristics:

---

[34] ISBN # 978-0071364300 - McGraw-Hill Publishing, 2000
[35] (c) 1927 (No. 962402)

- **Share credit**. Few managers realize that sharing the credit is a reflection on their effective management -- the right people know who leads an effort and that he/she has driven the individual contributors to achieve its goal.

- **Accept accountability**. If something's happened, acknowledge it with a plan that addresses it. Then act quickly to correct it and learn from the event.

- **Be the role model**. Set the example you want others to exhibit.

- **Friendly, fair, firm**. Know always that you have an objective. Be friendly about it, fair in handling that responsibility, and firm in ensuring that everyone is working toward the common goal.

The reality is that egotistical behavior underscores a deeper insecurity in the person exhibiting it. The person who is ready to be humble about their role and accomplishments doesn't have the same insecurities or self-esteem issues. It's a fact lost on most people because they'll usually believe the opposite is true. Trust me, it's not. It takes far more security and self-esteem to recognize that you're not the expert on every subject versus being the person who always has something to prove. Keeping this thought in mind will not only be empowering for you, it will empower your entire team and produce better results.

Let your actions and accomplishments tell your story.

Answer to Exercise 4-1:

Earlier in the book, in Exercise 4-1, I referenced a specific logic problem and asked you to think about the solution. By now, you've likely read on and forgotten the question, so let's take a moment and recap now:

Exercise 4-1:

Assemble a team of say 5 or 6 people, along with a canister of tennis balls. Give them the following assignment:

"Everyone in the group must touch each of the balls at least once in the shortest possible amount of time." Have a stopwatch ready to time 2 things (one won't really require a stopwatch, the other might). The first is how long it takes them to reach the solution with which they're satisfied. The second is how long it takes to execute the solution from start to finish.

This was an exercise predicated on "constraints" and the notion that we often impose nonexistent constraints on a solution. How many times have you heard the hackneyed phrase of "think outside the box"? What does that really mean?

The answer is that it's meaningless. It's analogous to suggesting that there are only 2 responses to any issue -- one predicated on conventional wisdom, and one that is simply a different source of conventional wisdom, since "thinking outside the box" implies that there is a "box", and that we exist either inside or outside of it.

Do we ever really question *why there's even a box*? I challenge anyone to develop a response to that question that doesn't imply that conventional thinking has immediately entered the picture, or that some constraint has limited his or her choices. With that in mind, please take a moment and again read the rules to the exercise. This time, only read the instructions and the rules. Nothing more.

If you read it differently this time, that's a good start. If you realized that the key phrase of "touch each of the balls at least once" could have different meanings, you've gone just a bit further.

Now when you originally read this exercise, you probably had in mind that you might need to form a line that passed balls from one person to another to complete the assignment. Or you might have had people putting the balls on a table to stagger hands across all of them at once, though even the thought of that would seem chaotic and disorganized. You might have gathered your group of 5 or 6 people to try a variety of solutions and resulted in times exceeding 4 or 5 seconds to complete the task. You probably never thought that you could complete it in less than 2 seconds.

You could complete it in under a second if you removed all constrained thinking. So let's think about how that's possible.

"Touch each of the balls at least once." How can that be achieved in such a short time? Gravity? Not using both hands? Not lifting more than one finger to each ball? Organizing the hands above and below one another? Is a picture of the solution becoming clearer?

Have one person hold the can with one hand, and the balls inside the can with the index finger of the other. On a signal, let them drop through a close ring formed by the hands of each person, each of whom has one finger extended. The balls will drop to the floor. If successful, the process should take about 1 second.

When you read that now, it seems so simple.

When you thought about it several chapters ago, you might have agonized over the thought process. Had I told you then that the entire process could be done in about 1 second, you might have suggested that it wasn't possible.

The other part of the exercise was to time your team on how long their solution took, and the duration of time to reach their conclusion. Now that you know the answer to this -- yes, I intentionally kept you hanging until the end of the book because I wanted you to understand the concepts and thought further before you attempted this with the new information -- you can use this as a thought-provoking exercise to better understand your performing teams in a few respects:

- How they perform as a team

- How they reach conclusions, including group dynamics

- Whether they impose constraints artificially

- How open they are to new concepts

I highly endorse this as an approach to better understand your team's dynamics. Here are a few additional suggestions to enhance the experience:

- Ask the team to report back their solution and rate it against your known baseline. When they've explained their solution, challenge them for a faster time and send them back until they return with their solution.

    - Note whether there is active resistance or complaint

    - Note whether the team finds working against a more challenging objective difficult

    - Note if there are personality conflicts in the team that start taking over when the new challenges are issued.

- When the team responds with a solution that doesn't match the one above, respond by questioning whether that's the best they could do, with an answer that "they're wrong". Note the responses, or any hostility that might evolve.

- Once you've suggested, "they're wrong", they'll likely ask, "how do you know" or "well, show me your solution." Respond indicating that you know a better way, but you're looking for them to creatively figure that out.

This is not designed to provoke hostile thinking, and if it emerges during the exercise, explain your objectives in engaging the team. It's important for them to understand that the intent was not to prove them wrong, but to challenge any false assumptions and constraints in solving the problem.

And of course, indicate to them that the exercise needs to be kept a secret now that they know it before they spoil the fun for future groups.

Lessons from the Trenches

Across a career that spans many years and many experiences, it's difficult to pick out only select experiences that express the right lessons and impart wisdom about both my chosen profession and contribute productively toward improving understanding and effectiveness.

I've selected several that I felt explain best, along with the rest of this publication.

The importance of listening.

Communication does not mean, "talking". It usually means listening, and more specifically actively listening to understand issues and develop solutions. The notion of knowing when to be silent and absorb information can be lost on the majority of people.

- If you have nothing of value to say or contribute, don't believe that you need to convince others of that fact.

- It's better to be thought of as stupid than to open your mouth and remove all doubt.

- We listen far more than we speak anyway.

Your customer will better appreciate the person who listens versus one who constantly rambles. Really. So don't think that you need to fill the silent void with useless chatter.

Know what you know, and especially know what you don't.

It's important to admit what you don't know, and people will generally respect that not everyone will know the answer to every question immediately. Your customer may be irate, but words in the heat of the battle will serve little to resolve their problem. Understanding their issue, and listening to better assess it will do more to satisfy their temporary anger. You don't know the root-cause yet, but in time you will. Your goal is to respond when you can do so intelligently with specific actions.

Talk is cheap. Speculation is rampant. Answers and actions speak volumes.

Admit your mistakes.

Everyone has made mistakes (Remember the egotist? He's made quite a few). Humans are fallible beings (so are machines, by the way). Nothing is perfect, and we're all entitled to a few mistakes provided that we understand and learn something from them. Hiding them does little. Covering them up degrades confidence. Denying them is disingenuous. Failure to admit to them shows a lack of character.

Get out in front of them, and take the action to correct them, learn from them, and hopefully don't repeat them in the future.

Hard work is noble -- get your hands dirty. Take initiative.

Even as I managed people who, in turn, were managing projects, I differed from some of my colleagues in that I wasn't afraid to get personally involved when someone was struggling. To those who might disagree, I'd argue this: If you saw a drowning man, would you throw him a life preserver or an anchor? Or would you walk by and ignore his pleas for help?

If it's in your power to make an impact and help others, besides just satisfying the customer, get involved! It counts under the heading of "takes initiative". Under that heading, if you see an area where you can be of value, take initiative to collaborate with your customers by sharing your thoughts and offering your attention, time, and effort.

If it's not ethical, walk away.

When all is said and done, all we that we truly have is our reputation. Perhaps we've been asked to do something that constitutes a breach of ethics, or violates either our own or our organization's principles (hopefully, our own principles exceed the standards of any organization). Be ready to walk away from it.

It won't be the toughest decision you'll need to make, because your conscience should be telling you that it's the only decision you can make. You cannot do what your ethics cannot support. Don't consider how costly it will be in the short-term. The damage to your reputation -- personally and professionally -- is permanent.

Have fun!

Our entire objective in life is to enjoy it while we're here. Find the right balance personally and professionally that makes you happy. The result will reflect in a renewed attitude toward work that filters out the unimportant items and focuses on goals that truly help the organization. Balancing both your personal and professional life will have a lasting impact on your ability to excel. The workaholic isn't always the person that gets ahead, and if he/she actually succeeds, at what personal cost has it been?

The moment that you find no joy in your job, your role, or your career is when you should walk away. With that in mind, that I'll present my last piece of advice.

Challenge yourself.

When I decided to write this, it was after I came to the realization that my prior role had become unrewarding to me, and I was no longer happy with the environment, the organization, or felt our values matched. We were slowly reaching the point of impasse beyond reconciliation. My personal life, my health, and my well being suffered. In a moment of extreme clarity, I stood up, gathered my things, and left with a goal of challenging myself and being happy with my life and career.

I have no regrets about my decision. I walked away satisfied that I'd done everything within my power.

I enjoyed the challenge of reflecting through my experiences, and contributing to a profession of over 2 decades that provided me with unparalleled opportunities. My challenge wasn't to change the world, but to impart my experience to improve it and help others. My goal was to do something that truly made me happy: To make a difference.

Now it's your turn to challenge yourself. It's your turn to challenge your own thinking, the way you've worked in the past, and to make a difference in your organization. It's your turn to be happy. It's your turn to think strategically and differently and to turn around our beliefs about projects, initiatives, and capabilities. Enjoy the journey. You only get to do it once.

Index

CPSIA information can be obtained at www.ICGtesting.com
Printed in the USA
BVOW041413061112

304827BV00007B/13/P